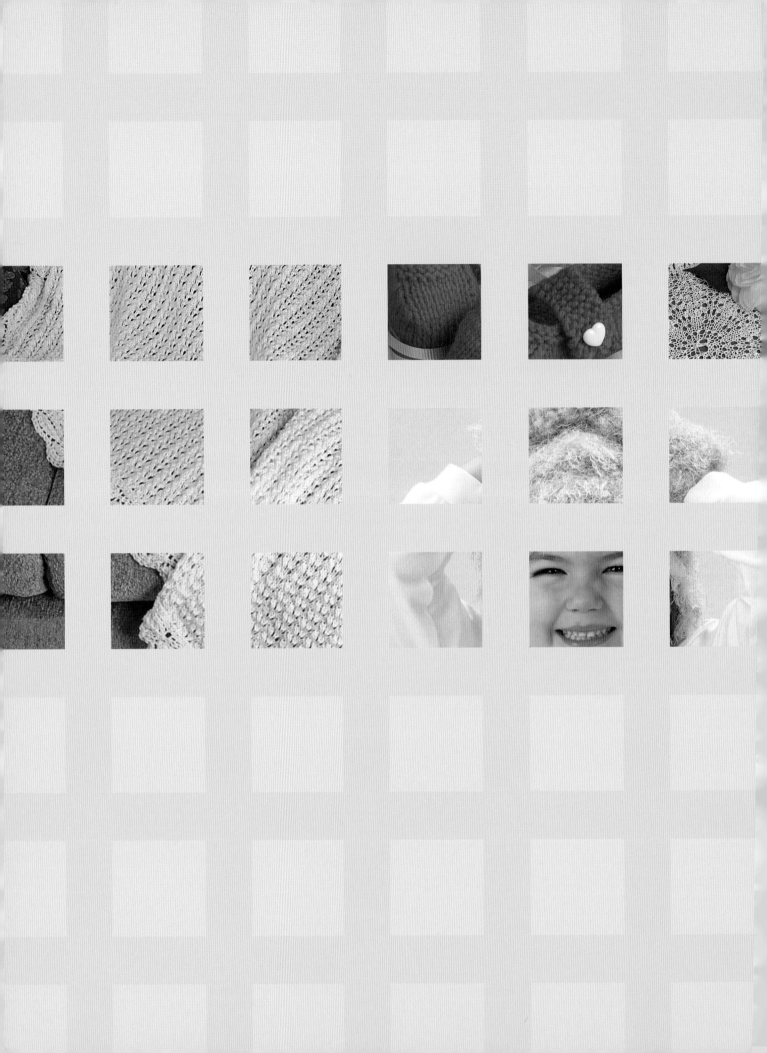

100 KNITTING PROJECTS

Jean Leinhauser and Rita Weiss

Sterling Publishing Co., Inc.
New York

Library of Congress Cataloging-in-Publication Data Available

2 4 6 8 10 9 7 5 3

Published by Sterling Publishing Co., Inc.
387 Park Avenue South, New York, NY 10016
© 2006 by The Creative Partners™ LLC
Distributed in Canada by Sterling Publishing
c/o Canadian Manda Group, 165 Dufferin Street,
Toronto, Ontario, Canada M6K 3H6
Distributed in the United Kingdom by GMC Distribution Services
Castle Place, 166 High Street, Lewes, East Sussex, England BN7 1XU
Distributed in Australia by Capricorn Link (Australia) Pty. Ltd.
P.O. Box 704, Windsor, NSW 2756, Australia

Printed in China
All rights reserved

Sterling ISBN-13: 978-1-4027-2310-0
ISBN-10: 1-4027-2310-5

For information about custom editions, special sales, premium
and corporate purchases, please contact Sterling Special Sales
Department at 800-805-5489 or specialsales@sterlingpub.com.

INTRODUCTION

What can you make with two sticks and some string?

Not much, but change that to two knitting needles and some yarn and a whole world of creative fun opens to you. The versatility of knitting is clearly demonstrated in this book of 100 delightful designs, ranging from intricate high-fashion sweaters to humble dishcloths.

Like most knitters you probably have that special need for more and more patterns. We've tried to meet that need by filling this book with 100 spectacular patterns, all designed to keep you busy making "just one more row".

Whether you're a new knitter ready to move on from scarves to something more interesting, or a knitter who's done it all but still loves a new challenge, you'll find designs perfect for you in this collection.

Knitted designs for women and little girls, babies, men and boys—they are all here in this book, and we've used a wide range of beautiful, up-to-the-minute yarns to make the projects stand out in a crowd.

So get out those "sticks", grab your favorite yarn and start knitting whether it's a simple afghan, a magnificent sweater, or even a lace doily. This book was a labor of love for us, and we know that each time you start one of this projects, it will be a labor of love for you.

Jean Leinhauser   *Rita Weiss*

CONTENTS

CONTENTS

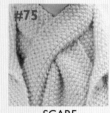

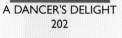

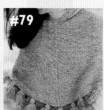

CABLE CARDIGAN

Designed by Donna Druchunas

MATERIALS

Bulky weight yarn
  1000 (1000, 1200, 1200) yards
  teal

Note: *Photographed model made with Plymouth Outback Mohair color #801, Teal*

Seven 1" diameter buttons

Size 7 (4.5 mm) straight knitting needles

16" Size 7 circular knitting needle

Size 9 (5.5 mm) straight knitting needles (or size required for gauge)

GAUGE

16 sts = 4" in stock st (knit 1 row, purl 1 row) with larger needles

Note: *Instructions are written for size Small; changes for sizes Medium, Large and X-Large are in parentheses. When only one number is listed, it applies to all sizes.*

SIZES	Small	Medium	Large	X-Large
Body Bust Measurments	32"	36"	40"	44"
Finished Bust Measurements	36"	40"	44"	48"

INSTRUCTIONS

Back

Starting at lower edge with smaller straight needles, CO 67 (75, 83, 91) sts.

Row 1 (right side): K1; *P1, K1; rep from * across.

Row 2: P1; *K1, P1; rep from * across.

Rep Rows 1 and 2 until piece measures 2 1/2", ending by working a right-side row.

Increase Row (wrong side): Continue in ribbing patt and inc 15 sts evenly spaced across row: 82 (90, 98, 106) sts.

Change to larger straight needles.

Body

Row 1 (right side): K4 (6, 8, 10); *P2, K6, P2 (these 10 sts form cable section); K6 (7, 8, 9); rep from * 3 more times; P2, K6, P2 (cable section); K4 (6, 8, 10).

Row 2: P4 (6, 8, 10); *K2, P6, K2, P6 (7, 8, 9); rep from * 3 more times; K2, P6, K2, P4 (6, 8, 10).

Row 3: K4 (6, 8, 10); *P2, sl next 3 sts to cable needle and hold in back, K3, K3 from cable needle, P2; K6 (7, 8, 9); rep from * 3 more times, *P2, sl next 3 sts to cable needle and hold in back, K3, K3 from cable needle, P2, K4 (6, 8, 10).

Row 4: Rep Row 2.

Rows 5 through 8: Rep Rows 1 through 4.

Rep Rows 1 through 8 until back measures 22" (23", 24", 25"). BO.

Left Front

Starting at lower edge and with smaller straight needles, CO 41 (45, 49, 53) sts.

Ribbing

Row 1 (right side): *P1, K1; rep from * to last 5 sts, place marker, K5.

Row 2: K5, sl marker, *P1, K1; rep from * across.

Rep Rows 1 and 2 until ribbing measures 2 1/2".

Increase Row (wrong side): Continue in ribbing patt as established and inc 4 sts evenly spaced across row: 45 (49, 53, 57) sts.

Change to larger straight needles.

Body

Row 1 (right side): K4 (6, 8, 10); P3, K6, P2; K6 (7, 8, 9) P2, K6, P2; K10 (11, 12, 13); sl marker, K5.

Row 2: K5, sl marker, P10 (11, 13, 13); K2, P6, K2; P6 (7, 8, 9); K2, P6, K2; P4 (6, 8, 10).

Row 3: K4 (6, 8, 10): P2, sl next 3 sts to cable needle and hold in back, K3, K3 from cable needle, P2; K6 (7, 8, 9); P2, sl next 3 sts to cable needle and hold in back, K3, K3 from cable needle, P2; K10 (11, 12, 13), sl marker, K5.

Row 4: Rep Row 2.

Rows 5 through 8: Rep Rows 1 through 4.

Rep Rows 1 through 8 until front measures 20" (21", 22", 23"). End by working a right-side row.

Neck Shaping

Row 1 (wrong side): BO 12 (12, 13, 13) sts, work in patts as established to end of row: 33 (37, 40, 44) sts.

Continue in patt as established and BO 2 sts at beg of every following wrong-side row 2 times. Then dec 1 st at beg of every wrong-side row 2 (2, 3, 3) times: 27 (31, 33, 37) sts at end of last row.

When front measures 22" (23", 24", 25"), BO rem sts.

Mark placement for 7 buttons, the first 1" above bottom and the last ½" below neck edge with the rest evenly spaced between.

Right Front

Starting at lower edge with smaller straight needles, CO 41 (45, 49, 53) sts.

Ribbing

Row 1 (right side): K5, place marker; *P1, K1, rep from * across.

Row 2: *P1, K1, rep from * to marker, sl marker, K5.

Rep Rows 1 and 2 until ribbing measures 1". End by working a wrong-side row.

Buttonhole (right side): K3, YO, K2tog, work to end of row.

Continue in patt as established until ribbing measures 2½".

Increase Row (wrong side): Continue in ribbing patt as established and inc 4 sts evenly spaced across row: 45 (49, 53, 57) sts.

Change to larger straight needles.

Body

Row 1 (right side): K5, slip marker, K10 (11, 12, 13); P2, K6, P2; K6 (7, 8, 9); P2, K6, P2; K4 (6, 8, 10).

Row 2: P4 (6, 8, 10); K2, P6, K2; P6 (7, 8, 9); K2, P6, K2; P10 (11, 12, 13), sl marker, K5.

Row 3: K4 (6, 8, 10); P2, sl next 3 sts to cable needle and hold in back, K3, K3 sts from cable needle, P2; K6 (7, 8, 9); P2, sl next 3 sts to cable needle and hold in back, K3, K3 sts from cable needle; K10 (11, 12, 13), sl marker, K5.

Row 4: Rep Row 2.

Rows 5 through 8: Rep Rows 1 through 4.

Rep Rows 1 through 8, working a buttonhole to correspond to each marker on left front edge until front measures 20" (21", 22", 23"), ending by working a wrong-side row.

Neck Shaping

Row 1 (right side): BO 12 (12, 13, 13) sts, work in patt as established to end of row: 33 (37, 40, 44) sts

Continue in patt as established and BO 2 sts at beg of every following right-side row 2 times, then K2tog at beg of every right-side row 2 (2, 3, 3) times: 27 (31, 33, 37) sts at end of last row.

When front measures 22" (23", 24", 25"). BO rem sts.

Sleeve (make 2)

Starting at lower edge with smaller straight needles, CO 29 (31, 33, 25) sts.

Cuff

Row 1 (right side): K1; *P1, K1, rep from * across.

Row 2: P1; *K1, P1, rep from * across.

Rep Rows 1 and 2 until ribbing measures 2 1/2". End by working a right-side row.

Increase Row (wrong side): Continue in ribbing patt as established and inc 3 sts spaced evenly across row: 32 (34, 36, 38) sts.

Change to larger straight needles.

Arm

Row 1 (right side): K11 (12, 13, 14); P2, K2, P2; K11 (12, 13, 14).

Row 2: P11 (12, 13, 14); K2, P6, K2; P11 (12, 13, 14).

Row 3: K11 (12, 13, 13); P2, sl next 3 sts to cable needle and hold in back; K3, K3 from cable needle, P2; K11 (12, 13, 14).

Row 4: Rep Row 2.

Rows 5 through 8: Rep Rows 1 through 4.

Rep Rows 1 through 8, and at same time, begin sleeve shaping: Inc at beg and end of every 3rd row 21 (22, 23, 23) times: 74 (78, 82, 84) sts at end of last row.

When sleeve measures 17" (17", 18", 18"). BO 32 (34, 36, 37) sts at beg of next 2 rows: 10 sts.

Continue working in patt as est until sleeve saddle measures 6" (6 3/4", 7 1/4", 8 1/4"). BO.

Finishing

Sew shoulders to saddle portion of sleeve.

Sew sleeves to armholes.

Sew side and underarm seams.

Collar

With right-side facing and circular needle, pick up and knit 85 (89, 93, 97) sts around neck edge between front bands.

Row 1 (right side): K1, *P1, K1; rep from * across.

Row 2: P1; *K1, P1; rep from * across.

Rep Rows 1 and 2 until collar measures 6 1/2", ending by working a wrong-side row.

BO loosely. Weave in ends.

Sew buttons on left band opposite buttonholes.

#2 RETRO SOAKER

Designed by Theresa Belville for Little Turtle Knits

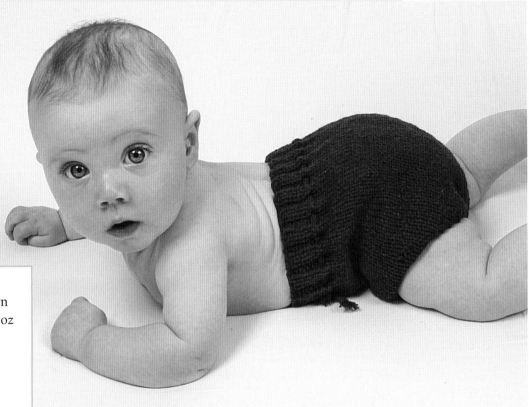

MATERIALS

DK weight 100% wool yarn
1 3/4 (2, 2, 5, 3, 3 1/2, 4) oz
crimson

Note: *Photographed model made with Chester Farms Cestari 3 ply, Crimson*

2 stitch markers

16" Size 6 (4 mm) circular knitting needle (or size required for gauge)

16" Size 4 (3.5 mm) circular knitting needle (or 2 sizes smaller than size required for gauge)

Size G (4 mm) crochet hook

GAUGE

22 sts and 30 rows = 4" with larger needles in stock st (knit 1 row, purl 1 row when working in rows; knit every row when working in rnds)

Note: *Instructions are written for size preemie; changes for larger sizes are in parentheses.*

SIZES	Preemie	Newborn	Small	Medium	Large	Toddler
Waist	15"	17"	18 1/2"	20"	21 1/2"	23"
Rise	10 1/2"	12 1/2"	14"	16"	18"	20"
Thigh	8"	9"	10"	11"	12"	14"
Weight range in pounds	under 8	8 - 12	10 - 18	16 - 22	20 - 26	over 25

INSTRUCTIONS

Waist Ribbing

With smaller needles, CO 80 (96, 104, 112, 120, 128) sts; join, being careful not to twist sts. Mark beg of rnd.

Work in K2, P2 rib for 6 (8, 10, 10, 10, 12) rnds.

Eyelet Rnd: K2; *K2tog, YO; rep from * until 2 sts rem, K2.

Body

Change to larger needles.

Rnd 1: K20 (24, 26, 28, 30, 32), place Marker A; K40 (48, 52, 56, 60, 64), place Marker B, K20 (24, 26, 28, 30, 32) sts.

Rnds 2 through 7: Knit.

Rnd 8 (Short Row Rnd): Knit to 1 st before Marker B, wrap next stitch and turn, purl to 1 st before Marker A, wrap next stitch and turn, knit to end of round.

Rep Rnds 2 through 8 until work measures 3 1/2" (4 1/2", 5 1/4", 6 1/2", 7 1/2", 8 1/2") from CO-edge, measured on the front, not over the short rows.

Crotch Flaps

Dividing Row: Knit to 3 (3, 4, 4, 5, 5) sts before Marker A, BO 4 (4, 6, 6, 7, 8) sts, remove marker; knit to 1 (1, 2, 2, 2, 3) sts before Marker B, BO 4 (4, 6, 6, 7, 8) sts, remove marker, knit to end. Do not join. From here on, work in rows.

There are now 34 (42, 44, 48, 50, 52) sts for the Front Flap and 38 (46, 48, 52, 56, 58) sts for the Back Flap.

Front Flap

Row 1 (wrong side): Sl 1, purl across.

Row 2: Sl 1, K1, SPO, knit until 3 sts rem, sl 1, K1, PSSO, K1.

Rep Rows 1 and 2 until 22 (24, 26, 28, 30, 32) sts rem.

Work 0 (2, 4, 6, 6, 8) rows even in stock st, ending by working a right-side row.

Leave rem sts on needle, but cut yarn, leaving a 12" yarn end.

Back Flap

With right side facing, join yarn and knit across.

Row 1: Sl 1, purl across.

Row 2: Sl 1, K1, SPO, knit until 3 sts rem, sl 1, K1, PSSO, K1.

Rep Rows 1 and 2, one (2, 2, 3, 4, 4) times more, then Row 1 one time.

Crotch

Row 1: Sl 1, K1, SP2O, knit until 4 sts rem, P2SSO, K1.

Row 2: Sl 1, purl across.

Rep Rows 1 and 2 until 22 (24, 26, 28, 30, 32) sts rem.

Work 0 (0, 2, 2, 2, 4) rows even in stock st, ending by working a right-side row.

Finishing

Hold front and back flaps together with wrong sides tog and sew.

Around each leg opening, with crochet hook sc in each sl st, and in every other bound-off st at top of the opening.

Make an I-cord drawstring (see Page 252) about twice the size of the waist opening. Weave drawstring through eyelets in ribbing at waist.

#3 ALLURING SCARF

Designed by Zena Low for Patons

SIZE
Approximately 7 ¹/₂" x 68"

MATERIALS
Fur-type yarn
  3 ¹/₂ oz red

Note: *Photographed model made with Patons® Allure #04532 Garnet*

Size 10 ¹/₂ (6.5 mm) knitting
  needles (or size required for
  gauge)

GAUGE
9 sts and 13 rows = 4" in stock st
  (knit 1 row, purl 1 row)

INSTRUCTIONS

CO 17 sts.

Rows 1 through 5: Knit.

Row 6 (wrong side): K2, P10, K2.

Row 7 (right side): Knit.

Rep Rows 6 and 7 until work measures 67" from CO row, ending by working a right-side row.

Knit 4 rows. BO.

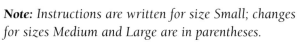

#4 KEYHOLE SWEATER

Designed by Bev Nimon for S.R. Kertzer Limited

Note: Instructions are written for size Small; changes for sizes Medium and Large are in parentheses.

SIZES	Small	Medium	Large
Body Bust Measurements	34"	36"	38"
Finished Bust Measurements	36"	39"	41"

MATERIALS

Faux fur type yarn
 9 (9, 9) oz blue

Ribbon yarn
 5 1/2 (5 1/2, 7 1/2) oz blue

Note: Photographed model made with S.R. Kertzer Baby Monkey #11 and Sari #55

Size 13 (9 mm) 36" long
 circular needle (or size
 required for gauge)

Size J (6 mm) crochet hook

4 stitch markers

One stitch holder

GAUGE

8 sts and 14 rows = 4" with one
 strand of each yarn held tog

INSTRUCTIONS

Body

Note: *Garment is worked in one piece to armholes.*

With one strand of each yarn held tog, CO 76 (84, 88) sts; join, being careful not to twist sts.

Rnd 1: Place marker; K38 (42, 44), place marker, knit to end of rnd. Markers indicate side seams.

Rnd 2: Purl.

Rnd 3: Knit.

Rnds 4 and 5: Rep Rnds 2 and 3.

Knit every rnd until piece measures 2 1/2".

Dec one st before and after each marker on next 2 rnds: 68 (76, 80) sts.

Work even until piece measures 4".

Inc one st before and after each marker: 72 (80, 84) sts.

Work even until piece measures 9 1/2" (9 1/2", 10").

Back Armhole Shaping

Place first 36 (40, 42) sts on a holder for Front.

Now work in rows:

Row 1 (wrong side): BO 3 (4, 4) sts, purl across: 33 (36, 38) sts.

Row 2: BO 3 (4, 4) sts, knit across: 30 (32, 34) sts.

Continue in stock st, dec one st each side, every other row 2 (3, 3) times: 26 (26, 28) sts.

Continue in stock st until piece measures 18" (18", 18 1/2"), ending by working a wrong-side row.

Dividing Row (right side): BO 2 (2, 2), K5 (5, 6) sts; attach a 2nd ball of yarn and BO12 (12, 12) back neck sts, knit across.

Left Back Shoulder and Neckline

Row 1 (wrong side): BO 2 (2, 2) sts, purl to last 2 sts, dec one st at neck edge: 4 (4, 5) sts.

Row 2: BO 2 (2, 2) sts, knit across.

Row 3: BO 2 (2, 3) sts.

Right Back Shoulder and Neckline

Row 1 (wrong side): Dec 1 st at neck edge, purl to end of row: 4 (4, 5) sts.

BO 2 (2, 2) sts at beg of next row.

BO rem 2 (2, 3) sts.

Front Armhole Shaping

Sl sts on holder onto left needle and hold with wrong side facing. Work now in rows.

Row 1 (wrong side): BO 3 (4, 4) sts, purl across: 33 (36, 38) sts.

19

Instructions continue on next page. →

Row 2: BO 3 (4, 4) sts, knit across: 30 (32, 34) sts.

Continue in stock st, dec one st each side, every other row 2 (3, 3) times: 26 (26, 28) sts.

Continue in stock st until piece measures 12" (12", 12½"), ending by working a wrong-side row.

Keyhole Opening

Row 1 (right side): K10 (10, 11) sts, BO 6 sts. Join a 2nd ball of yarn and knit across last 10 (10, 11) sts.

Work both sides of keyhole opening at same time, with each side being worked with separate ball of yarn.

Row 2: Purl.

Row 3: Knit.

Row 4: Purl.

Row 5 (right side): CO one st at each edge of keyhole, knit across.

Rows 6 through 9: Rep Rows 4 and 5.

Row 10: Purl across both sides of opening: 26 (26, 28) sts.

Continue working in stock st until piece measures 15½" (15½", 16"), ending by working a wrong-side row.

Front Neck Shaping

Knit 9 (9, 10) sts, attach another ball of yarn, BO center 8 (8, 8) sts, and knit across row.

Working both sides at once, dec one st at each neck edge, every other row 3 (3, 3) times.

Continue in stock st until piece measures 18" (18", 18½"), ending by working a wrong-side row.

Right Front Shoulder and Neckline

Row 1 (right side): BO 2 (2, 2) sts, knit across: 4 (4, 5) sts.

Row 2: BO 2 (2, 2) sts, purl across.

Row 3: BO 2 (2, 3) sts.

Left Front Shoulder and Neckline

Rep Rows 1 through 3 of Right Front and Neckline. Do not reverse shaping.

Finishing

Sew shoulder seams.

Armhole Edging

With crochet hook, work one row single crochet and one row of reverse single crochet around each armhole edge.

#5 RED, WHITE AND BLUE PUFFS

Designed by Rita Weiss

SIZE
45" x 60"

MATERIALS
Worsted weight yarn
  8 oz blue
  12 oz red
  12 oz white

Note: Photographed model made with Red Heart® Super Saver® #380 Windsor Blue and TLC® Amoré #3907 Red Velvet and #3001 White

36" Size 11 (8 mm) circular knitting needle (or size required for gauge)

GAUGE
16 sts = 5" in stock st (knit 1 row, purl 1 row)

INSTRUCTIONS

With blue, CO 142 sts; do not join, work back and forth in rows

Rows 1 through 4: Knit. At end of Row 4, finish off blue and join red.

Row 5 (right side): Knit.

Row 6: Purl

Rows 7 and 9: Rep Row 5.

Rows 8 and 10: Rep Row 6. At end of Row 10, finish off red and join blue.

Row 11 (right side): K4; *sl next st off left needle and unravel it 6 rows down to blue. Put right needle through blue lp from front of work, draw lp up and put it on left needle and knit lp off; K5; rep from * across.

Row 12: Purl. Finish off blue and join white.

Rows 13 through 18: Rep Rows 5 through 10.

At end of Row 18, finish off white and join blue.

Row 19: Rep Row 11.

Row 20: Purl. Finish off blue and join red.

Rep Rows 5 through 20 until afghan measures about 59", ending by working a Row 11.

On last rep do not finish off blue. Rep Rows 1 through 4 in blue.

BO; weave in all ends.

Fringe
Follow Single Knot Fringe Instructions on page 251. Cut blue strands 20" long and use one strand for each knot. Knot through each st across short ends of afghan.

21

#6 FOR THE SPECIAL MAN

Designed by Patons Design Staff

SIZES			
Scarf			
9" x 64 1/2"			
Socks	Medium	Large	X-Large
Finished Foot Length	9 1/2"	10 1/2"	11"

Sock Yarn

For Scarf

   1 3/4 oz medium grey (MC)

   1 3/4 oz dark grey (A)

   1 3/4 oz light grey (B)

   1 3/4 oz brown (C)

For Socks

   3 1/2 oz medium grey (MC)

   1 3/4 oz dark grey (A)

   1 3/4 oz light grey (B)

   1 3/4 oz brown (C)

For Gloves

   3 1/2 oz brown

Note: Photographed model made with Patons® Kroy Socks, #5401 Glencheck (MC), #5402 Gentry Grey (A), #54047 Windsor Tweed (B) and #54013 Hickory (C).

Size 2 (2.75 mm) knitting needles (or size required for gauge) for socks

One Size 2 (2.75 mm) spare knitting needle (for socks)

Size 3 (3.25 mm) knitting needles (or size required for gauge) for scarf and gloves

2 Stitch holders

Yarn bobbins (optional)

GAUGE

Scarf and Gloves

   28 sts and 36 rows = 4" with larger needles in stock st (knit 1 row, purl 1 row)

Socks

   34 sts and 44 rows = 4" with smaller needles in stock st (knit 1 row, purl 1 row)

STITCH GUIDE

M1: make one st by picking up horizontal lp lying before next st and knitting into back of lp: increase made

SCARF

INSTRUCTIONS

Note: When working color patt, wind bobbins or small balls of the colors to be used, one for each separate area of color in the design, Start new colors at appropriate points. To change colors, twist the two colors around each other where they meet, on wrong side, to avoid a hole.

With MC, CO 18 sts, With C, CO 18 sts, With B, cast CO 18 sts, With A, CO 18 sts: 72 sts.

Row 1 (right side): With A, K2, (P2, K4) twice, P2, K2; with B, K2, (P2, K4) twice, P2, K2; with C, K2, (P2, K4) twice, P2, K2; with MC, K2, (P2, K4) twice, P2, K2.

Row 2: With MC, P2, (K2, P4) twice; K2, P2; with C, P2, (K2, P4) twice, K2, P2; with B, P2, (K2, P4) twice, K2, P2; with A, P2, (K2, P4) twice, K2, P2.

Rows 3 through 20: Rep Rows 1 and 2.

Row 21: With MC, K18; with A, K18; with B, K18; with C, K18.

Row 22: With C, P2, (K2, P4) twice, K2, P2; with B, P2, (K2, P4) twice, K2, P2; with A, P2, (K2, P4) twice, K2, P2; with MC, P2, (K2, P4) twice, K2, P2.

Row 23: Rep Row 21.

Rows 24 through 39: Rep Rows 22 and 23.

Row 40: Rep Row 22.

Instructions continue on next page. ➡

Row 41: With C, K18; with MC, K18; with A, K18; with B, K18.

Row 42: With B, P2, (K2, P4) twice, K2, P2; with A, P2, (K2, P4) twice, K2, P2; with MC, P2, (K2, P4) twice, K2, P2; with C, P2, (K2, P4) twice, K2, P2.

Row 43: Rep Row 41.

Rows 44 through 59: Rep Rows 42 and 43.

Row 60: Rep Row 42.

Row 61: With B, K18; with C, K18; with MC, K18; with A, K18.

Row 62: With A, P2, (K2, P4) twice, K2, P2; with MC, P2, (K2, P4) twice, K2, P2; with C, P2, (K2, P4) twice, K2, P2; with B, P2, (K2, P4) twice, K2, P2.

Row 63: Rep Row 61.

Rows 64 through 79: Rep Rows 62 and 63.

Row 80: Rep Row 64.

Row 81: With C, K18; with MC, K18; with A, K18; with B, K18.

Row 82: With B, P2, (K2, P4) twice, K2, P2; with A, P2, (K2, P4) twice, K2, P2; with MC, P2, (K2, P4) twice, K2, P2; with C, P2, (K2, P4) twice, K2, P2.

Row 83: Rep Row 81.

Rows 84 through 99: Rep Rows 82 and 83.

Row 100: Rep Row 64.

Rep Rows 1 through 100 four more times; then rep Rows 1 through 80 once.

BO in patt.

SOCKS

INSTRUCTIONS (make 2)

Note: Instructions are written for size Medium; changes for Large and X-Large are in parentheses.

With MC, CO 72 sts loosely.

Row 1 (right side): *K1, P1; rep from * across.

Row 2: Rep Row 1.

Rep Rows 1 and 2 for 2 ½", ending by working a wrong-side row.

Work Rows 1 through 100 for scarf.

Divide for Instep and Heel

Sl first 18 sts onto a st holder for heel, Join yarn to rem sts and work even in patt across next 36 sts (instep or top of foot). Place rem 18 sts on a st holder for heel.

Instep

Work even in patt on the 36 instep sts until foot from divided row measures 6 ½", (7 ½", 8") ending by working a wrong-side row.

Shape Toe

Row 1: K1, sl 1, K1, PSSO; work even in patt to last 3 sts, K2tog, K1: 34 sts.

Row 2: P3, work even in patt to last 3 sts, P3.

Rep these 2 rows until 16 sts rem. Cut yarn and leave sts on spare needle.

Heel

Sl both sets of 18 sts onto needle, having back seam in center.

Join MC and with right side of work facing work across these 36 sts as follows:

Row 1: *Sl 1, K1; rep from * to end of row.

Row 2: Sl l, purl to end of row.

Rep Rows 1 and 2 until heel measures 2" (2 ¼", 2 ½") ending by working a Row 1.

Shape Heel

Row 1: Sl 1, P18, P2tog, P1, turn, leaving rem sts unworked.

Row 2: Sl l, K4, sl l, K1, PSSO, K1, turn.

Row 3: Sl l, P5, P2tog, P1, turn.

Row 4: Sl l, K6, sl l, K1, PSSO, K1, turn.

Cont in this manner, having one st more before dec, until there are 20 sts.

Pick Up Heel

Row 1: P20; pick up and K14 (16, 18) sts along side of heel, turn.

Row 2: K34 (36, 38); pick up and K14 (16, 18) sts along rem side of heel: 48 (52, 56) sts.

Row 3: Purl.

Shape Sole

Row 1: K1, sl l, K1, PSSO, knit to last 3 sts, K2tog, K1.

Row 2: Purl.

Rep Rows 1 and 2 until 36 sts rem.

Work even until sole measures same length as instep to beg of toe shaping, ending by working a purl row.

Shape Toe

Row 1: K1, sl 1, K1, PSSO; work even in patt to last 3 sts, K2tog, K1: 34 sts.

Row 2: P3, work even in patt to last 3 sts, P3.

Rep these 2 rows until 16 sts rem. Cut yarn and leave sts on needle.

Sew 2 sets of 16 sts tog. Sew foot and leg seams, Block on sock blockers or press lightly on wrong side using a damp cloth.

GLOVES

INSTRUCTIONS

Right Glove

With brown, CO 49 sts.

Cuff

Row 1 (right side): K1; *P1, K1; rep from * across.

Row 2: PI; *K1, P1; rep from * across.

Rep these 2 rows for 3 ½", ending by working a wrong-side row.

Next Row: Knit.

Next Row: Purl

Rep these 2 rows twice.

Thumb Gusset

Row 1: K26; (K1, M1) twice; knit across: 51sts.

Row 2: Purl

Row 3: Knit.

Row 4: Purl

Row 5: K27, M1, K3, MI; knit across: 53 sts.

Instructions continue on next page. →

Rows 6 through 8: Rep Rows 2 through 4.

Row 9: K27, M1, K5, M1; knit across: 55 sts.

Rows 10 through 12: Rep Rows 2 through 4.

Row 13: K27, M1, K7, M1; knit across: 57 sts.

Rows 14 through 16: Rep Rows 2 through 4.

Row 17: K27, M1, K9, M1; knit across: 59 sts.

Rows 18 through 20: Rep Rows 2 through 4.

Row 21: K27, M1, K11, M1; knit across: 61 sts.

Rows 22 through 24: Rep Rows 2 through 4.

Rows 25 and 26: Purl.

Thumb

Row 1: K40, turn, leaving rem sts unworked.

Row 2: P13, CO 4 sts, turn: 17 sts.

Row 3: Knit.

Row 4: Purl.

Rows 5 through 24: Rep Rows 3 and 4.

Row 25: K2tog, (K1, K2tog) 5 times: 11 sts.

Row 26: Purl.

Row 27: (K2tog) 5 times, K1: 6 sts.

Row 28: Purl.

Cut yarn. Thread end into a tapestry needle and through rem sts. Draw up and fasten securely. Sew seam.

With right side of work facing, pick up and knit 5 sts from CO sts at base of thumb, Knit to end of row: 53 sts.

Row 1 (wrong side): Purl.

Row 2: Knit.

Rows 3 through 16: Rep Rows 1 and 2.

Row 17: Purl.

First Finger

Row 1: With right side facing, K34, turn, leaving rem sts unworked.

Row 2: P15, turn, CO 2 sts, turn: 17 sts.

Row 3: Knit.

Row 4: Purl.

Rows 5 through 28: Rep Rows 3 and 4.

Row 29: (K2, K2tog) 4 times, K1: 13 sts.

Row 30: Purl.

Row 31: (K1, K2tog) 4 times, K1: 9 sts.

Row 32: Purl.

Cut yarn. Thread end into a tapestry needle and through rem sts. Draw up and fasten securely. Sew seam.

Second Finger

Row 1: With RS of work facing, pick up and knit 3 sts at base of first finger, K7, turn.

Row 2: P17, turn; CO 2 sts, turn: 19 sts.

Row 3: Knit.

Row 4: Purl.

Rows 5 through 30: Rep Rows 3 and 4.

Row 31: (K2, K2tog) 4 times, K3: 15 sts.

Row 32: Purl.

Row 33: (K1, K2tog) 5 times: 10 sts.

Row 34: Purl.

Cut yarn. Thread end into a tapestry needle and through rem sts. Draw up and fasten securely. Sew seam.

Third Finger

Row 1: With right side of work facing, pick up and knit 3 sts at base of second finger, K7, turn.

Row 2: P17, turn; CO 2 sts, turn: 19 sts.

Row 3: Knit.

Row 4: Purl.

Rows 5 through 28: Rep Rows 3 and 4.

Row 29: (K2, K2tog) 4 times, K3: 15 sts.

Row 30: Purl.

Row 31: (K1, K2tog) 5 times: 10 sts.

Row 32: Purl.

Cut yarn. Thread end into a tapestry needle and through rem sts. Draw up and fasten securely. Sew seam.

Fourth Finger

Row 1: With right side of work facing, pick up and knit 3 sts at base of 3rd finger, K5, turn.

Row 2: P13.

Row 3: Knit.

Row 4: Purl.

Rows 5 through 20: Rep Rows 3 and 4.

Row 21: (K1, K2tog) 4 times, K1: 9 sts.

Row 22: Purl.

Row 23: (K2tog) 4 times, K1: 5 sts.

Row 24: Purl.

Cut yarn. Thread end into a tapestry needle and through rem sts. Draw up and fasten securely.

Sew side and cuff seams, reversing seam for cuff turnback.

Left Glove

Work same as Right Glove to Thumb Gusset.

Left Glove Thumb Gusset

Row 1: K19, (M1, K1) twice, knit across: 51 sts.

Row 2: Purl.

Row 3: Knit.

Row 4: Purl.

Row 5: K21, MI, K3, MI, knit across: 53 sts.

Rows 6 through 8: Rep Rows 2 through 4.

Row 9: K21, M1, K5, M1, knit across: 55 sts.

Rows 10 through 12: Rep Rows 2 through 4.

Row 13: K21, M1, K7, M1, knit across: 57 sts.

Rows 14 through 16: Rep Rows 2 through 4.

Row 17: K21, M1, K9, M1; knit across: 59 sts.

Rows 18 through 20: Rep Rows 2 through 4.

Row 21: K21, M1, K11, M1; knit across: 61 sts.

Rows 22 through 24: Rep Rows 2 through 4.

Row 25 and 26: Purl.

Instructions continue on next page. →

Thumb

Row 1: K34, turn, CO 4 sts, turn.

Row 2: P17, turn.

Complete as given for thumb of Right Glove.

With right side of work facing, pick up and knit 5 sts from cast on sts at base of thumb, knit to end of row: 53 sts.

Row 1 (wrong side): Purl.

Row 2: Knit.

Rows 3 through 16: Rep Rows 1 and 2.

Row 17: Purl.

First Finger

Row 1: K34, turn. CO 2 sts, turn.

Row 2: P17, turn.

Complete as given for first finger of Right Glove.

Second Finger

Row 1: With right side of work facing, pick up and knit 3 sts at base of first finger, K7, CO 2 sts, turn.

Row 2: P19, turn.

Complete as for 2nd finger of Right Glove.

Third Finger

Row 1: With right side of work facing, pick up and knit 3 sts at base of 2nd finger, K7, CO 2 sts, turn.

Row 2: P19, turn.

Complete as for 3rd Finger of Right Glove.

Fourth Finger

Work as for 4th Finger of Right Glove.

Sew side and cuff seam, reversing seam for cuff turnback.

#9 FOR AN ENCHANTED EVENING

Designed by Bev Nimon for S.R. Kertzer Limited

SIZE
24" x 72" before fringing

MATERIALS
Eyelash yarn
   250 g (8 ¾ oz) black

Metallic novelty yarn
   75 g (2 ¾ oz) black

Note: Photographed model made with S.R. Kertzer Baby Monkey #12 Black and Baffi #100 Black

Size 17 (12.75 mm) knitting needles
   (or size required for gauge)

GAUGE
9 sts = 6" with 1 strand of each yarn
   held tog

PATTERN STITCH
Row 1 (right side): K2; *YO, K2 tog; rep from * to last st, K1.

Row 2: K1, purl to last 2 sts, K2.

Rep Rows 1 and 2 for patt.

INSTRUCTIONS

Note: Work with 1 strand of each yarn held tog throughout pattern.

CO 37 sts.

Rows 1 through 3: Knit.

Work in pattern stitch until piece measures 72". BO loosely.

Following fringe instructions on page 251, cut 11" lengths of yarn. With 3 strands in each knot, tie knots 3" apart across each short end of shawl.

#10 FUN AND FURRY VEST

Designed by Patons Design Staff

Note: *Instructions are written for size 2; changes for sizes 4 and 6 are in parentheses.*

SIZES	2	4	6
Body Chest Measurements	21 $^1/_2$"	23"	25"
Finished Chest Measurements	25"	27"	29"

MATERIALS

Eyelash type yarn
  3 $^1/_2$ (3 $^1/_2$, 5 $^1/_4$) oz variegated

Note: *Photographed model made with Patons® Cha Cha #2002 Vegas*

2 stitch holders

2 stitch markers

Size 11 (8 mm) knitting needles
  (or size required for gauge)

GAUGE

11 sts and 16 rows = 4" in stock
  st (knit 1 row, purl 1 row)

INSTRUCTIONS

Note: Vest is worked in one piece.

Starting at bottom, CO 62 (67, 72) sts loosely.

Rows 1 through 4: Knit.

Row 5: Knit, increasing 6 (7, 8) sts evenly spaced: 68 (74, 80) sts.

Row 6 (right side): Knit.

Row 7: K3, purl to last 3 sts, K3.

Rep Rows 6 and 7 until work measures 4" (4 1/2", 5") from CO edge, ending by working a wrong-side row.

Dividing Row: K15 (16,18) for Right front; place these sts on a st holder. BO 4 sts for underarm; K30 (34, 36) for Back and place these sts on a st holder. BO 4 sts for underarm; K15 (16, 18) for Left Front.

Left Front

Row 1 (wrong side): K3, purl to last 3 sts, K3.

Row 2: Knit to last 5 sts, K2tog, K3: 14 (15, 17) sts.

Row 3: Rep Row 1.

Row 4: Knit.

Rep last 4 rows 4 (3, 5) more times. At end of last row: 10 (12, 12) sts.

Rep Rows 3 and 4 until armhole measures 5" (5 1/2", 6") from underarm, ending by working Row 3. BO.

Back

With wrong side of work facing, place 30 (34, 36) sts from back holder on a needle and join yarn.

Row 1 (wrong side): K3, purl to last 3 sts, K3.

Row 2: Knit.

Rep Rows 1 and 2 until armhole measures 5" (5 1/2", 6"), ending by working Row 1. BO. Place markers 10 (12, 12) sts in from side edges for shoulders.

Right Front

With wrong side of work facing, place 15 (16, 18) sts from right front stitch holder on a needle.

Row 1 (wrong side): Join yarn and K3, purl to last 3 sts, K3.

Row 2: K3, K2tog, knit across: 14 (15, 17) sts.

Row 3: Rep Row 1.

Row 4: Knit.

Rep last 4 rows 4 (3, 5) more times. At end of last row: 10 (12, 12) sts.

Rep Rows 3 and 4 until armhole measures 5" (5 1/2", 6"), ending by working Row 3. BO.

Finishing

Sew shoulder seams.

Ties (make 2)

CO 30 sts. BO.

Sew ties to beg of V-neck shaping as shown in the photo.

#11 CABLES FROM THE TOP DOWN

Designed by Nazanin S. Fard

Note: *Instructions are written for size Small; changes for Medium and Large are in parentheses.*

SIZES	Small	Medium	Large
Body Bust Measurements	32"	36"	40"
Garment Bust Measurements	36"	40"	44"

MATERIALS

Worsted weight yarn
   21 (24 ½, 28) oz dark rose

Note: *Photographed model made with Plymouth Encore #1048 dark rose*

Cable needle

Stitch markers

Stitch holders

Four Size 8 (5 mm) double
   pointed knitting needles
   (dpn)

29" Size 8 (5 mm) circular
   knitting needle (or size
   required for gauge)

16" Size 8 (5 mm) circular
   knitting needle (or size
   required for gauge)

GAUGE

24 stitches = 4" in K2, P2 rib
   without stretching

STITCH GUIDE

T3B: Work to one st before 2 knit sts. Sl next st onto cable needle and leave in back; K2 , then purl st from cable needle.

T3F: Work up to 2 knit sts. Sl next 2 sts onto cable needle and hold in front. Purl next st, K2 from cable needle.

T4B: Work to 2 sts before 2 knit sts. Sl next 2 sts onto cable needle and leave it in the back; K2, P2 from cable needle.

T4F: Work up to 2 knit stitches. Sl next 2 sts onto cable needle and hold in front; P2, then K2 from cable needle.

C4B: Work up to 4 knit stitches. Sl next 2 sts onto cable needle and leave in back; K2, then K2 from cable needle.

C4F: Work up to 4 knit stitches. Sl next 2 sts onto cable needle and hold in front; K2, then K2 from cable needle.

PM: Place Marker

M1 stitch (M1): Pick up the horizontal bar between the next 2 sts with left needle and knit into the back of the stitch: inc made.

Front Cable Pattern (24-st panel)

Row 1: P2, C4B, (P4, C4B) twice, P2.

Row 2 and every even numbered row: Knit the knit sts and purl the purl sts.

Row 3: P1, T3B, (T4F, T4B) twice, T3F, P1.

Row 5: T3B, P3, C4F, P4, C4F, P3, T3F.

Row 7: K2, P3, T3B, T4F, T4B, T3F, P3, K2.

Row 9: (K2, P3) twice, C4B, (P3, K2) twice.

Row 11: K2, P3, T3F, T4B, T4F, T3B, P3, K2.

Row 13: T3F, P3, C4F, P4, C4F, P3, T3B.

Row 15: P1, T3F, (T4B, T4F) twice, T3B, P1.

Rep Rows 1-16 for pattern.

INSTRUCTIONS

Starting at neck edge with smaller circular needle, CO 76, (82, 90) sts. Join, being careful not to twist sts.

Purl one row.

For Size Small Only

Rnd 1: Divide for st pattern starting with front: (P4, K4) 3 times, P4, place marker, K2 (seam sts), place marker, [P2, K2, P2] (sleeve sts), place marker, K2, place marker, [(P2, K2) 6 times, P2] (back sts), place marker, K2 (seam sts), place marker, [P2, K2, P2] (sleeve sts), place marker, K2, place marker: 76 sts.

For Size Medium Only

Rnd 1: Divide for st pattern starting with front: K2, (P4, K4) 3 times, P4, K2, PM, K2 (seam sts), place marker, [P2, K2, P2] (sleeve sts), place marker, K2, place marker, [(P2, K2) 7 times, P2] (back sts), place marker, K2 (seam sts), place marker, [P2, K2, P2] (sleeve sts), place marker, K2, place marker: 82 sts.

For Size Large Only

Rnd 1: Divide for st pattern starting with front: K2, (P4, K4) 3 times, P4, K2, place marker, K2 (seam sts), place marker, [(P2, K2) twice, P2] (sleeve sts), place marker, K2, place marker, [(P2, K2) 7 times, P2] (back sts), place marker, K2 (seam sts), place marker, [(P2, K2) twice, P2] (sleeve sts), place marker, K2, place marker: 90 sts.

For All Sizes

Rnd 2: Knit the knit sts and purl the purl sts.

Rnds 3 through 18: Follow instructions for cable pattern on the 24 center front sts, keep rem sts in rib pattern.

Shape Back Neck
(worked in short rows)

Row 19: Turn; work in patt on next 28 (30, 34) sts, turn.

Row 20: Work in patt on next 10 (10, 10) sts, turn.

Instructions continue on next page. →

Row 21: Work in patt on next 18 (20, 20) sts, turn.

Row 22: Work in patt on next 26 (30, 30) sts, turn.

Row 23: Work in patt on next 36 (40, 44) sts, turn.

Row 24: Work in patt on next 46 (50, 58) sts, turn.

Join work and now work in rnds.

Rnds 25 and 26: Work in patt.

Begin Raglan Shaping

Keeping patt as established, M1 at each side of seam sts every other rnd, 34 (36, 40) times changing to larger circular needle when you have enough sts:

96 (104, 112) sts for Front + 2 seam sts;

74 (78, 90) sts for Sleeve + 2 seam sts;

96 (102, 110) sts for Back + 2 seam sts;

74 (78, 90) sts for Sleeve + 2 seam sts.

Place sleeve sts plus one st on each side on a st holder.

Body

Rnd 1: Work Front sts in patt, CO 12 sts for underarm, work back sts in patt, CO 12 sts for underarm, place marker: 220 (234, 250) sts.

Work even in patt until piece measures 24" (24", 26") end by working Cable Patt Row 2.

Next Rnd: Work in patt to cable patt, then: P2, (K2tog) twice, [(P2tog) twice, (K2tog) twice] 2 times, P2: 14 sts of cable panel rem. Finish rnd in patt. BO in patt.

Sleeve (make 2)

Place 76 (80, 92) sleeve sts onto smaller circular needle. CO 5 sts for underarm, work across these 5 sts, place marker, inc 1, work in patt across sleeve sts, inc 1 in last st, place marker, turn, CO 5 more sts for underarm, turn. Work in rounds: 88 (92, 104) sts.

Note: *When necessary as dec progresses, move sts to dpns from circular needle.*

Work sleeve in patt, dec one st after first marker and one st before 2nd marker every 6th rnd 10 times: 68 (72, 84) stitches; then every 4th rnd 10 times: 48 (52, 64) stitches. Work even until Sleeve measures 16 1/2", (16 3/4", 17 1/2") from underarm. BO. Sew underarm seam.

#12 ELEGANT SHAWL

Designed by Patons Design Staff

SIZE
23" x 62"

MATERIALS
DK or sport weight yarn
  31 ¹/₂ oz lilac

Note: Photographed model made with Patons® Katrina #10305 Lilac

Size 9 (5.5 mm) knitting needles
  (or size required for gauge)

Cable Needle

GAUGE
18 sts and 24 rows = 4"

STITCH GUIDE
C4B: Slip next 2 sts onto cable needle and hold at back of work; K2, then K2 from cable needle.

INSTRUCTIONS

CO 104 sts.

Row 1 (right side): *K5; (YO, K2tog) 10 times; rep from * to last 4 sts, K4.

Row 2 (and all even rows): Purl.

Row 3: *K4; (sl 1, K1, PSSO, YO) 10 times, K1; rep from * to last 4 sts, K4.

Row 5: Rep Row 1.

Row 7: C4B, (sl 1, K1, PSSO, YO) 10 times, K1; rep from * to last 4 sts, C4B.

Row 8: Purl.

Rep Rows 1 through 8 until shawl measures 62" from CO edge ending by working a wrong-side row. BO.

Fringe
Following fringe instructions on page 251, cut 14" lengths of yarn. Taking 3 strands tog, knot into fringe along CO and BO edges as shown in photograph. Trim evenly.

#13 LADY VICTORIA'S FANCY HAT

Designed by Sheila Jones

SIZE
Fits up to 23" head

MATERIALS
Bulky weight mohair novelty yarn
150 yds red mix (A)

Worsted weight yarn
75 yards orchid (B)
75 yards fuchsia (C)

Note: Photographed model made with Trendsetter Dune #95 (A); and Brown Sheep Lamb's Pride Worsted #M102 Orchid Twist (B) and #M23 Fuchsia (C)

16" Size 10 (6 mm) circular knitting needles (or size required for gauge)

Four Size 10 (6 mm) double-point knitting needles

Size H (5 mm) crochet hook

Yarn needle

1 stitch marker

GAUGE
12 sts = 4" with one strand of color A and one strand of color B held tog in stock st (knit 1 row, purl 1 row).

Note: Hat is knit with two strands held tog throughout.

INSTRUCTIONS

With one strand of A and one strand of B held tog, CO 70 sts; join, place marker to indicate beg of rnd.

Rnd 1: Starting at bottom rolled edge, knit.

Knit until piece measures 4 1/2". Purl 3 rnds.

Next Rnd: Drop B and join C. With A and C, on wrong side with right side facing, *pick up the back lp of the last knit rnd (directly below the next st on needle) and sl this stitch to left needle. Knit the lifted stitch tog with the next stitch; rep from * around: 70 sts.

Shape Top

Note: Change to double point needles when necessary.

Rnds 1 through 3: Knit.

Rnd 4: *K5, K2tog; rep from* around: 60 sts.

Rnds 5 and 6: Knit

Rnd 7: *K4, SSK; rep from * around: 50 sts.

Rnd 8: Knit.

Rnd 9: * K3, K2tog; rep from * around: 40 sts.

Rnd 10: Knit.

Rnd 11: *K2, SSK; rep from * around: 30 sts.

Rnd 12: Knit.

Rnd 13: *K1, K2tog; rep from * around: 20 sts.

Rnd 14: *SSK; rep from * around: 10 sts.

Rnd 15: *K2tog; rep from * around: 5 sts. Finish off, leaving a long yarn end. Thread end into a yarn needle and draw through rem sts; draw up tightly and secure. Weave in ends.

With A and B held tog, with crochet hook work one rnd sc around bottom edge of hat.

Flower

With 2 strands of C, CO 54 sts.

Row 1: *P1, P2tog; rep from * across to last 2 sts, P2: 36 sts.

Row 2: *K3tog; rep from * across: 24 sts.

Row 3: *P3tog, rep from * across: 8 sts.

Row 4: (K2tog) 4 times: 4 sts.

Row 5: P2tog twice: 2 sts. BO, leaving a long end. Thread end into a yarn needle and draw up, fasten securely. Sew short edges of flower tog; sew flower to side of hat.

Cord Button

With 2 strands of A, CO 3 sts on one double-point needle. With another double-point, K3; *do not turn, slide sts to opposite end of needle. Take yarn around back of sts and with 2nd needle, K3; rep from * until piece measures 2 1/2". Finish off, leaving a long yarn end. Thread end into a yarn needle and draw through rem sts. Sew to center of flower, making a circle button.

#14 HUGS AND KISSES LAYETTE

SIZE
Instructions are written for one
 size, infant to 6 months.

MATERIALS
Sport or DK weight yarn
 10 oz pink

*Note: Photographed model made
with Lion Brand® MicroSpun #101
Peppermint Pink*

5 stitch holders

4 stitch markers

3 small buttons

Size 3 (3.25 mm) knitting needles

Size 4 (3.5 mm) knitting needles
 (or size required for gauge)

GAUGE
24 sts and 32 rows = 4" with
 larger needles in patt st.

SWEATER

INSTRUCTIONS

Back
With smaller needles, CO 55 sts. Work in
K1, P1 rib for ³/₄". Change to larger needles
and work in patt st until piece measures
8¹/₂" from beg, end by working a patt Row 4.

Shape Armholes
Row 1: BO 3 sts, knit across.

Row 2: BO 3 sts, purl across. Place rem 49
sts on a st holder.

Left Front
With smaller needles, CO 25 sts. Work as
for Back to armhole shaping.

Shape Armhole
Row 1: BO 3 sts, knit across.

Row 2: Purl.

Place rem 22 sts on a st holder.

Right Front
With smaller needles, CO 25 sts. Work as
for Back to Armhole Shaping.

Shape Armhole

Row 1: Knit.

Row 2: BO 3 sts, purl across.

Place rem 22 sts on a st holder.

Sleeve (make 2)

With smaller needles, CO 37 sts. Work in K1, P1 rib for ³⁄₄".

Change to larger needles and work in patt st for 6", ending by working a patt Row 4.

Shape Sleeve Cap

Row 1: BO 3 sts, knit across.

Row 2: BO 3 sts, purl across. Place rem 31 sts on a st holder.

Joining Row

With larger needles and wrong side facing, sl 22 sts from Left Front holder to needle, place marker; sl 31 sts from Sleeve holder to needle, place marker; sl 49 sts from Back holder to needle, place marker; sl 31 sts from Sleeve holder to needle, place marker; sl 22 sts from Right Front holder to needle: 155 sts.

Shape Raglans

Row 1: *Knit to within 2 sts of next marker, K2tog tbl (through the back loop), sl marker, K2tog; rep from * across, knit to end: 147 sts.

Row 2: Purl.

Rep Rows 1 and 2 thirteen times more; at same time, when raglan measures 2 ¹⁄₂", shape neck.

Shape Neck

Continue in Stock st and keeping raglan shaping as established, at beg of next 2 rows work first 4 sts, then place these 4 sts on a holder; then dec one st at beg and end of every other row at neck edge twice. On last purl row, P2tog before and after each marker. Place rem 23 sts on a st holder.

Neckband

With smaller needles and right side facing, pick up 49 sts along neck edge, including sts on holders, and work in K1, P1 rib for 6 rows. BO in rib.

Left Front Button Band

With right side facing and smaller needles, pick up and knit 79 sts along Left Front center edge (including neckband). Work in K1, P1 rib for 6 rows. BO in rib. Mark for 3 buttons as foll: First button at 5th st from top, next 2 buttons 8 sts apart.

Right Front Buttonhole Band

Work as for Left Front Button Band for 2 rows. On next row, work buttonholes opposite each marker as follows: BO one st; on following row CO one st over each BO st. Rib for 2 more rows. BO in rib.

Finishing

Sew side and sleeve seams. Sew on buttons.

BOOTIES

INSTRUCTIONS (make 2)

Starting at top of cuff, with smaller needles, CO 27 sts.

Work in K1, P1 rib for 4 rows. Change to larger needles.

Row 1 (right side): Knit.

Row 2: Purl

Row 3: K2; *YO, P1, P3tog, P1, YO, K1; rep from * across, ending last rep with K2.

Row 4: Purl.

Rows 5 through 8: Rep Rows 1 through 4.

Row 9: BO 9 sts, knit across.

Row 10: BO 9 sts, purl across: 9 sts rem.

Instep

Work even in stock st on 9 sts for 1 ½", ending by working a purl row. Cut yarn and place sts on a st holder.

With right side facing, join yarn and pick up 9 sts along the BO sts; pick up 8 sts along the instep; K9 sts from holder, pick up 8 sts along instep; pick up 9 sts along BO sts: 43 sts. Work even in stock st for 1", ending by working a purl row.

Shape Toe

Row 1: K2tog tbl, K18, sl 1, K2tog, PSSO, K18, K2tog: 39 sts.

Row 2: Purl.

Row 3: K2tog tbl, K16, sl 1, K2tog, PSSO, K16, k2tog: 35 sts.

Row 4: Purl.

Row 5: K2tog tbl, K14, sl 1, K2tog, PSSO, K14, K2tog: 31 sts.

BO as to purl. Sew back seam and sole.

HAT

INSTRUCTIONS

With smaller needles, CO 85 sts. Work in K1, P1 rib for 6 rows. Change to larger needles and begin to work in Patt St, inc 12 sts evenly spaced across Row 1: 97 sts.

Work Patt Rows 1 through 4 six times, dec 1 st at end of last row: 96 sts.

Dec Row 1: *K10, K2tog; rep from * across.

Dec Row 2: *P2tog, P9; rep from * across.

Dec Row 3: *K8, K2tog; rep from * across.

Dec Row 4: *P2tog, P7; rep from * across.

Cont dec every row, having one st fewer between decreases, until 16 sts rem. Cut yarn, leaving a long end. Thread yarn into a tapestry needle and draw through rem sts; pull up tightly and secure; sew back seam.

#15 BABY AFGHAN TOTE

Designed by Cynthia G. Grosch

SIZE
30" x 40" open

20" x 30" folded

MATERIALS
Chunky weight yarn
 900 grams blue

Note: *Photographed model made with Sirdar Yarn Denim Chunky #5165 Denim Blue Marl*

18 Size/No. 10 (21 mm) Sew-On Snaps

24" Size 15 circular knitting needle (or size required for gauge)

Two Size 15 double-point knitting needles (dpn)

GAUGE
11 sts and 18 rows = 4" over patt st

PATTERN STITCH
Row 1: *K1, yf, sl 1, yb; rep from * across

Row 2: P2; *yb, sl 1, yf, P1; rep from * across

Rep Rows 1 and 2 for patt.

INSTRUCTIONS

Starting at bottom, with circular needle CO 82 sts. Do not join; work back and forth in rows. Work in patt until piece measures 43". BO.

Finishing
With dpn CO 3sts. Following I-cord instructions on page 252, make two 38" lengths.

Fold each end of afghan 1 ½" to the wrong side and whipstitch to form casing for threading I-cord. Thread cords through casing. Knot each end of each cord. Pull cord on one 30" end and tie two ends tog to form bag handles. Rep at other 30" end for second handle.

Fold afghan in half (20" x 30") and sew top half of 9 snaps from one (30") end to fold, then sew bottom half of 9 snaps along same side of afghan from fold to other (30") end. Rep for other side of afghan. To form tote, snap the sides closed.

#16 RAGLAN TOP

Designed by Bernat Design Staff

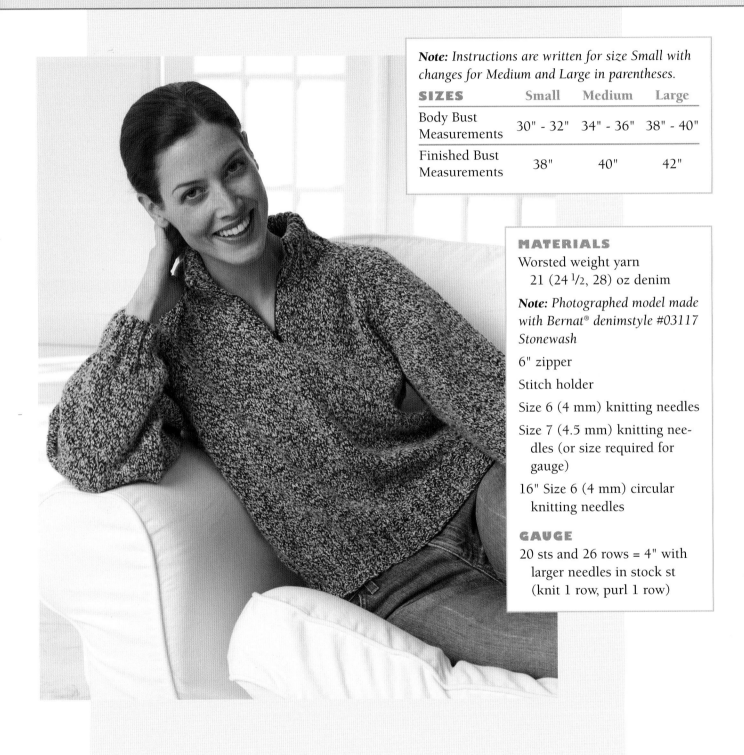

Note: *Instructions are written for size Small with changes for Medium and Large in parentheses.*

SIZES	Small	Medium	Large
Body Bust Measurements	30" - 32"	34" - 36"	38" - 40"
Finished Bust Measurements	38"	40"	42"

MATERIALS

Worsted weight yarn
   21 (24 ½, 28) oz denim

Note: *Photographed model made with Bernat® denimstyle #03117 Stonewash*

6" zipper

Stitch holder

Size 6 (4 mm) knitting needles

Size 7 (4.5 mm) knitting needles (or size required for gauge)

16" Size 6 (4 mm) circular knitting needles

GAUGE

20 sts and 26 rows = 4" with larger needles in stock st (knit 1 row, purl 1 row)

INSTRUCTIONS

Note: *Slip all sts as to knit unless otherwise specified.*

Back

With smaller straight needles CO 94 (98, 102) sts.

Row 1 (right side): K2; *P2, K2; rep from * across.

Row 2: P2; *K2, P2; rep from * across.

Rep Rows 1 and 2 for 2", ending by working a Row 2. On last row, inc 0 (2, 2) sts: 94 (100, 104 sts).

Change to larger straight needles and work in stock st until piece measures 11", ending by working a wrong-side (purl) row. BO 5 sts for underarms at beg of next 2 rows.

Raglan Shaping

Row 1: K2, sl 1, K1, PSSO; knit to last 4 sts, K2tog, K2.

Row 2: Purl.

Rep last 2 rows until 32 (34, 38) sts rem, ending by working a wrong-side row.

Work 0 (2, 0) rows even.

For Size Large Only
Next row: K2, sl 1, K1, PSSO, knit to last 4 sts, K2tog, K2.

Work 3 rows even.

Rep last 4 rows once more: 34 sts.

For All Sizes
BO

Front

Work as for back through Row 2 of Raglan Shaping.

Rep last 2 rows until 68 (66, 64) sts rem; ending by working a wrong-side row.

Divide for Neck Opening

Row 1: K2, sl 1, K1, PSSO; knit 30 (29, 28) sts (neck edge). Place rem sts on a stitch holder.

Row 2: Purl.

Row 3: K2, sl 1, K1, PSSO; knit across.

Rep last 2 rows, 8 times more: 24 (23, 22) sts.

Next row: Purl.

Shape Neck

Row 1: K2, sl 1, K1, PSSO, K14 (13, 12) sts (neck edge); turn. Place rem 6 sts onto a stitch holder.

Row 2: P2tog, purl across.

Row 3: K2, sl 1, K1, PSSO; knit to last 2 sts, K2tog.

Rep last 2 rows 0 (1, 1) more time.

Next row: Dec 0 (0, 1) st at beg of row. Purl to end of row: 14 (10, 8)

43

Instructions continue on next page. →

For Sizes Small and Medium Only

Row 1: K2, sl 1, K1, PSSO; knit to last 2 sts, K2tog.

Row 2: Purl.

Rep last 2 rows 4 (2) more times: 4 sts rem.

For Size Small Only

Next row: K2, sl 1, K1, PSSO.

For Size Medium Only

Next row: Knit to last 2 sts, K2tog.

For Size Large Only

Row 1: Knit to last 2 sts, K2tog.

Row 2: Purl.

Row 3: K2, sl 1, K1, PSSO; Knit to last 2 sts, K2tog.

Row 4: Purl.

Row 5: Knit.

Rep Rows 2 through 4 once more: 3 sts rem.

For All Sizes

Work 1 (1, 2) rows even.

Next row: Sl 1, K2tog, PSSO. Finish off.

Join yarn to rem sts.

Row 1: Knit to last 4 sts, K2tog, K2.

Row 2: Purl.

Row 3: Knit to last 4 sts, K2tog, K2.

Rep last 2 rows 8 times more: 24 (23, 22) sts.

Shape Neck

Row 1: Purl to last 6 sts (neck edge), turn. Place rem 6 sts onto st holder.

Row 2: Knit to last 4 sts, K2tog, K2.

Row 3: Purl to last 2 sts, P2tog.

Row 4: K2tog, knit to last 4 sts, K2tog, K2.

Rep last 2 rows 0 (1, 1) more time.

Next row: Dec 0 (0, 1) st at beg of row. Purl to end of row.

For Sizes Small and Medium Only

Next row: K2tog, knit to last 4 sts, K2tog, K2

Next row: Purl.

Rep last 2 rows 4 (2) more times: 4 sts.

Next row: K2tog, K2.

For Size Large Only

Row 1: K2tog, knit to end of row.

Row 2: Purl.

Row 3: K2tog, knit to last 4 sts, K2, K2tog.

Row 4: Purl.

Row 5: Knit.

Rep Rows 2 through 4 once more: 3 sts.

For All Sizes

Work 1 (1, 2) row(s) even.

Next row: Sl 1, K2tog, PSSO. Finish off.

Sleeve (make 2)

With smaller needles CO 46 (46, 50) sts.

Row 1 (right side): K2; *P2, K2; rep from * across.

Row 2: P2; *K2, P2; rep from * across.

Rep Rows 1 and 2 for 2 1/2", ending by working a Row 2, and inc 14 (16, 14) sts evenly spaced across last row: 60 (62, 64) sts.

Change to larger needles and proceed in stock st, inc 1 st each end of the 9th row and every 8th row until there are 82 (84, 86) sts.

Work even until sleeve from beg measures 17 ½" (18", 18") , ending by working a wrong-side row.

Raglan Shaping

Rows 1 and 2: BO 5 sts at beg of row.

Row 3: K2, sl 1, K1, PSSO; knit to last 4 sts, K2tog, K2.

Row 4: P2, P2tog, purl to last 4 sts, P2togtbl, P2.

Rep last 2 rows 4 (2, 0) times more: 52 (62, 72) sts.

Next Row: K2, sl 1, K1, PSSO, knit to last 4 sts, K2tog, K2.

Next Row: Purl.

Rep last 2 rows until 10 sts rem. BO.

Finishing
Neckband

Sew raglan seams. With right side facing and circular needle, knit across 6 sts from right front. Pick up and knit 12 sts up right front neck edge, 10 sts from right sleeve. Knit across 32 (34, 36) sts from back st holder, inc 2 (0, 2) sts evenly across. Pick up and knit 10 sts from left sleeve and 12 sts down left neck edge. Knit across 6 sts from left front: 90 (90, 94) sts. Do not join; work in rows.

Beg with a Row 2, work in K2, P2 ribbing as for back for 5". BO in ribbing.

Fold collar in half to wrong side and sew into neck.

Sew in sleeves. Sew side and sleeve seams. Sew in zipper.

#17 BEAUTIFUL BOBBLES

Designed by Rita Weiss

SIZE
45" x 60"

MATERIALS
Bulky weight mohair-type yarn
37 1/2 oz blue multicolor

Note: *Photographed model made with Lion Brand® Jiffy® #360 Midnight Blues*

36" Size 10 1/2 (6.5 mm) circular knitting needle (or size required for gauge)

GAUGE
4 sts = 1" in stock st (knit 1 row, purl 1 row)

INSTRUCTIONS

Note: Always slip stitches as to knit.

CO 181 sts; do not join, work back and forth in rows.

Row 1 and all wrong-side rows: K4; *P23, K2; rep from * to last 2 sts, K2.

Row 2 (right side): K2, P2; *sl 1, K1, PSSO; K6, (YO, K1) twice; sl 1, K2tog, PSSO; (K1, YO) twice; K6, K2tog, P2; rep from * across to last 2 sts, K2.

Row 4: K2, P2; *sl 1, K1, PSSO; K5, YO, K1, YO, K2, sl 1, K2tog, PSSO; K2, YO, K1, YO, K5, K2tog, P2; rep from * to last 2 sts, K2.

Row 6: K2, P2; *sl 1, K1, PSSO; K4, YO, K1, YO, Bobble; K2, sl 1, K2tog, PSSO; K2, Bobble; YO, K1, YO, K4, K2tog, P2; rep from * to last 2 sts, K2.

Row 8: K2, P2; *sl 1, K1, PSSO; K3, YO, K1, YO, Bobble; K3, sl 1, K2tog, PSSO; K3, Bobble; YO, K1, YO, K3, K2tog, P2; rep from * to last 2 sts, K2.

Row 10: K2, P2; *sl 1, K1, PSSO; K2, YO, K1, YO, Bobble; K4, sl 1, K2tog, PSSO; K4, Bobble; YO, K1, YO, K2, K2tog, P2; rep from * to last 2 sts, K2.

Row 12: K2, P2; *sl 1, K1, PSSO; (K1, YO) twice, Bobble; K5, sl 1, K2tog, PSSO; K5, Bobble; (YO, K1) twice; K2tog, P2; rep from * to last 2 sts, K2.

Row 14: K2, P2; *sl 1, K1, PSSO; YO, K1,YO, Bobble; K6, sl 1, K2tog, PSSO; K6, Bobble; YO, K1, YO, K2tog, P2; rep from * to last 2 sts, K2.

Rep Rows 1 through 14 until afghan measures approx 60". BO loosely.

#18 SHAKER STITCH PULLOVER

Designed by Sandy Scoville for Coats & Clark

Note: *Instructions are written for size Small; changes for sizes Medium and Large are in parentheses.*

SIZES	Small	Medium	Large
Body Bust Measurements	30 - 32"	34 - 36"	38 - 40"
Finished Bust Measurements	36"	39 $^1/_2$"	43"

MATERIALS

Worsted weight yarn
   20 (22, 25) oz cream

Note: *Photographed model made with Red Heart® Plush™ #9103 Cream*

Size 5 (3.75 mm) knitting needles

Size 7 (4.5 mm) knitting needles
   (or size required for gauge)

2 stitch markers or small safety pins

GAUGE

18 sts and 30 rows = 4" with
   larger needles in patt

INSTRUCTIONS

Back

Starting at bottom with smaller needles, CO 81 (89, 97) sts.

Ribbing

Row 1 (wrong side): K1; * P1, K1; rep from * across.

Row 2: P1; *K1B, P1; rep from * across.

Rows 3 through 12: Rep Rows 1 and 2. Change to larger needles and work in patt as follows:

Body

Row 1 (wrong side): K2 (3, 7); [P1, K1, P1] 0 (1, 1) time; [K5, P1, K1, P1, K7, P1, K1, P1] 4 times; [K5, P1, K1, P1] 0 (1, 1) time; K7 (3, 7).

Row 2: P2 (3, 7); [K1B, P1, K1B] 0 (1, 1) time; [P5, K1B, P1, K1B, P7, K1B, P1, K1B] 4 times; [P5, K1B, P1, K1B] 0 (1, 1) time; P7 (3, 7).

Rep Rows 1 and 2 until piece measures 13" from CO row, ending by working a wrong-side row.

Shape Armholes

Keeping continuity of patt, BO 5 (8, 8) sts at beg of next 2 rows: 71 (73, 81) sts. Work even in patt until armhole measures 6" (6", 7"), ending by working a wrong-side row.

Divide for Neck

Work in patt across 24 (24, 28) sts for right shoulder; with a 2nd skein of yarn, BO center 23 (25, 25) sts for neck; and work in patt across rem 24 (24, 28) sts for left shoulder. Working in pattern on both sides at once with separate yarn, dec 1 st at neck edge every right-side row until 17 (17, 19) sts rem on each side. BO all sts.

Front

Work same as back until armholes measure 5" (5", 6"), ending by working a wrong-side row.

Divide for Neck

Work in patt across 24 (24, 28) sts for left shoulder; with a 2nd skein of yarn, BO center 23 (25, 25) sts for neck; work in patt across rem 24 (24, 28) sts for right shoulder. Now work same as back, working even until front measures same as back to shoulders. BO all sts.

Sleeve (make 2)

Beginning at lower edge with smaller needles, CO 35 (35, 39) sts. Work 12 rows of ribbing same as Back. Change to larger needles and work as follows:

Row 1 (wrong side): K12 (12, 14), place marker; P1, K1, P1, K5, P1, K1, P1, place marker; K12 (12, 14).

Row 2: P12 (12, 14), K1B, P1, K1B, P5, K1B, P1, K1B, P12 (12, 14).

Row 3: K1; inc in next st, knit to first marker, P1, K1, P1, K5, P1, K1, P1, knit to last 3 sts, inc in next st, K2: 37 (37, 41) sts.

Row 4: Purl to first marker, K1B, P1, K1B, P5, K1B, P1, K1B, purl to end of row.

Row 5: Knit to first marker, P1, K1, P1, K5, P1, K1, P1, knit to end of row.

Row 6: Rep Row 4.

Rep Rows 3 through 6 until there are 81 (81, 85) sts. Work even in patt until sleeve measures 20" (20", 21") from CO row, ending by working a right-side row. BO.

Finishing

Collar

Sew right shoulder seam. With right side facing and smaller needles, pick up and K95 (99, 105) sts around neck. Beg with Row 1 of Back Ribbing, work in ribbing for 4". Change to larger needles and continue in ribbing until collar measures 8". BO in patt.

Sew rem shoulder and collar seam reversing seam on collar for turn-back. Sew side and sleeve seams. Set in sleeves and sew, easing to fit.

#12 STARBURST DOILY

Designed by Rita Weiss

SIZE
10" diameter

MATERIALS
Bedspread weight size 10
  crochet thread
  80 yds ecru

*Note: Photographed model made
with J&P Coats® Opera® #50 Ecru*

Stitch marker or safety pin

Four size 3 (3.25 mm) double-
  point knitting needles (or size
  required for gauge)

24" Size 3 (3.25 mm) circular
  knitting needle (or size
  required for gauge)

*Note: Begin doily with double
point needles and switch to circular needle when the number of sts
increases.*

GAUGE
16 sts = 2" in circular stock st
  (knit each row)

INSTRUCTIONS

*Note: Always mark the start of each rnd by
placing a stitch marker or small safety pin.
Replace the marker at the start of each rnd.*

Note: Always slip stitches as if to purl.

CO 9 sts onto one double-point needle.
Divide the sts onto three needles; join,
being careful not to twist sts.

Rnds 1 and 2: Knit.

Rnd 3: *YO, K1; rep from * around: 18 sts.

Rnds 4: Knit.

Rnd 5: Rep Rnd 3: 36 sts.

Rnd 6: Knit.

Rnd 7: *K1B, YO, K5, YO; rep from
* around: 48 sts.

Rnd 8: Knit.

Rnd 9: *K1B, YO, K7, YO; rep from
* around: 60 sts.

Rnd 10: Knit.

Rnd 11: *K1B, YO, K9, YO; rep from
* around: 72 sts.

Rnd 12: Knit.

Rnd 13: *K1B, YO, K11, YO; rep from
* around: 84 sts.

Rnd 14: Knit.

Rnd 15: *K1B, (YO, K2tog) 3 times, YO, K1,
(YO, sl 1, K1, PSSO) 3 times, YO; rep from
* around: 96 sts.

Rnd 16: Knit.

Rnd 17: *K1B, (YO, K2tog) 3 times, YO, K3, (YO, sl 1, K1, PSSO) 3 times, YO; rep from * around: 108 sts.

Rnd 18: Knit.

Rnd 19: K1B, (YO, K2tog) 4 times, YO, K1, (YO, sl 1, K1, PSSO) 4 times, YO; rep from * around: 120 sts.

Rnd 20: Knit.

Rnd 21: *YO, K1B, (YO, K2tog) 4 times, YO, K3 tog, (YO, sl 1, K1, PSSO) 4 times; rep from * around: 120 sts.

Rnd 22: Knit.

Rnd 23: *YO, K3, YO, sl 1, K1, PSSO, YO, K3tog, YO, K2tog; rep from * around: 120 sts.

Rnd 24: Knit.

Rnd 25: *YO, K5, YO, sl 1, K1, PSSO, K1, K2tog; rep from * around: 120 sts.

Rnd 26: Knit.

Rnd 27: *YO, K7, YO, K3tog; rep from * around: 120 sts.

Rnd 28: Knit.

Rnd 29: *K5, (YO) 4 times, K5; rep from * around: 168 sts.

Rnd 30: *K5, M9 in first YO, allow the 3 other YO's to slip off left-hand needle, K5; rep from * around: 228 sts.

Rnd 31: *K5, YO, K9, YO, K5; rep from * around: 252 sts.

Rnd 32: Knit.

Rnd 33: *K5, YO, K11, YO, K5; rep from * around: 276 sts.

Rnd 34: Knit.

Rnd 35: *K3, (K2tog, YO) 4 times, K1, (YO, sl 1, K1, PSSO) 4 times, K3; rep from * around: 276 sts.

Rnd 36: Knit.

Rnd 37: *K2, (K2tog, YO) 4 times, K3, (YO, sl 1, K2, PSSO) 4 times, K2; rep from * around: 276 sts.

Rnd 38: Knit.

Rnd 39: *K1, (K2 tog, YO) 5 times, M3, (YO, sl 1, K1, PSSO) 5 times, K1; rep from * around: 300 sts.

Rnd 40: Knit.

Rnd 41: *(K2tog, YO) 5 times, K5, (YO, sl 1, K1, PSSO) 5 times; rep from * around: 300 sts.

Rnd 42: Knit.

BO loosely.

Finishing

Carefully block doily, gently pulling the twelve little points until the star shape is in position.

#20 RAGLAN COWL

Designed by Patons Design Staff

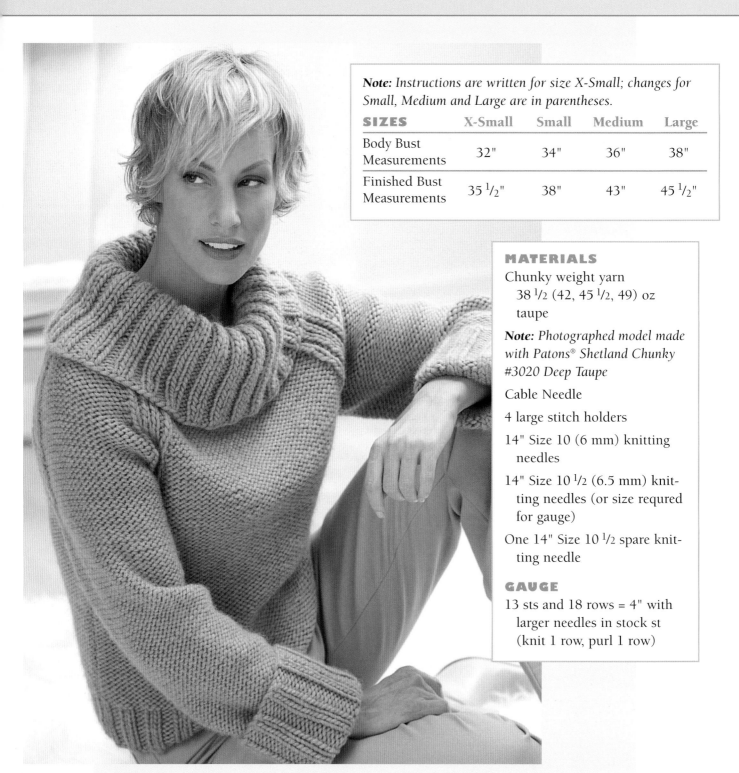

Note: *Instructions are written for size X-Small; changes for Small, Medium and Large are in parentheses.*

SIZES	X-Small	Small	Medium	Large
Body Bust Measurements	32"	34"	36"	38"
Finished Bust Measurements	35 1/2"	38"	43"	45 1/2"

MATERIALS

Chunky weight yarn
  38 1/2 (42, 45 1/2, 49) oz
  taupe

Note: *Photographed model made with Patons® Shetland Chunky #3020 Deep Taupe*

Cable Needle

4 large stitch holders

14" Size 10 (6 mm) knitting
  needles

14" Size 10 1/2 (6.5 mm) knitting needles (or size requred
  for gauge)

One 14" Size 10 1/2 spare knitting needle

GAUGE

13 sts and 18 rows = 4" with
  larger needles in stock st
  (knit 1 row, purl 1 row)

INSTRUCTIONS

Back

Bottom Ribbing

With smaller needles, CO 58 (62, 70, 74) sts.

Row 1 (right side): K2; *P2, K2; rep from * across.

Row 2: P2; *K2, P2; rep from * across.

Rows 3 through 10: Rep Rows 1 and 2 four more times, ending by working a wrong-side row.

Sweater Body

Change to larger needles and work in rev stock st until piece measures 12 1/2" from CO row, ending by working a wrong-side row.

Shape Raglan Armholes

Row 1: BO 3 sts, T3F, purl to last 7 sts, T3B, P1, K3.

Row 2: BO 3 sts, (K1, P1) twice; knit to last 4 sts, (P1, K1) twice: 52 (56, 64, 68) sts.

Row 3: P1, K1, P1, sl 1, K1, PSSO, purl to last 5 sts, K2tog, P1, K1, P1.

Row 4: (K1, P1) twice; knit to last 4 sts, (P1, K1) twice.

Row 5: (P1, K1) twice; purl to last 4 sts, (K1, P1) twice.

Row 6: Rep Row 4.

Rep last 4 rows 5 (6, 4, 3) more times: 40 (42, 54, 60) sts.

Top Shaping

Row 1: P1, K1, P1, sl 1, K1, PSSO, purl to last 5 sts, K2tog, P1, K1, P1.

Row 2: (K1, P1) twice; knit to last 4 sts, (P1, K1) twice.

Rep last 2 rows 3 (2, 7, 9) times more. Place rem 32 (36, 38, 40) sts on a st holder.

Front

Work same as Back to Top Shaping.

Front Top Shaping

For Sizes X-Small, Medium and Large Only

Row 1: P1, K1, P1, sl 1, K1, PSSO; purl to last 5 sts, K2tog, P1, K1, P1.

Row 2: (K1, P1) twice; knit to last 4 sts, (P1, K1) twice.

Rep Rows 1 and two 0 (4, 6) times more: 38 (44, 44, 46) sts.

Left Neck Shaping

For All Sizes

Row 1 (right side): P1, K1, P1, sl 1, K1, PSSO, P2tog (neck edge); leave rem 31 (35, 37, 39) sts on needle, and pick up spare needle to continue.

Row 2: K2tog, K1, P1, K1.

Row 3: Sl 1, K1, PSSO, P2tog.

Row 4: K2.

Row 5: Sl 1, K1, PSSO; finish off.

Right Neck Shaping

Row 1: With right side of work facing, sl next 24 (28, 30, 32) sts to a stitch holder; join yarn to rem 7 sts and P2tog, K2tog, P1, K1, P1.

Row 2: K1, P1, K1, K2tog.

Row 3: P2tog, K2tog.

Row 4: K2.

Row 5: K2tog. Finish off; weave in ends.

Sleeve (make 2)

Cuff

With smaller needles, CO 34 sts and work in K2, P2 ribbing for 5", inc 1 st at each end of needle on last row: 36 sts.

Body of Sleeve

Change to larger needles and work in rev stock st, inc 1 st at each end of needle on 7th row and then every 8 rows thereafter until there are 46 (48, 50, 54) sts.

Work even in rev stock st until work measures 20" (21", 21 1/2", 22") from cast-on row, ending by working wrong-side row.

Shape Raglans

Row 1: Bind off 3 sts, T3F, purl to last 7 sts, T3B, P1, K3.

Row 2: Bind off 3 sts, (K1, P1) twice; knit to last 4 sts, (P1, K1) twice: 40 (42, 44, 48) sts.

Row 3: P1, K1, P1, sl 1, K1, PSSO, purl to last 5 sts, K2tog, P1, K1, P1.

Row 4: (K1, P1) twice; knit to last 4 sts, (P1, K1) twice.

Row 5: (P1, K1) twice; purl to last 4 sts, (K1, P1) twice.

Row 6: Rep Row 4.

Rep Rows 3 through six 4 (4, 5, 3) more times: 30 (32, 32, 40) sts.

Top Shaping

Row 1: P1, K1, P1, sl 1, K1, PSSO, purl to last 5 sts, K2tog, P1, K1, P1.

Row 2: (K1, P1) twice; knit to last 4 sts, (P1, K1) twice.

Rep Rows 1 and two 5 (6, 5, 9) times more.

Place rem 18 (18, 20, 20) sts on a st holder.

Finishing

Sew raglan seams, leaving left back raglan seam open.

Collar

With right side facing and with larger needles, K18 (18, 20, 20) from left sleeve st holder. Pick up and knit 5 sts down left front neck edge. K24 (28, 30, 32) sts from front st holder. Pick up and knit 5 sts up right front neck edge. K18 (18, 20, 20) from right sleeve st holder. K32 (36, 38, 40) from back st holder: 102 (110, 118, 122) sts.

Work in K2, P2 ribbing for 12", ending by working a wrong-side row. Bind off in ribbing.

Sew left back raglan and collar seams, reversing seam on Collar for turn-back. Sew side and sleeve seams, reversing seams on cuffs for turn-back.

Weave in all ends.

#21 ROUND DISHCLOTH

Designed by Rita Weiss

STITCH GUIDE

Make 5 (M5): (K1, P1) twice, K1 all in same stitch: M5 made.

INSTRUCTIONS

Note: Mark beg of rnds with stitch marker or small safety pin.

CO 9 sts onto one double-point needle. Divide the sts evenly onto 3 needles; join, being careful not to twist sts.

Rnd 1: Knit.

Rnd 2: Knit and purl into each stitch:18 sts.

Rnd 3: *K1, P1; rep from * around.

Rnd 4: *P1, K1; rep from * around

Rnd 5: Rep Rnd 3.

Rnd 6: Rep Rnd 2: 36 sts.

Rnds 7 through 12: Rep Rows 3 and 4.

Rnd 14: Rep Rnd 2: 72 sts.

Rnds 15 through 19: Rep Rnds 3 and 4.

Rnd 20: Rep Rnd 2: 144 sts.

Rnds 21 and 23: Rep Rnd 4.

Rnd 22: Rep Rnd 3.

Rnd 24: Rep Rnd 2: 288 sts.

Rnd 25: Rep Rnd 4.

Rnd 26: *K2tog, YO, K2tog; turn; P1, M5, P1, sl 1 as to purl, turn; BO 7 sts (one st remains on right needle); rep from * around. Finish off; weave in yarn ends.

#22 LIZZIE'S PONCHO

Designed by Sheila Jones

MATERIALS

Worsted weight yarn
   500 (600, 850) yds pink
   (MC)

Medium weight eyelash
   or fur yarn
   200 (220, 310) yds pastel
   multicolor (A)

Note: *Photographed model made with Plymouth Encore Worsted #029 (MC) and Plymouth Italian Collection Firenze #441 (A)*

Size 11 (8 mm) knitting
   needles (or size required
   for gauge)

Yarn needle

GAUGE

12 sts = 4" with two strands
   held tog in stock st (knit
   1 row, purl 1 row)

Note: *Instructions are written for 2 year size; changes for larger sizes are in parentheses.*

SIZES	2 years	4 - 6 years	8 - 10 years
Finished Rectangle	11" x 21"	13" x 22"	15" x 23"

INSTRUCTIONS

Rectangle (make 2)

With one strand of MC and one strand of A held tog, CO 63 (66, 69) sts.

Rows 1 through 5: Knit.

At end of Row 5, cut Color A and attach one more strand of MC. With two strands of MC held tog:

Row 6 (right side): Knit.

Row 7: Purl.

Row 8: Knit.

Row 9: Purl.

Row 10: Knit.

Rep Rows 1 through 10 four (5, 6) times.

Rep Rows 1 through 5 once more for eleven (13, 15) stripes.

BO; weave in ends.

Sew together according to diagram.

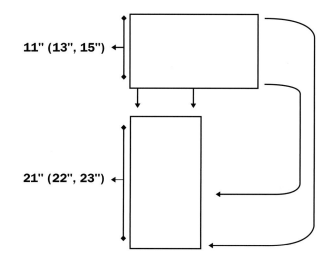

11" (13", 15")

21" (22", 23")

#23 SUMMER TOP

MATERIALS

DK or sport weight cotton yarn
350g (400 g, 450 g, 500 g) white

*Note: Photographed model made
with Twilleys Freedom Cotton #1
Pure White*

Size 5 (3.75 mm) knitting needles

Size 6 (4 mm) knitting needles
(or size required for gauge)

GAUGE

21 sts and 30 rows = 4" with
larger needles in patt st

*Note: Instructions are written for size X-Small; changes for
Small, Medium and Large are in parentheses.*

SIZES	X-Small	Small	Medium	Large
Body Bust Measurements	32"	34"	36"	38"
Finished Bust Measurements	36"	38"	39"	41"

INSTRUCTIONS

Back

With smaller needles, CO 95 (99, 103, 107) sts.

Row 1 (right side): Knit

Row 2: P1; * K1, P1; rep from * across.

Change to larger needles and continue to work in patt st until piece measures 9" from cast-on edge, ending by working a Row 2.

Eyelet Row: K5 (7, 9, 11); *YO, K2tog, K10; rep from * to last 6 (8, 10, 12) sts, YO, K2tog, K4 (6, 8, 10).

Work even in stock st (P1 row, K1 row), until piece measures 13" from beg, ending by working a purl row.

Shape Armholes

Row 1: BO 5 sts, knit across.

Row 2: BO 5 sts, purl across

Row 3: K1, K2tog tbl, knit to last 3 sts, K2 tog, K1.

Row 4: Purl.

Row 5: Knit

Row 6: Purl.

Rep Rows 3 through 6, three times more: 77 (81, 85, 89) sts.

Work even in stock st until piece measures 7" (7" 7 1/2" 7 1/2") from start of armhole shaping, ending by working a wrong-side row.

Shape Shoulders

Continuing in stock st, BO 9 (9, 10, 10) sts at the beg of each of the the next 4 rows.

Place rem 41 (45, 45, 49) sts on a st holder for neck.

Front

Work same as Back until armhole measures 4 1/2" (4 1/2", 5", 5") from start of armhole shaping, ending by working a wrong-side row.

Shape Left Neck

Row 1: K32 (32, 34, 34) sts; place rem sts on a st holder.

Row 2: BO 3 sts, purl across.

Row 3: Knit to last 4 sts, K2tog, K2.

Rep the last 2 rows until 20 (20, 22, 22) sts rem.

Next Row: P2, P2tog, purl to end.

Next Row: Knit to last 4 sts, K2tog, K2.

Work even in stock st until Front is same length as Back to shoulder shaping, ending by working a purl row.

Instructions continue on next page. →

Shoulder Shaping

Row 1: BO 9 (9, 10, 10) sts, knit across.

Row 2: BO 9 (9, 10, 10) sts, purl across.

Shape Right Neck

With right side facing, place center 13 (17, 17, 21) sts on a st holder; rejoin yarn to rem sts.

Row 1: BO 3 sts, knit across.

Row 2: Purl to last 4 sts, P2tog tbl, P2.

Work as given for left neck reversing shaping.

Neckband

Sew right shoulder seam. With right side facing and smaller needles pick up and knit 21 sts along left side of neck, knit 13 (17, 17, 21) sts from holder at center front, pick up and knit 21 sts along right side of neck and knit across 41 (45, 45, 49) sts from center back holder: 96 (104, 104, 112) sts.

Row 1 (wrong side): * K1, P1; rep from * across.

Row 2: Knit.

Row 3: Rep Row 1.

Row 4: K18, K3tog tbl, K13: (17, 17, 21) sts, K3tog, knit to end.

Rows 5 through 7: Work even in patt.

Row 8: K16, K3tog tbl, K13 (17, 17, 21), K3tog, knit to end.

Rows 9 through 11: Work even in patt.

Row 12: K14, K3tog tbl, K13 (17, 17, 21) K3tog, knit to end.

Cont in patt without shaping until neck measures 3" ending by working a wrong side row. BO loosely.

Left Armhole Edging

Sew left shoulder seam and neck edge. With right side facing and smaller needles pick up and knit 41 (41, 43, 43) sts along left front armhole edge, pick up and knit 41 (41, 43, 43) sts along left back armhole: 82 (82, 86, 86) sts

Row 1 (wrong side): *K1, P1; rep from * across.

Row 2: Knit.

Rows 3 and 4: Rep Rows 1 and 2.

Row 5: Rep Row 1. BO.

Right Armhole Edging

Work same as Left Armhole Edging.

Sew side and sleeve seams.

Tie

With smaller needles, CO 2 sts.

Knit until tie measures 47" long. BO and weave in ends. Thread tie through Eyelet Row and tie in a bow at center front.

#24 HOODED CAPELET

SIZE
27" around; 19" long

MATERIALS
Eyelash yarn
  7 oz variegated

Note: Photographed model made with Patons® Cha Cha #2006 Jazz

Stitch marker

16" Size 11 (8 mm) circular knitting needle
  (or size required for gauge)

GAUGE
12 sts and 16 rows = 4" in stock st
  (knit 1 row, purl 1 row)

INSTRUCTIONS

Loosely CO 83 sts; join, place marker at beg of rnd and move up as you work.

Knit even in rnds until work measures 19" from CO edge.

BO loosely.

#25 LITTLE RED SHOES

Designed by Patons Design Staff

Note: *Instructions are written for smaller size; changes for larger size are in parentheses*

SIZE

3 to 6 months

12 to 18 months

MATERIALS

DK weight yarn
1 ³/₄ oz red

Note: *Photographed model made with Patons® Astra #02762 Cardinal*

Two ¹/₂" shank buttons

Size 3 (3.25 mm) knitting needles (or size required for gauge)

GAUGE

26 sts and 36 rows = 4" in stock st (knit 1 row, purl 1 row)

INSTRUCTIONS (make 2)

Sole

CO 45 (55) sts.

Row 1 (wrong side): Knit.

Row 2: Inc in first st, K21 (26), M2, K20 (25), inc, K1: 49 (59) sts.

Row 3 and all uneven rows: Knit.

Row 4: Inc in first st, K23 (28), M2, K22 (27), inc, K1: 53 (63) sts.

Row 6: Inc in first st, K25 (30), M2, K24 (29), inc, K1: 57 (67) sts.

Row 8: Inc in first st, K27 (32), M2, K26 (31), inc, K1: 61 (71) sts.

Row 9: Knit.

For Size 12 to 18 Months Only
Row 10: Inc in first st, K34, M2, K33, inc, K1: 75 sts.

Row 11: Knit.

Sides

Row 1 (wrong side): Purl.

Row 2: Knit.

Rows 3 through 6: Rep Rows 1 and 2.

Row 7: Rep Row 1.

Instep

Row 1 (right side): K35 (43), sl 1K, turn, leave rem sts on needle.

Row 2: P2togtbl, P7 (9), P2tog, sl 1P, turn.

Row 3: K2tog, K7 (9), sl 1, K1, PSSO, sl 1K, turn.

Row 4: Rep Row 2.

Row 5: Rep Row 3.

For Size 12 to 18 Months Only
Row 6: Rep Row 2.

Row 7: Rep Row 3.

For All Sizes
Next Row: Rep Row 2.

Next Row: K2tog, K7 (9), sl 1, K1, PSSO, knit across.

Knit 2 rows. BO.

Sew back and sole seam.

Strap (make 2)

CO 5 sts.

Work 1 1/2" in garter st (knit each row).

Row 1 (buttonhole row): K2, YO, K2tog, K1.

Rows 2 through 4: Knit.

Row 5: K2tog, K2, K2tog: 3 sts.

Row 6: K3.

Row 7: Sl 1K, K2tog, PSSO. BO.

Sew strap in position. Sew button to correspond to buttonhole.

#26 WARM AND WONDERFUL

Note: Instructions are written for size Small; changes for sizes Medium, Large, 1X and 2X are in parentheses.

SIZES	Small	Medium	Large	1X	2X
Body Bust Measurements	36"	40"	44"	48"	52"
Finished Bust Measurements	38"	42"	46"	50"	54"

MATERIALS

Chunky weight yarn
   25 (25, 30, 30, 35) oz

Note: Photographed model made with Lion Brand® Wool-Ease® Chunky #141 Appleton

Size 10 ½ (6.5 mm) straight knitting needles (or size required for gauge)

16" Size 10 (6 mm) circular knitting needle

Five ⅞" buttons

GAUGE

12 sts and 18 rows = 4" with larger needles in stock st (knit 1 row, purl 1 row)

INSTRUCTIONS

Back

CO 57 (63, 69, 75, 81) sts.

Row 1 (right side): *K3, P3; rep from * to last 3 sts, K3.

Row 2: *P3, K3; rep from * to last 3 sts, P3.

Rep Rows 1 and 2 until piece measures 6". Change to Pattern Stitch and work even until piece measures 14" from beginning.

Shape Armholes

Rows 1 and 2: BO 5 (6, 6, 7, 8) sts at beg of each row.

Row 3: K1, SSK, work to last 3 sts, K2tog, K1.

Row 4: Purl.

Rep Rows 3 and 4 three (4, 5, 6, 6) times more: 39 (41, 45, 47, 51) sts. Work even until piece measures 22" (22½", 23", 23½", 24½") from beg.

Shape Shoulders and Back Neck

Row 1: BO 4 (4, 4, 5, 5) sts at beg of row, work across.

Row 2: BO 4 (4, 4, 5, 5) sts, work 7 (8, 9, 9, 10) sts, attach 2nd ball of yarn and BO center 17 (17, 19, 19, 21) sts, work across.

Row 3: BO 3 (4, 4, 4, 5) sts at beg of row, dec one st at each neck edge, work across.

Row 4: BO 3 (4, 4, 4, 5) sts at beg of row.

BO 4 (4, 5, 5, 5) sts at beg of next two rows.

Front

Work same as Back until piece measures 20" (20½", 21", 21", 22"), ending by working a wrong-side row.

Front Neck and Shoulder Shaping

Row 1: Work 14 (15, 16, 18, 19) sts, attach another ball of yarn, BO center 11 (11, 13, 11, 13) sts, work to end of row.

Working both sides at once, dec one st at each neck edge every other row 3 (3, 3, 4, 4) times. Continue in patt until piece measures 22" (22½", 23", 23½", 24"). Work shoulders as for Back.

Sleeve (make 2)

CO 27 (27, 33, 33, 39) sts and work K3, P3 rib as for Back for 4", ending by working a wrong-side row and inc 0 (0, 0, 2, 0) sts evenly across last row. Change to Patt Stitch and work 4 rows even.

Then inc one st each side on next row and every 4th rows 0 (9, 0, 5, 10) times, and every 5th row 10 (3, 10, 6, 2) times: 49 (53, 55, 59, 65) sts.

Work even until sleeve measures 17".

Shape Sleeve Cap

BO 5 (6, 6, 7, 8) sts at beg of next 2 rows. Dec one st each side every row 4 (2, 2, 0, 0) times and then every other row 7 (9, 10, 12, 13) times. BO rem 17 (19, 19, 21, 23) sts.

Finishing

Sew shoulder seams.

Collar

With smaller circular needle and with right side facing, start at front left shoulder and pick up 56 (56, 62, 62, 68) sts evenly around neck; CO 5 more sts: 61 (61, 67, 67, 73) sts; do not join, work back and forth in rows.

Row 1: P2;* K3, P3; rep from * to last 5 sts, K3, P2.

Row 2 (buttonhole row): K2, P1, M1, P2tog, work in rib as established across.

Continue in rib pattern as established, and rep buttonhole row every 6 rows 4 more times, and change to larger straight needles after 14 rows are worked. Work one row after last buttonhole row. BO in patt. Sew buttons in purl channel on left side opposite buttonholes. Turn down collar and sew down at BO edge.

Sew in sleeves. Sew side and sleeve seams.

#27 TUTTI FRUTTI

Designed by Laura Gebhardt

MATERIALS

Worsted weight yarn
  14 (14, 17 ¹/₂, 17 ¹/₂) oz
  light yellow (A)
  8 ¹/₂ (8 ¹/₂, 11 ¹/₂ , 11 ¹/₂) oz
  variegated (B)

Note: *Photographed model made with Bernat® Satin #04615 Banana #05733 Bermuda*

Size 8 (5 mm) straight knitting needles (or size required for gauge)

Four size 8 (5 mm) double-point knitting needles

Four size 7 (4.5 mm) double-point knitting needles

2 stitch holders

GAUGE

22 sts and 34 rows = 4" with larger needles in stock stitch (knit 1 row, purl 1 row)

Note: *Instructions are written for size 6; changes for larger sizes are in parentheses*

CHILDREN'S SIZES	6	8	10	12
Finished Chest Measurements	29 ¹/₂"	31 ¹/₂"	32 ¹/₄"	33 ³/₄"

INSTRUCTIONS

Back

With straight knitting needles and A, CO 81 (87, 89, 93) sts.

Row 1 (right side): With A, knit.

Row 2: Purl.

Row 3: With B, K1; *sl 1, K1; rep from * across.

Row 4: K1; *sl 1, K1; rep from * across.

These 4 rows form patt. Work in pattern until piece measures 10" (10 1/2", 11 1/2", 11 1/2") from CO edge, ending by working a wrong-side row.

Armhole Shaping

Continue in patt, BO 5 (6, 6, 7) sts at beg next 2 rows: 71 (75, 77, 79) sts.

Dec 1 st at beginning and end next 5 (6, 6, 6) right-side rows: 61 (63, 65, 67) sts.

Work even in patt until back measures 6" (6 1/2", 6 1/2", 7") from beg of armhole shaping, end by working a wrong-side row.

Shape Neck and Shoulders

Continuing in patt, BO 6 sts at beg of next 6 (6, 4, 4) rows: 25 (27, 41, 43) sts.

BO 0 (0, 7, 8) sts at beg of next 0 (0, 2, 2) rows: 25 (27, 27, 27) sts. Place rem sts on holder for back of neck.

Front

Work same as Back to Armhole Shaping

Front Armhole Shaping

Continue in patt, BO 5 (6, 6, 7) sts at beg of next 2 rows: 71 (75, 77, 79) sts.

Dec 1 st at beg and end of next 5 (6, 6, 6) right-side rows: 61 (63, 65, 67) sts.

Work even in patt until piece measures 4 1/2" (5", 5", 5 1/2") from beg of armhole shaping, ending by working a wrong-side row.

Shape Neck and Shoulders

Work in patt across 26 (26, 27, 28) sts, sl next 9 (11, 11, 11) sts onto holder for front of neck; join separate ball of yarn and work in patt across last 26 (26, 27, 28) sts.

Working both shoulders at same time, dec one st at neck edge every row 8 times: 18 (18, 19, 20) sts rem on each shoulder.

Continue even in patt until work measures 16" (17", 17 1/2", 18 1/2") from CO edge, ending by working a wrong-side row.

BO 6 sts at beg of next 6 (6, 4, 4) rows. BO 0 (0, 7, 8) sts at beg of next 0 (0, 2, 2) rows.

Instructions continue on next page. →

Sleeve (make 2)

Using straight needles and A, CO 43 (43, 45, 45) sts.

Work in pattern, inc one st each side on 5th row and every 6th row thereafter until there are 61 (59, 55, 55) sts; then inc one st each side every 8th row until there are 71 (73, 73, 77) sts. Work even until sleeve measures 12" (13", 14", 15") from CO edge.

Shape Sleeve Cap

BO 5 (6, 6, 7) sts at beg of next 2 rows: 61 (61, 61, 63) sts.

Dec one st each side every right-side row 7 (8, 8, 12) times: 47 (45, 45, 39) sts.

Continue in patt, dec one st each side every row until 11 (9, 9, 11) sts rem. BO rem sts.

Collar

Sew shoulder seams.

Using smaller double-point needles, pick up and knit 25 (27, 27, 27) sts from back holder, 15 sts down left front neck, knit 9 (11, 11, 11) sts from holder and pick up and knit 15 sts up right front neck to shoulder: 64 (68, 68, 68) sts.

Work in K1, P1 rib for 3". Change to larger double point needles and work in rib for another 3".

BO loosely in rib.

Fold collar over to form turtleneck.

Finishing

Sew sleeves in place having center of sleeve at shoulder seam. Join sleeve and side seams.

Weave in all ends.

#28 A PAIR OF PONCHOS AND A PURSE

Designed By Patons Design Staff

Note: *Instructions are written for child's size; changes for mother's size are in parentheses*

SIZE
Mother's Version fits 32" to 38" bust

Child's Version fits 4 to 8 years

MATERIALS
Worsted weight yarn

Mother's version

   17 $\frac{1}{2}$ oz brown (MC)

   3 $\frac{1}{2}$ oz cream (A)

   3 $\frac{1}{2}$ oz tan (B)

   3 $\frac{1}{2}$ oz grey (C)

Child's version

   7 oz dk blue (MC)

   3 $\frac{1}{2}$ oz cream(A)

   3 $\frac{1}{2}$ oz blue (B)

   3 $\frac{1}{2}$ oz tan (C)

Note: *Mother's photographed model made with Patons® Décor #1633 chocolate taupe (MC),#1602 Aran (A), #1661 taupe, #1673 grey heather (C); child's photographed model made with Patons® Décor #1622 Rich Country Blue (MC), #1602 Aran (A), #1621 Country Blue (B), #1631 Taupe (C).*

Four Size 7 (4.5 mm) double-point knitting needles (or size required for gauge)

29" Size 7 circular knitting needle (or size required for gauge)

4 Stitch markers

GAUGE
20 sts and 26 rows = 4" in stock st (knit 1 row, purl 1 row)

Instructions continue on next page. →

PONCHO

INSTRUCTIONS

Starting at neck with double-point needles, CO 25 (28) sts on first and 2nd needles and 26 (28) sts on third needle: 76 (84) sts. Join, being careful not to twist sts. Mark beg of rnd and move marker up as you work.

Collar

Knit in rounds until work measures 3" (3 ½") from CO edge.

Body Dividing Rnd: Mark first st and knit it, K18 (20) for back; [mark next st and knit it, K18 (20)] 3 times.

Note: Change to circular needle when needed to accommodate sts.

Rnd 1: (M1, knit marked st, M1, knit to next marked st) 4 times: 84 (92) sts.

Rnd 2: Knit.

Rep last 2 rounds 12 (20) more times. At end of last rnd: 180 (252) sts.

Next round: Knit to 3rd marked st and knit it, K22 (31), turn.

From now on work in rows. Do not join.

Row 1 (right side): M1 in first st, knit to last st, M1 in last st: 182 (254) sts.

Row 2: P1, purl across, inc 27 (24) sts evenly spaced: 209 (278) sts.

Row 3: With MC, K1; work Row 1 of 23-st rep chart 9 (12) times , reading knit row from right to left; with MC, K1.

Row 4: With MC, P1; work Row 2 of chart 9 (12) times, reading purl row from left to right; with MC, P1.

Continue to work all rows of chart, keeping first and last sts of each row in MC.

Next row (right side): With MC, knit, dec 27 (24) sts evenly spaced across: 182 (254) sts.

Work in stock st until piece measures 14" (19") from CO row, ending by working a right-side row.

Last Body Row: Purl, dec 9 (13) sts evenly spaced across: 173 (241) sts.

Border

Row 1: K1; *P1, K1; rep from * to end of row.

Rows 2 through 8: Rep Row 1. BO in patt. Sew back seam.

Fringe

Following fringe instructions on page 251, cut 13" lengths of MC. Work single knot fringe across BO edge with 3 strands of yarn in each knot.

Chart

23 st rep

Start Here

Key

☐ = Contrast A

⊙ = Contrast B

■ = Contrast C

Note: When working from chart, use separate balls of Colors B and C for each area of color in the design to avoid carrying colors not in use across long areas.

PURSE

INSTRUCTIONS

Front

Body

With MC and circular needle, CO 42 sts. Do not join; work back and forth in rows.

Work in stock st until piece measures 1 ½" from CO edge, ending with a right-side row.

Next row: P1, purl across, inc 4 sts evenly spaced, P1: 46 sts.

Work chart twice in stock st to end of chart, reading knit rows from right to left and purl rows from left to right.

Next Row (right side): With MC, dec 4 sts evenly spaced across row: 42 sts.

Work in stock st until work measures 9" from CO edge.

Last Row: Purl, dec 5 sts evenly spaced across: 37 sts.

Border

Row 1: K1; *P1, K1; rep from * to end of row.

Rows 2 through 8: Rep Row 1. BO in patt.

Back

Work same as Front.

Sew bottom and side edges tog reversing seam for turn back. Fold border to right side.

Strap

Following I-cord instructions on page 252, with MC make 36" I-cord and sew to top of purse.

Fringe

Following fringe instructions on page 251, cut 9" lengths of MC. Work single knot fringe across BO edge with 3 strands of yarn in each knot.

#3 TIMELY TANK

Designed by Bev Nimon for S.R. Kertzer Limited

Note: *Instructions are written for size Small with changes for sizes Medium and Large in parentheses.*

SIZES	Small	Medium	Large
Body Bust Measurements	34"	37"	40"
Garment Bust Measurements	38"	42 $\frac{1}{4}$"	45 $\frac{3}{4}$"

MATERIALS

DK or sport weight cotton yarn
  3 $\frac{1}{2}$ (3 $\frac{1}{2}$, 5 $\frac{1}{4}$, 5 $\frac{1}{4}$) oz pink

Note: *Photographed model made with S.R. Kertzer Limited Super 10 Cotton, #3486 Tiger Lily*

14" Size 6 (4 mm) straight knitting needles (or size required for gauge)

16" Size 6 (4 mm) circular knitting needle

16" Size 5 (3.5 mm) circular knitting needle

GAUGE

22 sts and 28 rows = 4" with larger needles in stock stitch (knit 1 row, purl 1 row)

INSTRUCTIONS

Back

With straight needles, starting at bottom of garment, CO 104 (116, 126) sts.

Rows 1 through 3: Knit.

Work even in patt for 3"ending by working a wrong-side row.

Back Decreases

Row 1: K2 tog, work to last 2 sts, SSK: 102 (114, 124) sts.

Rows 2 through 4: Work even in patt.

Row 5: Rep Row 1: 100 (112, 122) sts.

Rep Rows 1 through 5 until there are 92 (104, 114) sts.

Work 12 rows even in patt, ending by working a wrong-side row.

PATTERN

Row 1 (right side): Knit.

Row 2: Purl.

Row 3: Knit.

Row 4: Purl.

Row 5: Knit.

Row 6: Knit.

Repeat these 6 rows for pattern.

STITCH GUIDE

Slip, slip, knit decrease (SSK): Sl 2 sts as if to knit, one at a time to right-hand needle. Insert tip of left-hand needle into fronts of these 2 sts and knit them together: SSK made.

Increase (inc): knit in front and in back of same st.

Back Increases

Row 1 (right side): Inc in first st, work in patt to last st, inc in last st: 84 (94, 106, 116) sts.

Rows 2 through 6: Work even in patt.

Row 7: Rep Row 1: 96 (108, 118) sts.

Rep Rows 2 through 7 until there are 104 (116, 126) sts.

Work even in patt until piece measures 13" (13", 13") from CO edge.

Armhole Shaping

Row 1: BO 8 (9, 10) sts at beg of row; work even in patt across: 96 (107, 116) sts.

Row 2: Rep Row 1: 88 (98, 106) sts.

Rows 3 through 5: Work even in patt.

Row 6: K2 tog, work in patt to last two sts, SSK: 86 (96, 104) sts.

Rep Rows 3 through 6 until there are 76 (78, 94) sts.

Next Row: Rep Row 6: 74 (76, 92) sts.

Next Row: Work even in patt.

Rep last two rows until there are 38 (44, 44) sts. BO.

Front

Work same as back until piece measures 19" (19 3/4", 19 3/4").

Neck Shaping

Work in patt to center 24 (26, 24) sts. Attach another ball of yarn. BO center 24 (26, 24) sts, and work across row. Working both sides at once and continuing armhole decs as for back, dec 1 st at each neck edge, every other row 7 (9, 10) times.

Continue shaping as for back until all sts are decreased.

Finishing

Sew side seams and shoulders at neck edge.

Turtleneck

With smaller circular needle and right side facing, pick up 23 (25, 27) sts from right neck edge, pick up 24 (26, 24) front neck sts, pick up 23 (25, 27) sts from left neck edge, pick up 38 (44, 44) back neck sts, place marker, join: 108 (120, 122) sts.

Note: When working in the round, knit 4 rows for stock st, knit 1 row, purl 1 row for garter stitch.

Work in patt for 2".

Change to larger circular needles and work in patt for 3". BO loosely.

#32 BRIGHT AND EASY CARDIGAN

Designed by Donna Druchunas

Note: *Instructions are written for size Small; changes for sizes Medium and Large are in parentheses*

SIZES	Small	Medium	Large
Body Bust Measurements	32"	36"	40"
Finished Bust Measurements	39"	43 1/2"	47"

MATERIALS

Bulky weight yarn
   700 (780, 900) yds teal tweed (A)

Worsted weight yarn
   200 (200, 200) yds light green (B)

Note: *Photographed model made with Classic Elite Gatsby #2146 Tangiers Teal tweed (A), and Classic Elite Bazic Wool #2902 Wintergreen (B)*

Size 9 (5.5 mm) knitting needles

Size 10 (6 mm) knitting needles (or size required for gauge)

16" Size 10 circular knitting needle (or size required for gauge)

Size J (6 mm) crochet hook

Six 7/8" diameter buttons

Sewing needle and thread

GAUGE

12 sts = 4" in Seed st with larger needles

INSTRUCTIONS

Note: *Throughout pattern, when working with B use 2 strands held tog.*

Back

Starting at bottom with one strand of A and smaller needles, CO 54 (58, 66) sts.

Finish off A and attach 2 strands of B.

Ribbing

Work in K2, P2 ribbing until piece measures 2".

Increase Row (wrong side): Work in ribbing as established, inc 4 (6, 4) sts evenly spaced across row: 58 (64, 70) sts.

Change to larger needles.

Body

Attach A. Do not cut B.

Work stripe pattern:

Rows 1 through 4: Work seed stitch with A

Rows 5 through 8: Work stock stitch (knit 1 row, purl 1 row) with B.

Rep rows 1 through 8 once more. Finish off B.

Work in seed stitch with A until back measures 14 1/2" (15", 15 1/2").

Armhole Shaping

Continuing in seed st, BO 5 sts at beg of next 2 rows: 48 (54, 60) sts.

Dec 1 st at beg and end of every other row 4 times: 40 (46, 52) sts. Continue in seed stitch until piece measures 22 1/2" (23 1/2", 24 1/2").

Shape Shoulders

BO 3 (3, 4) sts at beg of next 2 rows: 34 (40, 44) sts.

BO 3 (4, 4) sts at beg of next 2 rows: 28 (32, 36) sts.

BO 4 sts at beg of next 2 rows: 20 (24, 28) sts.

BO rem sts.

Right Front

Starting at bottom with A and smaller needles, CO 26 (30, 32) sts. Finish off A, attach a double strand of B.

Ribbing

Work in K2, P2 ribbing until piece measures 2".

Increase Row (wrong side): Continue in ribbing as established, inc 2 sts evenly spaced: 28 (32, 34) sts.

Change to larger needles.

Body

Attach A. Do not cut B.

Work stripe patt:

Instructions continue on next page. →

Rows 1 through 4: Work seed stitch with A.

Rows 5 through 8: Work stock stitch with B.

Rep Rows 1 through 8 once more; finish off B.

Work in seed stitch with A until piece measures 14 1/2" (15", 15 1/2"); end by working a right-side row.

Armhole Shaping
BO 5 sts at beg of next row: 23 (27, 29) sts.

Dec 1 st at beg of next wrong-side row 4 times: 19 (23, 25) sts.

At the same time, when piece measures 20 1/2" (21 1/2", 23 1/2"), ending by working a wrong-side row and begin neck shaping.

Neck Shaping
BO 7 (8, 9) sts at beg of next right-side row: 12 (15, 16) sts

Dec 1 st at beg of next right-side row 2 (4, 4) times: 10 (11, 12) sts.

Work even in seed stitch until piece measures 22 1/2" (23 1/2", 24 1/2"); ending by working a right-side row.

Shape Shoulders
BO 3 (3, 4) sts beg of next row: 7 (8, 8) sts. Work 1 row even.

BO 3 (4, 4) sts beg of next row: 4 (4, 4) sts. Work 1 row even.

BO rem sts.

Left Front
Work as for right front until piece measures 14 1/2" (15", 15 1/2"); ending by working a wrong-side row.

Armhole shaping
BO 5 sts at beg of next right-side row: 23 (27, 29) sts.

Dec 1 st at beg of next right-side row 4 times: 19 (23, 25) sts.

At the same time, when piece measures 20 1/2" (21 1/2", 23 1/2")", ending by working a right-side row and begin neck shaping.

Neck Shaping
BO 7 (8, 9) sts at beg of next wrong-side row: 12 (15, 16) sts.

Dec 1 st at beg of next wrong-side row 2 (4, 4) times: 10 (11, 12) sts.

Work even in seed stitch until piece measures 22 1/2" (23 1/2" , 24 1/2"); ending by working a wrong-side row.

Shape Shoulders
BO 3 (3, 4) sts beg of next row: 7 (8, 8) sts. Work 1 row even.

BO 3 (4, 4) sts beg of next row: 4 (4, 4) sts. Work 1 row even.

BO rem sts.

Sleeve (make 2)
Cuff
Starting at cuff with A and smaller needles, CO 22 (26, 30) sts. Finish off A, attach a double strand of B.

Ribbing
Work in K2, P2 ribbing until piece measures 2". Change to larger needles.

Arm

Attach A, finish off B.

Work in seed stitch with A and at same time, begin sleeve increases:

Inc one st at each end of every 4th row 9 (8, 7) times, then every 5th row 6 (7, 8) times: 52 (56, 60) sts.

Work even in patt until piece measures 17" (17 ½", 18"); ending by working a wrong-side row.

Sleeve Cap Shaping

BO 5 sts at beg of next 2 rows: 42 (46, 50) sts.

Dec one st at each end of every row 4 times: 34 (38, 42) sts. BO rem sts.

Finishing

Sew shoulder seams. Sew sleeves into arm-holes.

Sew side and underarm seams.

Buttonhole Band

On right front, use pins to mark buttonhole placement starting ½" from bottom and at neck edge, with rem four buttons evenly spaced between.

On right front, with right side facing, using smaller needles and B, pick up 54 (58, 62) sts. Work 2 rows of K2, P2 rib.

Buttonhole Row: Work in K2, P2 rib; when you come to a buttonhole marker YO, work 2tog.

Continue to work K2, P2 rib until band measures 1". Attach A, finish off B. BO in patt.

Button Band

On left front, with right side facing and B, pick up 54 (58, 62) sts. Work in K2, P2 rib until band measures 1". Attach A, finish off B. BO in patt.

Sew on buttons to correspond to button-holes.

Work 1 row of single crochet with A along bottom of button bands.

Collar

With circular needle and right-side facing, with A pick up 18 (22, 26) right front neck sts, 24 (28, 32) back neck sts, and 18 (22, 26) front neck sts: 60 (72, 84) sts. Do not join, work back and forth in rows. Work in seed stitch until collar measures 3". BO loosely.

#33 HOODED CARDIGAN

Designed by Donna Druchunas

MATERIALS

Bulky weight yarn (A)
340 (410, 490) yds

Worsted weight yarn (B)
100 (100, 100) yds

Note: Photographed model made with Classic Elite Gatsby #2146 Tangiers Teal tweed (A), and Classic Elite Bazic Wool #2902 Wintergreen (B)

Size 9 (5.5 mm) knitting needles

Size 10 (6 mm) knitting needles

16" Size 10 (6 mm) circular knitting needle (or size required for gauge)

Size J (6 mm) crochet hook

Six 7/8" diameter buttons

Sewing needle and thread

6 stitch markers or small safety pins

GAUGE

12 sts = 4" with larger needles in Seed st

Note: Instructions are written for size 4; changes for larger sizes are in parentheses.

SIZE	4	6	8
Body Chest Measurement	23"	25"	27"
Finished Chest Measurement	27"	31"	35"

INSTRUCTIONS

Note: Throughout pattern, when working with B use 2 strands held tog.

Back

Starting at bottom with one strand of A and smaller needles, CO 42 (46, 50) sts.

Finish off A and attach 2 strands of B.

Ribbing

Work in K2, P2 ribbing until piece measures 2". Change to larger needles.

Body

Finish off B and attach A. Work in Seed st until back measures 16" (18", 20"). BO.

Right Front

Starting at lower edge with A and smaller needles, CO 18 (22, 26) sts. Finish off A and attach 2 strands of B.

Ribbing

Work in K2, P2 ribbing until piece measures 2". Change to larger needles.

Body

Attach A, finish off B.

Work in Seed st until front measures 13 1/2" (15 1/2", 17 1/2"), endng by working a wrong-side row.

Shape Neck

Keeping continuity of patt, BO 3 (4, 5) sts at beg of next right-side row: 15 (18, 21) sts.

BO 2 sts at beg of following right-side row: 13 (16, 19) sts.

Dec 1 st at beg of following right-side row 2 times: 11 (14, 17) sts at end of last row.

Work even in patt until front measures same as back. BO rem sts.

Left Front

Work as for Right Front to neck shaping.

Shape Neck

Keeping continuity of patt, BO 3 (4, 5) sts at beg of next wrong-side row: 15 (18, 21) sts.

BO 2 sts at beg of following wrong-side row: 13 (16, 19) sts.

Dec 1 st at beg of following wrong-side row 2 times: 11 (14, 17) sts at end of last row.

Work even in patt until front measures same as back. BO rem sts.

Sleeve (make 2)
Cuff

With A and smaller needles, CO 22 (26, 26) sts.

Finish off A; attach 2 strands of B.

Ribbing

Work in K2, P2 rib until piece measures 2". Change to larger needles.

Arm

Attach A. Do not finish off B.

Begin stripe pattern as follows, and at the same time, inc 1 st at beg and end of every 4th row 8 (6, 5) times, then at beg and end of every 6th row 2 (4, 6) times: 42 (46, 48) sts at end of last row.

Stripe Pattern

Rows 1 through 4: Work Seed st with A.

Rows 5 through 8: Work Stock st with 2 strands of B.

Rep Rows 1 through 8 once more. Finish off B. Continue working Seed st with A and continue working sleeve increases until sleeve measures 14" (15 1/2", 17"). BO.

Finishing
Seams

Sew shoulder seams.

Sew sleeves to armholes.

Sew side and underarm seams.

Buttonhole Band

On right front, use pins to mark buttonhole placement 1/2" from bottom and at neck edge, with remaining four buttons evenly spaced between.

On right front, with right side facing, using smaller needles and 2 strands of B, pick up 46 (50, 54) sts. Work 2 rows of K2, P2 Ribbing.

Work buttonhole row: Work in K2, P2 ribbing, and when you come to a buttonhole marker, YO, K2tog.

Continue to work K2, P2 Ribbing until band measures 1". Attach A, finish off B. BO in patt.

Button Band

On left front, with right side facing and 2 strands of B, pick up 46 (50, 54) sts. Work in K2, P2 Ribbing until band measures 1". Attach A, finish off B. BO in patt.

Sew on buttons to correspond to buttonholes.

Work 1 row of single crochet with A along bottom of button bands.

Hood

With right-side facing, using circular needle and A, pick up and knit 4 sts at top of right button band, 14 (16, 18) sts across right front neck, 12 (14, 16) back neck sts, place marker, pick up and knit remaining 12 (14, 16) back sts, 14 (16, 18) left front neck sts, and 4 sts at top of left button band: 60 (68, 76) sts. Do not join; work back and forth in rows.

Work even in Seed st for 2 1/2" (2 3/4", 3").

Continue to work in Seed st and inc 1 st on each side of center back marker every 5 rows 2 (4, 2) times, then every 6 rows 4 (2, 4) times: 72 (80, 88) sts.

Work even in patt until piece measures 10 1/2" (11", 12"). BO loosely. Sew top BO edges tog from center back to front edges to form hood.

#34 BLUE LEAVES

Designed by Rita Weiss

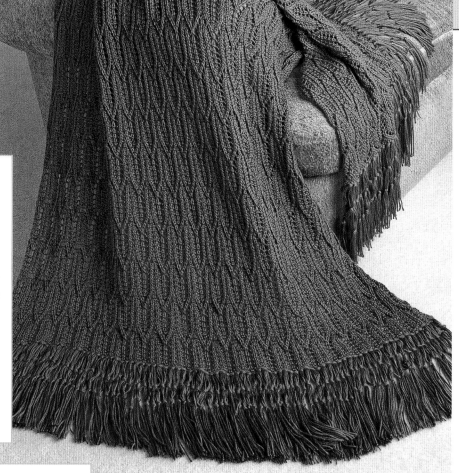

SIZE
44" x 60"

MATERIALS
Worsted weight yarn
   36 oz blue

Note: Photographed model made with Caron® Simply Soft® #9710 Country Blue

36" Size 9 (5.5 mm) circular
   knitting needle (or size
   required for gauge)

GAUGE
17 sts = 4" in patt

PATTERN
Note: Always slip stitches as if to knit.

Row 1 (right side): K1; *YO, sl 1, K1, PSSO; K3, K2tog, YO, K1; rep from * across.

Row 2 and all wrong-side rows: Purl.

Row 3: K2; *YO, sl 1, K1, PSSO; K1, K2tog, YO, K3; rep from * across, ending last rep with K2.

Row 5: P1; *K2, YO, sl 1, K2tog, PSSO; YO, K2, P1; rep from * across.

Rows 7, 9, 11, 13 and 15: P1; *sl 1, K1, PSSO; K1, (YO, K1) twice, K2tog, P1; rep from * across.

Row 16: Purl.

INSTRUCTIONS

CO 185 sts. Do not join; work back and forth in rows.

Work Rows 1 through 16 of Patt until piece measures about 60", ending with Row 16.

BO loosely.

Fringe
Follow Triple Knot Fringe instructions on page 251. Cut strands 22" long and use 4 strands in each knot. Tie knot through every other CO or BO stitch across each short end of afghan.

#35 A LITTLE BIT OF IRELAND

Designed by Patons Design Staff

MATERIALS

Chunky weight yarn
   70 (70, 73 ¹/₂, 77) oz cream

Note: *Photographed model made with Patons® Shetland Chunky #3008 Aran*

14" Size 15 (10 mm) knitting needles
   (or size required for gauge)

One 14" Size 15 (10 mm) spare knitting
   needle

Two stitch holders

Cable needle

GAUGE

9 sts and 13 rows = 4" with 2 strands of
   yarn held tog in stock st (knit 1 row,
   purl 1 row)

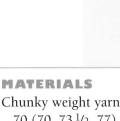

Note: *Instructions are written for size Small; changes for sizes Medium, Large and X-Large are in parentheses.*

Sizes	Small	Medium	Large	X-Large
Body Bust Measurements	30" - 32"	34" - 36"	38" - 40"	42" - 44"
Finished Bust Measurements	37"	41"	45"	48"

INSTRUCTIONS

Back

Bottom Border

Starting at bottom edge with 2 strands of yarn held tog, CO 48 (53, 58, 58) sts.

Row 1 (wrong side): K3; *P2, K3, rep from * across.

Row 2: P3; *Tw2R, P3, rep from * across.

Rows 3 through 10: Rep last 2 rows 4 times more.

Row 11: Rep Row 1, increasing 3 (2, 1, 5) st(s) evenly across: 51 (55, 59, 63) sts.

Body

Row 1 (right side): P2 (4, 6, 8), Tw2R, P2; *Work Row 1 of Cable Panel Patt; P2, Tw2R, P2; rep from * one time, work Row 1 of Cable Panel Patt, P2, Tw2R, P2 (4, 6, 8).

Row 2: K2 (4, 6, 8), P2, K2; *work Row 2 of Cable Panel, K2, P2, K2; rep from * one time, work Row 2 of Cable Panel, K2, P2, K2 (4, 6, 8).

These 2 rows form patt. Cable Panel is now in position.

Work in established patt, working corresponding rows of cable panel, until work measures 12 1/2" (13", 13", 13 1/2") from CO edge, ending by working a wrong-side row.

Armhole Shaping

Row 1: BO 3 sts, work in established patt across: 48 (52, 56, 60) sts.

Row 2: BO 3 sts, work in established patt across: 45 (49, 53, 57) sts.

Row 3: Dec 1 st at each edge, work in established pattern.

Row 4: Work in established pattern.

Rep Rows 3 and 4 until there are 41 (41, 41, 43) sts.

Work even in patt until armhole measures 8" (8 1/2", 8 1/2", 9"), ending by working a wrong-side row.

Shoulder Shaping

Row 1: BO 10 sts, work in established pattern.

Row 2: BO 10 sts, work in established pattern.

Place rem 21 (21, 21, 23) sts on a stitch holder.

Instructions continue on next page. →

Front

Work as for back to armhole shaping.

Armhole Shaping

Row 1: BO 3 sts, work in established patt across: 48 (52, 56, 60) sts.

Row 2: BO 3 sts, work in established patt across: 45 (49, 53, 57) sts.

Row 3: Dec 1 st at each edge, work in established pattern.

Row 4: Work in established pattern.

Repeat Rows 3 and 4 until there are 41 (41, 41, 43) sts.

Work even in patt until armhole measures 5" (5 ½", 5 ½" 6"), ending by working a wrong-side row.

Left Neck Shaping

Row 1: Work in patt across 15 sts (neck edge), turn, place rem sts on a spare needle.

Row 2: Work even in patt.

Row 3: Work in patt across 14 sts, dec 1 st at neck edge.

Row 4: Work even in patt.

Rep rows 3 and 4 until there are 10 sts.

Work even in patt until armhole measures same length as Back, ending by working a wrong-side row. BO all sts.

Right Neck Shaping

Row 1: With right side of work facing. Sl next 11 (11, 11, 13) sts from spare needle onto a st holder. Join yarn to rem 15 sts and work in patt across.

Row 2: Work even in patt.

Row 3: Dec 1 st, work in patt across.

Row 4: Work even in patt.

Rep rows 3 and 4 until there are 10 sts.

Work even in patt until armhole measures same length as Back, ending by working a wrong-side row. BO all sts.

Sleeves (make 2)

With 2 strands of yarn held tog, CO 38 sts.

Row 1 (wrong side): K3; *P2, K3, rep from * across.

Row 2: P3; *Tw2R, P3, rep from * across.

Rows 3 through 22: Rep Rows 1 and 2.

Row 23: K3; *P2, K2tog, K1, rep from * 5 times; P2, K3: 32 sts.

Row 24: P3; *Tw2R, P2, rep from * to last 5 sts, Tw2R, P3.

Row 25: K3; *P2, K2, rep from * to last 5 sts, P2, K3.

Row 26: Inc 1, P3; *Tw2R, P2, rep from * to last 5 sts, Tw2R, P3, inc 1.

Rows 27 through 31: Rep Rows 24 and 25, working inc sts into the reverse stock st pattern.

Rep Rows 26 through 31 until there are 40 (42, 42, 44) sts.

Work even in patt until work measures 18½" (19½", 20", 20") from CO edge, ending by working a wrong-side row.

Shape Sleeve Cap

Row 1: BO 3 sts, work in est patt: 37 (39, 39, 41) sts.

Row 2: BO 3 sts, work in est patt: 34 (36, 36, 38) sts.

Row 3: Dec 1 st, work in est patt to last 2 sts, dec 1 st.

Row 4: Work in est patt.

Rep Rows 3 and 4 until 32 sts rem for all sizes.

Next Row: Dec 1 st, work in est patt to last 2 sts, dec 1 st.

Rep this row until 4 sts rem. BO all sts.

Collar

Sew right shoulder seam.

With right side of work facing and 2 strands of yarn held tog, pick up and knit 10 sts down Left Front neck edge; K11 (11, 11, 13) from front st holder and dec 1 st at center. Pick up and knit 10 sts up Right Front neck edge and K21 (21, 21, 23) from Back st holder and dec 5 (5, 5, 4) sts evenly across: 46 (46, 46, 51) sts.

Row 1 (wrong side): K2; *P2, K3, rep from * to last 4 sts, P2, K2.

Row 2: P2, *Tw2R, P3; rep from * to last 4 sts, Tw2R, P2.

Rep last 2 rows until Collar measures 5", ending by working a wrong-side row. BO in patt.

Finishing

Sew left shoulder and collar seam. Sew side and sleeve seams. Sew in sleeves. Weave in all ends.

#36 CLOSE TO MY HEART SCARF

Designed by Suzanne Atkinson

SIZE
6" x 60"

MATERIALS
Worsted weight yarn
  7 oz red

Note: *Photographed model made with Patons® Classic Merino Wool #230 Bright Red*

Size 7 (4.5 mm) knitting needles (or size required for gauge)

Cable needle

GAUGE
28 sts and 34 rows = 4"
  worked over Chart A

M1: Lift strand between st just worked and next st and knit into back of it: M1 inc made.

Inc2: Inc two sts by knitting into front, back and front of next st.

Dec4: Sl 3 sts as to knit, one at at time, to right needle; *pass 2nd st on right needle over last st and off needle; sl last st back to left needle; sl 2nd st on left needle over first st and off needle;* sl first st back to right needle; rep from * to * once; K1.

T2B (Twist 2 Back): Sl next st to cable needle and hold behind work; K1, then P1 from cable needle.

T2F (Twist 2 Front): Sl next st to cable needle and hold in front of work; P1, then K1 from cable needle.

C2F (Cable 2 Front) [worked on wrong side]: Sl next st to cable needle and hold in front of work; K1, then K1 from cable needle.

C2B (Cable 2 Back) [worked on wrong side]: Sl next st to cable needle and hold in back of work; K1, then K1 from cable needle.

T3B (Twist 3 Back): Sl next st to cable needle and hold behind work; K2, then P1 from cable needle.

T3F (Twist 3 Front): Sl next 2 sts to cable needle and hold in front of work; P1, then K2 from cable needle.

C4B (Cable 4 Back): Sl next 2 sts to cable needle and hold behind work; K1, then K2 from cable needle.

C4F (Cable 4 Front): Sl next 2 sts to cable needle and hold in front of work; K2, then K2 from cable needle.

T4B (Twist 4 Back): Sl next 2 sts to cable needle and hold behind work; K2, then P2 from cable needle.

T4F (Twist 4 Front): Sl next 2 sts to cable needle and hold in front of work; P2, then K2 from cable needle.

T5B (Twist 5 Back): Sl next 3 stitches to cable needle and hold behind work; K2, then P3 from cable needle.

T5F (Twist 5 Front): Sl next 2 sts to cable needle and hold in front of work; P3, then K2 from cable needle.

INSTRUCTIONS

CO 38 sts.

First Seed Stitch Border

Row 1 (wrong side): Sl 1 as to purl with yarn in front; *K1, P1; rep from * to last st, K1.

Row 2: Sl 1 as to purl with yarn in front; *P1, K1; rep from * to last st, K1.

Rep Rows 1 and 2 three more times.

Foundation Pattern Row (wrong side): Sl 1 as to purl with yarn in front; (K1, P1) twice; K12, P4, K12, (K1, P1) twice, K1.

Note 1: Keep 5 sts in seed st border on each side edge for the entire length of scarf.

Note 2: Each row begins with sl 1 as to purl with yarn in front; each row ends with a knit st.

Note 3: Charts are provided for ease of working cable patts. Beg in lower right corner, read charts from right to left on right side rows, and from left to right on wrong-side rows. Use legend to interpret symbols on each chart.

Note 4: On Chart A, stitch count will vary. Chart begins with 28 sts, increases to 36 sts on Row 3, then decreases back to 28 sts on Row 26.

Instructions continue on next page. →

Start Pattern

*Beginning on Row 1, work Chart A until all 34 rows of chart have been completed. Work Chart B until all 26 rows of chart have been completed.

Rep from * two more times, then work Chart A once more until all 34 rows of chart have been completed.

**Work Chart C until all 26 rows of chart have been completed. Work Chart A until all 34 rows of chart have been completed.

Rep from ** once more.

Work Chart C until all 26 rows of chart have been completed.

Work Chart A until all 34 rows of chart have been completed, end by working a wrong-side row.

Chart A

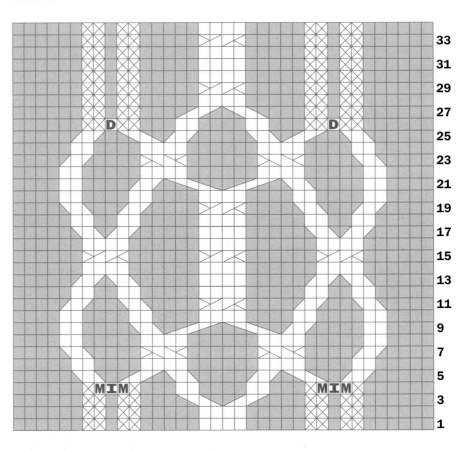

Second Seed Stitch Border

Work as for First Seed Stitch Border. BO in seed st.

Finishing

Block by pinning scarf out to finished dimensions and misting with cool water. Allow to dry.

KEY

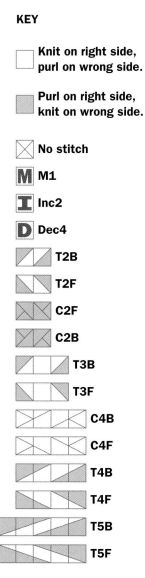

Knit on right side,
purl on wrong side.

Purl on right side,
knit on wrong side.

No stitch

M1

Inc2

Dec4

T2B

T2F

C2F

C2B

T3B

T3F

C4B

C4F

T4B

T4F

T5B

T5F

Chart B

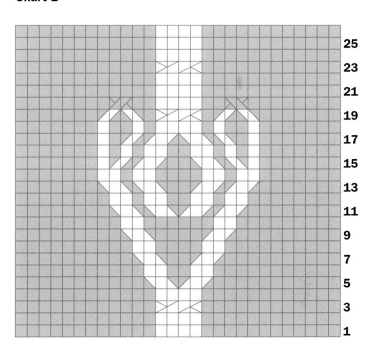

Chart C

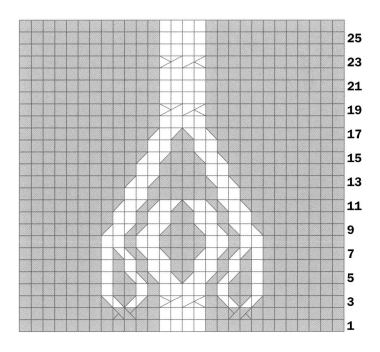

#37 LOVELY IN LACE

Note: Instructions are written for size Small; changes for sizes Medium and Large are in parentheses.

SIZES	Small	Medium	Large
Body Bust Measurements	32" - 34"	36" - 38"	40" - 42"
Finished Bust Measurements	35"	39"	44"

MATERIALS

Worsted weight yarn
22 3/4 (26 1/4, 31 1/2) oz rose

Note: Photographed model made with Naturally Merino et Soie #100 Rose

Size 7 (4.5 mm) knitting needles (or size required for gauge)

Stitch holder

Markers

GAUGE

20 sts and 20 rows = 4" in stock st (knit 1 row, purl 1 row)

INSTRUCTIONS

Back

Starting at bottom, CO 103 (123, 143) sts.

Ribbing

Row 1 (right side): K2, P2, K4, P2, (K3, P2, K4, P2, K1, P2, K4, P2) 4 (5, 6) times; K3, P2, K4, P2, K2.

Row 2: Knit the knit sts and purl the purl sts.

Rep Rows 1 and 2 twice.

Body

Row 1 (right side): K2, YO, P2, K4, P2; (P3tog, P2, K4, P2, YO, K1, YO, P2, K4, P2) 4 (5, 6) times; P3tog, P2, K4, P2, YO, K2.

Row 2 and all wrong side rows: Knit the knit sts and purl the purl sts and the YOs.

Row 3: K2, YO, K1, P2, K4, P1; (P3tog, P1, K4, P2, K1, YO, K1, YO, K1, P2, K4, P1) 4 (5, 6) times; P3tog, P1, K4, P2, K1, YO, K2.

Row 5: K2, YO, K2, P2, K4; (P3tog, K4, P2, K2, YO, K1, YO, K2, P2, K4) 4 (5, 6) times; P3tog, K4, P2, K2, YO, K2.

Row 7: K2, YO, K3, P2, K3; (sl 1, K2tog, PSSO, K3, P2, K3, YO, K1, YO, K3, P2, K3) 4 (5, 6) times; sl 1, K2tog, PSSO, K3, P2, K3, YO, K2.

Row 9: K2, YO, K4, P2, K2; (sl 1, K2tog, PSSO, K2, P2, K4, YO, K1, YO, K4, P2, K2) 4 (5, 6) times; sl 1, K2tog, PSSO, K2, P2, K4, YO, K2.

Row 11: K2, YO, P1, K4, P2, K1; (sl 1, K2tog, PSSO, K1, P2, K4, P1, YO, K1, YO, P1, K4, P2, K1) 4, (5, 6) times; sl 1, K2tog, PSSO, K1, P2, K4, P1, YO, K2.

Row 13: K2, YO, P2, K4, P2; (sl 1, K2tog, PSSO, P2, K4, P2, YO, K1, YO, P2, K4, P2) 4 (5, 6) times; sl 1, K2tog, PSSO, P2, K4, P2, YO, K2.

Row 15: K1, P2tog, P2, K4, P2, YO; (K1, YO, P2, K4, P2, P3tog, P2, K4, P2, YO) 4 (5, 6) times; K1, YO, P2, K4, P2, P2tog, K1.

Row 17: K1, P2tog, P1, K4, P2, K1, YO; (K1, YO, K1, P2, K4, P1, P3tog, P1, K4, P2, K1, YO) 4 (5, 6) times; K1, YO, K1, P2, K4, P1, P2tog, K1.

Row 19: K1, P2tog, K4, P2, K2, YO; (K1, YO, K2, P2, K4, P3tog, K4, P2, K2, YO) 4 (5, 6) times; K1, YO, K2, P2, K4, P2tog, K1.

Row 21: K1, K2tog, K3, P2, K3, YO; (K1, YO, K3, P2, K3, sl 1, K2tog, PSSO, K3, P2, K3, YO) 4 (5, 6) times; K1, YO, K3, P2, K3, sl 1, K1, PSSO, K1.

Row 23: K1, K2tog, K2, P2, K4, YO; (K1, YO, K4, P2, K2, sl 1, K2tog, PSSO, K2, P2, K4, YO) 4 (5, 6) times; K1, YO, K4, P2, K2, sl 1, K1, PSSO, K1.

Instructions continue on next page. →

Row 25: K1, K2tog, K1, P2, K4, P1, YO; (K1, YO, P1, K4, P2, K1, sl 1, K2tog, PSSO, K1, P2, K4, P1, YO) 4 (5, 6) times; K1, YO, P1, K4, P2, K1, sl 1, K1, PSSO, K1.

Row 27: K1, K2tog, P2, K4, P2, YO; (K1, YO, P2, K4, P2, sl 1, K2tog, PSSO, P2, K4, P2, YO) 4 (5, 6) times; K1, YO, P2, K4, P2, sl 1, K1, PSSO, K1.

Row 28: Knit the knit sts and purl the purl sts and the YOs.

Rep Rows 1 through 28 until piece measures 24" (25", 26") from CO edge, ending by working a wrong-side row.

BO loosely in patt.

Front

Work same as back.

Sleeve (make 2)

Starting at bottom edge, CO 63 sts.

Ribbing

Row 1 (right side): K2, P2, K4, P2; (K3, P2, K4, P2, K1, P2, K4, P2) twice; K3, P2, K4, P2, K2.

Row 2 (wrong side): Knit the knit sts and purl the purl sts.

Rep Rows 1 and 2 twice.

Next Row: Inc 1 st at each end of row: 65 sts.

Continue in patt as established, increasing 1 st at each end of every 10th (8th, 8th) row 7 (9, 8) times more: 79 (83, 81) sts, taking inc sts into rib patt.

For Large Size Only

Inc 1 st at each end of every 6th row 3 times more: 87 sts.

Work even until sleeve measures 17 1/2" (18", 18 1/2") from CO edge, ending by working a wrong-side row.

BO loosely in patt.

Mark center 11" at top of front and back for neck opening. Join left shoulder seam.

Collar

With right side facing, pick up and knit 80 sts along back neck and 80 sts along front neck: 160 sts.

Row 1 (right side of collar; wrong side of sweater): P1; (K3, P2, K4, P2, K1, P2, K4, P2) 7 times; K3, P2, K4, P2, K1, P2, K4, P1.

Row 2: Knit the knit sts and purl the purl sts.

Rep Rows 1 and 2 until piece measures 4 3/4", ending by working a Row 2.

BO loosely in patt.

Finishing

Join right shoulder and collar seams.

Place markers 7 1/2" (8", 8 1/2") down from shoulder seam on back and front. Sew sleeve top between markers. Join side and sleeve seams.

#38 PURE ELEGANCE

Designed by Bev Nimon for S.R. Kertzer Limited

SIZE
72" x 30" before fringe

MATERIALS
Railroad ribbon yarn
  10 1/2 oz red

Note: Photographed model made with S.R. Kertzer Ranee #50 Ruby

Size 13 (9 mm) knitting
  needles (or size required
  for gauge)

GAUGE
4 sts = 2" in Pattern Stitch

PATTERN STITCH
Row 1 (right side): K2; * YO, K2tog; rep from *to last st, K1.

Row 2: K1, purl to last 2 sts, K2.

Rep Rows 1 and 2 for patt.

INSTRUCTIONS

Starting at one short end, loosely CO 57 sts.

Rows 1 through 3: Knit.

Work in Patt Stitch until piece measures 70", ending by working a Row 2. Knit 3 rows. BO loosely.

Fringe

Following fringe instructions on page 251, cut 22" lengths of yarn. With 3 strands in each knot, tie knots 3" apart across CO edge and each short end.

#3 TOASTY WARM

Designed by Patons Design Staff

SIZES

Scarf
 5 1/2" x 28"

Hat
 Fits ages 2 (4, 6) yrs

Mittens
 Fit ages 2 (4, 6) yrs

MATERIALS

Eyelash yarn

Scarf
 1 3/4 (1 3/4, 3 1/2) oz variegated

Mittens
 1 3/4 oz variegated (for all sizes)

Note: *Photographed model made with Patons® Cha Cha #2001 Bunny Hop*

Size 10 1/2 (6.5 mm) knitting needles (or size required for gauge) for hat

Four Size 10 1/2 (6.5 mm) double-point knitting needles (or size required for gauge) for mittens

Size 11 (8 mm) knitting needles (or size required for gauge) for scarf

Small stitch holder or safety pin

Tapestry needle

GAUGE

Scarf
 11 sts and 16 rows = 4" in stock st (knit 1 row, purl 1 row)

Hat
 13 sts and 19 rows = 4" in stock st

Mittens
 12 sts = 4" with 2 strands in stock st

SCARF

INSTRUCTIONS

Note: Scarf is knit sideways.

With Size 11 needles, loosely CO 77 sts.

Row 1: Knit.

Row 2: Knit.

Rep Rows 1 and 2 until work measures 5 1/2" from CO edge. BO loosely.

HAT

INSTRUCTIONS

First Earflap

Starting at bottom with Size 10 1/2 needles, CO 3 sts.

Row 1 (wrong side): Knit.

Row 2: (Inc one st in next st) two times, K1: 5 sts.

Row 3: Inc one st in first st, knit to last 2 sts, inc one st in next st, K1: 7sts.

Row 4: Rep Row 3: 9 sts.

Row 5: Knit.

Row 6: Inc one st in first st, knit to last 2 sts, inc one st in next st, K1: 11 sts.

Row 7: Rep Row 5.

Row 8: Rep Row 6: 13 sts.

For 6-Year Size Only

Row 9: Rep Row 5.

Row 10: Rep Row 8: 15 sts.

For All Sizes

Work even in garter st (knit every row) until work measures 3" (3 1/2", 3 1/2") from CO row, ending by working a wrong-side row. BO.

Second Earflap

Work as for First Earflap. Do not cut yarn. Proceed as follows for remainder of Hat.

Next row (joining row): CO 4 sts and knit these 4 sts; K13 (13, 15) from Second Earflap. Turn and CO 20 (22, 22) sts. Turn and K13 (13, 15) from First Earflap. Turn and CO 4 sts: 54 (56, 60) sts.

Rows 1 through 4: Knit.

Row 5: Knit, inc 2 sts evenly across row: 56 (58, 62) sts.

Row 6: Knit.

Row 7: Purl.

Rep Rows 6 and 7, working in rev stock st until work measures 3 1/2" (4", 4 1/2") from joining row ending by working a knit row and dec 0 (2, 4) sts evenly across last row: 56 (56, 58) sts.

Top shaping

Row 1: K1 (1, 2), *K7, K2tog; rep from * to last 1 (1, 2) st(s), K1 (1, 2): 50 (50, 52) sts.

Row 2 and all even rows: Purl.

Row 3: K1 (1, 2), *K6, K2tog; rep from * to last 1 (1, 2) st(s), K1 (1, 2): 44 (44, 46) sts.

Row 5: K1 (1, 2) *K5, K2tog; rep from * to last 1(1, 2) st(s), K1 (1,2): 38 (38, 40) sts.

Row 6: K1 (1, 2) *K4, K2tog; rep from * to last 1 (1, 2) st(s), K1 (1, 2): 32 (32, 34) sts.

Row 8: K1 (1, 2) *K3, K2tog; rep from * to last 1 (1, 2) st(s), K1 (1, 2): 26 (26, 28) sts.

Row 10: K1 (1, 2) *K2, K2tog; rep from * to last 1 (1, 2) st(s), K1 (1, 2): 20 (20, 22) sts.

Row 12: K1 (1, 2) *K1, K2tog; rep from * to last 1 (1, 2) st(s), K1 (1, 2): 14 (14, 16) sts.

Finish off, leaving a long end, Thread yarn through tapestry needle and pull through rem sts and tighten. Fasten securely. Sew back seam.

MITTENS

INSTRUCTIONS

Right Mitten

With 2 strands of yarn, on one double-point needle, CO 14 (16, 18) sts. Divide sts on 3 needles; join and work in rnds. Place marker on first st, move marker up as you work.

Rnd 1 (right side): *K1, P1; rep from * around.

For 2-Year Size Only

Rnds 2 through 5: Rep Rnd 1.

Rnds 6 through 9: Knit.

For 4-Year Size Only

Rnds 2 through 6: Rep Rnd 1.

Rnds 7 through 12: Knit.

For 6-Year Size Only

Rnds 2 through 6: Rep Rnd 1.

Rnds 7 through 13: Knit.

For All Sizes

Shape Thumb Gusset

Rnd 1: K7 (8, 9), M1, K1, M1, knit to end of rnd: 16 (18, 20) sts.

Rnd 2: K7 (8, 9), M1, K3, M1, knit to end of rnd: 18 (20, 22) sts.

Rnd 3: K7 (8, 9), M1, K5, M1, knit to end of rnd: 20 (22, 24) sts.

Rnd 4: K14 (15, 16), sl last 7 sts just worked onto safety pin (for thumb opening) knit to end of rnd.

Rnd 5: Knit and CO 1 st over slipped sts: 14 (16, 18) sts.

Knit in rnds until work measures 4 1/2"
(4 3/4", 5 1/4") from start of thumb gusset.
Rearrange sts as follows: 7 (8, 9) sts on first
needle, 4 sts on 2nd needle, 3 (4, 5) sts on
3rd needle.

Shape Top
Rnd 1: First Needle: Sl 1, K1, PSSO, Knit to
last 2 sts, K2tog. 2nd Needle: Sl 1, K1, PSSO,
knit to end of needle. 3rd Needle: Knit to last
2 sts, K2tog: 10 (12, 14 sts).

Rnd 2: Rep Rnd 1: 6 (8, 10) sts.

For Sizes 4 and 6 Only
Rnd 3: Rep Rnd 1: 4 (6) sts.

For All Sizes
Finish off. Thread yarn end into a tapestry
needle and through rem 6 (4, 6) sts. Draw up
and fasten securely.

Thumb
K7 from safety pin. Pick up and knit 1 st at
base of thumb. Divide these 8 sts onto 3 needles; join. Knit 4 (5, 5) rnds even.

Next rnd: (K2, K2tog) twice.

Next rnd: (K1, K2tog) twice. Cut yarn; thread
end into a tapestry needle and draw through
rem 4 sts. Draw up and fasten securely.

Left Mitten
Work same as Right Mitten to Shape Thumb
Gusset.

Shape Thumb Gusset
Rnd 1: K6 (7, 8), M1, K1, M1, knit to end of
rnd: 16 (18, 20) sts.

Rnd 2: K6 (7, 8), M1, K3, M1, knit to end of
rnd: 18 (20, 22) sts.

Rnd 3: K6 (7, 8), M1, K5, M1, knit to end of
rnd: 20 (22, 24) sts.

Rnd 4: K13 (14, 15), sl last 7 sts just worked
onto a safety pin (for thumb opening).

Rnd 5: Knit, CO 1 st over slipped sts: 14 (16,
18) sts.

Continue working Left Mitten as for Right
Mitten.

#42 BEST IN BLACK

MATERIALS

DK Yarn

12 1/2 (14 1/4, 14 1/4, 16, 17 3/4) oz black

Note: Photographed model made with Twilleys of Stamford Freedom #14 Black.

Size 3 (3.25 mm) knitting needles

Size 5 (3.75 mm) knitting needles (or size required for gauge)

GAUGE

21 sts and 30 rows = 4" with larger needles in stock st (knit 1 row, purl 1 row)

24 sts and 25 rows = 4" with larger needles in pattern

Note: Instructions are written for size X-Small; changes Small, Medium, Large and X-Large are in parentheses.

SIZES	X-Small	Small	Medium	Large	X-Large
Body Bust Measurements	32"	34"	36"	38"	40"
Finished Bust Measurements	34"	36"	38"	40"	42"

INSTRUCTIONS

Back

With smaller needles, CO 81 (87, 91, 97, 103) sts.

Rows 1 (right side) through 16: Knit.

Row 17: *K3, M1; rep from * 8 (5, 7, 4, 1) time(s); ** K4, M1; rep from ** 5 (11, 9, 15, 21) times; *** K3, M1; rep from *** 8 (5, 7, 4, 1) time(s), K3: 105 (111, 117, 123, 129) sts.

Change to larger needles and work in patt until piece measures 14", ending by working a Row 2.

Shape Armholes

Row 1: BO 6 sts, K1, YO , K1; *YO, K1, sl 1, K2tog, PSSO, K1, YO, K1; rep from * across, ending with K1: 99 (105, 111, 117, 123) sts.

Row 2: BO 6 sts, purl to end of row: 93 (99, 105, 111, 117) sts.

Keeping continuity of patt as established, dec 1 st at each end of next 3 (5, 5, 9, 9) rows: 87 (89, 95, 93, 99) sts.

Work even for one row.

Dec 1 st at each end of next row, then every other row 2 (3, 3, 2, 2) times more: 81 (81, 87, 87, 93) sts.

Continue in patt until armhole measures 7" (7 1/2", 8", 8 1/2", 9" ending by working a Row 2.

Change to smaller needles

Decrease Row: *K4, K2tog; rep from * 3 (3, 5, 5, 5) times; **K5 (5, 3, 3, 5), K2tog; rep from ** 3 (3, 1, 1, 1) time(s); ***K4, K2tog; rep from *** 3 (3, 5, 5, 5) times, K5 (5, 5, 5, 7): 69 (69, 73, 73, 79) sts.

Knit 8 rows and BO evenly. Finish off; weave in ends.

Front

Work same as back.

Assembly

Steam work lightly over wrong side avoiding garter stitch borders. Sew shoulder seams for 1 1/2".

Armhole Borders

With right side facing and larger needles, pick up and knit 84 (88, 92, 98, 100) sts evenly around edge of armhole.

Knit one row and BO evenly.

Finishing

Sew side seams and armhole borders. Weave in all ends.

#43 BORDERING ON LACE

Designed by Rita Weiss

SIZE
40" x 36" before border

MATERIALS
Sport weight yarn
   17 ¹/₂ oz off white

Note: *Photographed model made with Patons® Astra #02783 Aran*

Yarn needle

29" size 8 (5 mm) circular
   knitting needle (or size
   required for gauge)

10" size 10 (6 mm) straight
   knitting needles (for border)

GAUGE
18 sts = 4" with smaller
   needles in lace patt

PATTERN STITCHES

Lace Pattern

Note: Always slip as to knit.

Row 1 (right side): K1; *YO, K3, YO, K1; rep from * across.

Row 2: Purl.

Row 3: K2; *sl 1, K2tog, PSSO, K3; rep from * across, ending last rep with K2.

Row 4: Purl.

Border Pattern

Row 1 and all wrong-side rows: Purl

Row 2 (right side): Sl 1, K2tog, YO, K3tog, YO, K2tog: 6 sts.

Row 4: Sl 1, (YO, K1) 3 times; YO, K2tog: 9 sts.

Row 6: Sl 1, K2tog, YO, K1, YO, K2, YO, K1, YO, K2tog: 11 sts.

Row 8: Sl 1, K2tog, (YO, K1) twice, K2tog, (K1, YO) twice, K2tog: 12 sts.

Row 10: Sl 1, K2tog, (YO, K1) twice, K3 tog, (K1, YO) twice, K2tog: 12 sts.

Row 12: Sl 1, K2tog, YO, K2, K3tog, K2, YO, K2tog: 10 sts.

Row 14: Sl 1, K2tog, YO, K1, K3tog, K1, YO, K2tog: 8 sts.

Border Corner

Rows 1 and 2: Work Rows 1 and 2 of Border Patt.

Row 3 (wrong side): P5, turn, leaving rem st on needle unworked.

Row 4: Sl 1, P2, YO, K2 tog.

Row 5: P4, turn, leaving rem sts on needle unworked.

Row 6: Sl 1, K1, YO, K2tog.

Row 7: P3, turn, leaving rem sts on needle unworked.

Row 8: Sl 1, YO, K2tog.

Row 9: Purl: 6 sts.

INSTRUCTIONS

With circular needle, CO 181 sts; do not join; work back and forth in rows.

Rep Rows 1 through 4 of Lace Pattern until piece measures about 36" from CO edge, ending by working a Row 4. BO all sts as to purl.

Border

With straight needles, CO 8 sts.

Work Rows 1 through 14 of Border Patt until border measures about 18" from CO edge, ending by working a Row 2. Then work corner patt.

Work Rows 4 through 14 of border once; then rep Rows 1 through 14 of border until border measures approx 40" from prev corner shaping, ending by working a Row 2. Work rem corners and next short and following longer edges in same manner, then ending on last edge approx 18" from 4th corner by working Row 14. BO all sts as to purl.

Finishing

Weave CO and BO edges of border tog. Pin border to afghan, having joining seam of border at side edge of afghan. Using yarn needle and same yarn, join border to afghan using an overcast st. Weave in all ends.

#44 DRAGON HOODIE

Designed by Marnie MacLean

SIZES	18 months	24 months	3 years
Body Chest Measurements	20 - 21"	22 - 23"	24 - 25"
Finished Chest Measurements	22 ¹/₂"	24 ¹/₂"	26 ¹/₂"

MATERIALS

Worsted weight yarn
  5 ¹/₂ oz green
  2 ³/₄ oz purple

Note: *Photographed model made with TLC® Amoré™ #3534 Light Thyme and #3627 Purple*

2 stitch markers

1 large stitch holder

10" separating plastic zipper, lavender or purple

18" (20", 21") round elastic for hood

Size 9 (6.5 mm) knitting needles

Size 10 ¹/₂ (6.5 mm) knitting needles (or size required for gauge)

GAUGE

15 sts and 20 rows = 4" in stock st (knit 1 row, purl 1 row)

INSTRUCTIONS

Note: Fronts and Back are worked in one piece to armholes.

Starting at bottom with smaller needles and purple, CO 81 (90, 97) sts.

Place a st marker between sts 20 and 21 (22 and 23, 24 and 25) and another marker between sts 61 and 62 (68 and 69, 73 and 74).

Seed Stitch Border

Work 5 rows in seed st (see Stitch Guide).

Body

Change to larger needles and green yarn.

Note: From here on, piece is worked entirely in stock st unless otherwise specified.

Rows 1 through 22 (26, 30): Work even in stock st, beg with a knit row (right side) and ending by working a wrong-side row.

Right Front Armhole and Neck

Row 1 (right side): Knit to first st marker; place rem sts on large st holder for Back and Left front.

Row 2: BO 2 sts for underarm, purl across: 18 (20, 22) sts.

Row 3: Knit

Row 4: Purl.

Row 5: Knit.

Row 6: P2 tog, purl across: 17 (19, 21) sts.

For Size Small Only
Dec one st at armhole edge every 3rd row 5 times, and on the 5th time also BO 4 sts at neck edge: 8 sts.

Then dec one st at neck edge every row, and at the same time, dec one st every other row at armhole edge until 2 sts rem. Work one row even. Work last 2 sts tog; finish off.

For Size Medium Only
Dec one st at armhole edge every 3rd row 3 times: 16 sts. Then dec one st at armhole every other row 2 times. On last row BO 4 sts at neck edge: 10 sts rem.

Continue dec every other row on armhole edge and at the same time, dec one st every row at neck edge for 4 rows: 4 sts. Then dec one st every other row at neck edge until 2 sts rem.

Work one row even. Work last 2 sts tog; finish off.

For Size Large Only
Work 3 rows even in stock st. Continuing in stock st, dec one st at armhole edge every other row 4 times: 16 sts.

Instructions continue on next page. ➔

BO 4 sts at neck edge: 12 sts.

Next Row: Dec one st at each edge: 10 sts.

Continue in stock st, dec one st at armhole edge every other row 5 times and at the same time, dec one st at neck edge every row 3 times: 2 sts.

Work one row even. Work last 2 sts tog. Finish off.

Left Front Armhole and Neck

With right side facing, leave center 41 (46, 47) sts on st holder for Back and place rem 20 (22, 24) sts on a needle for Left Front.

With knit side facing, join yarn and BO 2 sts for underarm; work across: 18 (20, 22) sts).

Work as for Right Front Armhole and Neck, reversing shaping.

Back Armholes and Neck

Move Back sts from st holder to a needle. With right side facing, join yarn.

Row 1: BO 2 sts for underarm, work across.

Row 2: Rep Row 1: 37 (42, 45) sts.

Work 3 rows even.

Dec one st at each end of next row: 35 (40, 43) sts.

Dec one st at each end every 3rd row 5 (2, 0) times: 25 (36, 43) sts

Dec one st at each end of every other row 1 (6, 9) times: 23 (24, 25) sts.

Work 4 sts, BO next 15 (16, 17) sts for neck, work 4 sts: 8 sts.

For Size Small Only

Working only on the last 4 sts, dec one st at each end: 2 sts. Work 1 row even; work last 2 sts tog. Return to other 4 rem sts on opposite side, join yarn and dec one st at each end: 2 sts. Work 1 row even, work last 2 sts tog. Finish off.

For Sizes Medium and Large Only

Working only on the last 4 sts , dec one st on neck edge every row until 2 sts rem. Work one row even, work last 2 sts tog. Finish off. Return to other 4 rem sts on opposite side ; join yarn and dec one st on neck edge every row until 2 sts rem. Work one row even, work last 2 sts tog. Finish off.

Sleeve (make 2)

With smaller needles and purple, CO 25 (26, 28) sts.

Work in seed st ribbing as before for 2" (2 1/2", 3").

Change to larger needles and green yarn and work 26 (30, 32) rows of stock st, beg by working a knit row.

Shape Armhole

BO 2 sts at beg of next 2 rows for underarms: 21 (22, 24) sts.

Work 3 rows even.

Next Row: Dec one st at each end: 19 (20, 22) sts.

Then dec one st at each end every 3rd row 5 (3, 1) times: 9 (14, 20) sts.

Then dec one st at each end of every other row 2 (6, 9) times: 5 (2, 2) sts. Work one row even.

BO.

Hood

Starting at front edge with smaller needles and purple, CO 68 (72, 76) sts.

Row 1: Knit.

Row 2: Purl.

Rows 3 through 8: Rep Rows 1 and 2.

Row 9: Knit.

Change to larger needles and green.

For Sizes Small and Medium Only
Continuing in stock st, work 3 (4) rows even. Then dec 1 at each end of next row and every other row 7 (7) times more: 52 (56) sts.

For Size Large Only
Dec one st at each end of every 3rd row 8 times: 60 sts.

For All Sizes
Continuing in stock st, work 5 (5, 3) rows even.

BO 19 (21, 22) sts at beg of next 2 rows: 14 (14, 16) sts.

Work even for 24 (27, 30) rows. BO.

Elastic Casing

With right side facing fold the purple area of the hood in half to the wrong side along the long edge. Sew in place to make casing, leaving ends open for insertion of elastic.

Form Top

With wrong sides tog, fold narrow piece of hood over wide piece and sew ends of rows of narrow piece to BO edges of wide piece, easing to fit. This forms a cup shape.

Finishing

Sew shoulder seams; sew sleeve seams and sew sleeves into armholes.

Zipper Placket

With smaller needles and purple yarn, with right side facing pick up 36 (38, 39) sts along front edge of Right Front. Work 5 rows in seed stitch. BO.

Work Left Front placket in same manner. Pin zipper in place in placket, letting any excess extend over the top. If needed, sew thread over zipper at point where it should stop. Test that zipper will not zip past this point. Cut excess zipper above this point, making sure zipper pull is below the point you are cutting.

Sew hood into neck opening, aligning placket with hood casing and centering back of hood to back of sweater. Thread round elastic through hood casing and draw up to desired size; cut off unneeded length, knot and sew ends securely.

Ears (make 2)

With smaller needles and green yarn, CO 3 sts.

Row 1: K1, inc, knit to next to last st, inc, K1: 5 sts.

Row 2: P1, inc in next st, purl to next to last st, inc in next st, P1: 7 sts.

Row 3: Rep Row 1: 9 sts.

Row 4: Purl.

Row 5: Knit.

Row 6: P2tog, purl to last 2 sts, P2tog.

Row 7: K2tog, knit to last 2 sts, K2tog.

Instructions continue on next page. →

Rep Rows 6 and 7 until one st remains. BO, leaving a long yarn end for sewing.

Spine

With smaller needles and purple yarn, CO 60 (64, 64) sts

First Peak

Row 1: Knit 10 (8, 10) sts, leaving rem sts unworked on left needle.

Row 2: Working only on these 10 (8, 10) sts, knit, dec one st at beg and end of row: 8 (6, 8) sts.

Rep Row 2 until 2 sts rem; K2tog. Finish off.

Next Peaks

Work as for First Peak across rem sts, working 10 (8, 10) sts at a time.

Spots

Note: *All spots are worked in stock st with purple yarn. When finishing off, leave a long yarn end for sewing.*

Spot 1 (make 2)

CO 2 sts.

Row 1: Knit.

Row 2: Purl, inc one st at each end.

Row 3: Knit, inc one st at each end: 6 sts.

Work even for 11 rows, then dec one st at each end of every row twice: 2 sts. Work one row even. BO.

Spot 2 (make 2)

CO 3 sts.

Row 1: Knit, inc one st at each end of row.

Row 2: Purl, inc one st at each end of row.

Row 3: Rep Row 1: 9 sts.

Work even for 8 rows, then dec one st at each end of every row 3 times: 3 sts. Work one row even. BO.

Spot 3 (make 2)

CO 3 sts.

Row 1: Knit, inc one st at beg and end of row: 5 sts.

Rows 2 through 9: Work even.

Row 10: Purl, dec one st at each end of row: 3 sts.

Row 11: Knit. BO.

Spot 4 (make 1)

CO 2 sts.

Row 1: Knit, inc one st at beg and end of row: 4 sts.

Rows 2 through 5: Work even.

Row 6: Purl, dec one st at each end of row.

Row 7: Knit. BO.

Spot 5 (make 1)

CO 3 sts.

Row 1: Knit, inc one st at beg and end of row: 5 sts.

Rows 2 through 6: Work even.

Row 7: Knit, dec one st at each end of row: 3 sts.

Row 8: Purl. BO.

Spot 6 (make 1)

CO 3 sts.

Row 1: Knit, inc one st at each end of row: 5 sts.

Rows 2 through 8: Work even.

Row 9: Purl, dec one st at each end of row: 3 sts.

Row 10: Knit. BO.

Finishing

Sew spots on sweater, following placement as shown in photo, or as desired.

Sew ears at top of hood seams as shown in photo.

Starting at center back, sew spine from top of lower seed stitch border to just between the ears, keeping spine straight and centered on back.

Sew zipper to placket.

ANCHORS AWAY

Designed by Patons Design Staff

MATERIALS

DK or sport weight yarn

    5 1/4 (5 1/4, 7) oz blue (MC)

    5 1/4 (5 1/4, 7) oz white (A)

    small quantity dark blue (for embroidery)

Note: *Photographed model made with Patons® Grace #60104 Azure (MC), #60005 Snow (A) and #60110 Marine (for embroidery)*

14" Size 3 (3.25 mm) knitting needles

14" Size 5 (3.75 mm) knitting needles (or size required for gauge)

One 14" Size 5 (3.75 mm) spare knitting needle

4 stitch holders

6 buttons.

GAUGE

24 sts and 32 rows = 4" with larger needles in stock st (knit 1 row, purl 1 row)

Note: *Instructions are written for size 3 months, changes for sizes 6 months and 12 months are in parentheses.*

SIZES	3 months	6 months	12 months
Body Chest Measurements	16"	17"	19"
Finished chest Measurements	22"	24"	26"

INSTRUCTIONS

Back

Left Side

Starting at cuff with MC and smaller needles, CO 27 (29, 31) sts.

Row 1 (right side): *K1, P1; rep from * to last st, K1.

Row 2: *P1, K1, rep from * to last st, P1.

Rows 3 and 4: Rep Rows 1 and 2.

Row 5: Rep Row 1.

Row 6: Inc 1 (0, 1) st, rib across, inc 0 (0, 1): 28 (29, 33) sts.

Change to larger needles and color A and begin stripe patt. (Note: Remember to change colors every six rows.)

Row 1: Knit.

Row 2: Purl.

Continue in stock st and stripe pattern, and at same time inc one st at each end of needle of 7th and every following 6th (6th, 8th) row until there are 36 (39, 43) sts.

Work even in stripe patt until piece measures 5" (6", 7 1/2") from CO edge, ending by working a wrong-side row. Cut yarn; leave sts on needle.

Right Side

Work as for Left Side; at end of last row, do not cut yarn.

Joining Row

Row 1 (right side): Work in patt across 36 (39, 43) sts of Right side, turn; cast on 4

sts; turn and work in patt across 36 (39, 43) sts of Left side: 76 (82, 90) sts.

Work even in patt until piece measures 3" (3 1/2", 4") from joining row, ending by working a wrong-side row.

Back Body Shaping

Continuing in patt, dec 1 st at each end of needle on next and on every following 10th (12th, 12th) rows until there are 66 (72, 78) sts. Work even in patt until piece measures 12 1/2" (13 3/4", 15") from joining row, ending by working a wrong-side row.

Back Neck Shaping

Row 1: K22 (24, 27), turn; leave rem sts on needle and continue with spare needle.

Row 2: P2tog, purl across: 21 (23, 26) sts.

Row 3: Knit to last two sts, K2 tog: 20 (22, 25) sts.

Row 4: Purl. Place rem sts on a st holder.

With right side of work facing, sl next 22 (24, 24) sts onto a st holder.

Row 1: Join yarn to rem 22 (24, 27) sts and work in patt across.

Row 2: Purl to last two sts, P2tog: 21 (23, 26) sts.

Row 3: K2tog, knit across: 20 (22, 25) sts.

Row 4: Purl. Place rem sts on a st holder.

Front

Work as for Back until piece measures 11 1/4" (12 1/2", 13 1/2") from joining row, ending by working a wrong-side row: 66 (72, 78) sts.

109

Instructions continue on next page. →

Front Neck Shaping
First Side

Row 1: Work in patt across 26 (29, 32) sts, turn, leaving rem sts on needle.

Row 2: With spare needle, P2tog (neck edge), purl across: 25 (28, 31) sts.

Row 3: Knit to last 2 sts, K2 tog: 24 (27, 30) sts.

Row 4: Dec 0 (1, 1) sts; purl across: 24 (26, 29) sts.

Row 5: Knit.

Row 6: P2tog, purl across: 23 (25, 28) sts.

Rows 7 through 12: Rep Rows 5 and 6: 20 (22, 25) sts.

Work even until work measures same length as Back from beg to shoulder. Place sts on a st holder.

Second Side

With right side facing, slip next 14 sts onto a st holder.

Row 1: Join yarn to rem 26 (29, 32) sts and work in patt across.

Row 2: Purl to last 2 sts, P2tog (neck edge): 25 (28, 31) sts,

Row 3: K2tog, knit across: 24 (27, 30) sts.

Row 4: Purl across to last 0 (2, 2) sts, P2tog on larger sizes: 24 (26, 29) sts.

Row 5: Knit.

Row 6: Purl across to last 2 sts, P2tog: 23 (25, 28) sts.

Rows 7 through 12: Rep Rows 5 and 6: 20 (22, 25) sts.

Work even until work measures same length as other side. Place sts on a holder.

Sleeves (make 2)

With MC and smaller needles, cast on 39 (41, 43) sts

Row 1: *K1, P1; rep from * across, ending with K1.

Row 2: *P1, K1; rep from * across, ending with P1.

Rows 3 and 4: Rep Rows 1 and 2.

Row 5: Rep Row 1:

Row 6: Knit 1 (2, 1); *inc 1 st, K8 (8, 9); rep from * 3 times more; inc 1 st, knit 1 (2, 1): 44 (46, 48) sts.

Change to larger needles. Continuing in stripe pattern, inc one st at each end of needle on 5th. Then inc every 6 (4, 4) rows until there are 54 (54, 56) sts.

For Sizes 6 Months and 12 Months Only
Inc 1 st at each end of needle on following 6th rows from prev inc until there are (60, 66) sts.

For All Sizes
Work even until piece measures 5 1/2" (6 1/2", 7 1/2") from beg, ending by working a wrong-side row. BO.

Finishing
Back Neckband

Row 1: With right side of work facing, with MC and smaller needles pick up and knit 3 sts down right back neck edge, K22 (24, 24) from back st holder, dec 1 st at center; pick up and knit 3 sts up left back neck edge: 27 (29, 29) sts.

Rows 2 through 6: Work in (K1, P1) ribbing. At end of last row, BO in ribbing.

Right Back Shoulder Band

Row 1: With right side of work facing, with MC and smaller needles, K20 (22, 25) from right back shoulder st holder, increasing 2 (2, 3) sts evenly across; then pick up and knit 5 sts across side of Back neckband: 27 (29, 33) sts.

Rows 2 through 6: Work in (K1, P1) ribbing. At end of last row, BO in ribbing.

Left Back Shoulder Band

Row 1: With right side of work facing, with MC and smaller needles, pick up and knit 5 sts across side of Back neckband, then K20 (22, 25) from left back shoulder st holder, increasing 2 (2, 3) sts evenly across: 27 (29, 33) sts.

Rows 2 through 6: Work in (K1, P1) ribbing. At end of last row, BO in ribbing.

Front Neckband

Row 1: With right side of work facing, with MC and smaller needles, pick up and knit 14 sts down left front neck edge; K14 (14, 14) from Back st holder, decreasing 1 st at center; pick up and knit 14 sts up right front neck edge: 41 sts.

Rows 2 through 6: Work 5 rows in (K1, PI) ribbing. At end of last row, BO in ribbing.

Left Front Shoulder Buttonhole Band

Row 1: With right side of work facing, with MC and smaller needles, K20 (22, 25) from left front shoulder st holder, increasing 2 (2, 3) sts evenly across, then pick up and knit 5 sts across side of Front neckband: 27 (29, 33) sts.

Rows 2 through 4: Work in (K1, P1) ribbing.

Row 5: Work in ribbing across 5 sts; *BO 2 sts; work in ribbing across 6 (7, 9) sts (including st on needle after BO); rep from * once more; BO 2 sts; work in ribbing to end of row: 3 buttonholes made.

Row 6: Work in ribbing, CO 2 sts over each set of BO sts; BO in ribbing.

Right Front Shoulder Buttonhole Band

Row 1: With right side of work facing, with MC and smaller needles, pick up and knit 5 sts across side of Front neckband; K20 (22, 25) from right front shoulder st holder, increasing 2 (2, 3) sts evenly across: 27 (29, 33) sts.

Rows 2 through 4: Work in (K1, P1) ribbing.

Row 5: Work in ribbing across 2 sts; *BO 2 sts, work in ribbing across 6 (7, 9) sts (including st on needle after BO); rep from * once more; BO 2 sts; work in ribbing to end of row: 3 buttonholes made.

Row 6: Work in ribbing, CO 2 sts over each set of 2 BO sts.

BO in ribbing.

Finishing

Weave in all ends.

Lap Front Shoulder Bands over Back Shoulder Bands and sew tog at sleeve edge. Place markers on side edges of Front and Back 4 1/2" (5, 5 1/2)" down from top of shoulder. Sew in sleeves between markers. Sew side and sleeve seams. Sew leg inseams. Sew buttons to correspond to buttonholes.

Embroidery

Using Duplicate Stitch (see page 252), work Chart with dark blue at center front as illustrated, placing top of row of sts 5 sts down from center front neck edge.

Chart

#46 DELIGHTFUL DOILY

Designed by Rita Weiss

SIZE
9 ¹/₂" diameter

MATERIALS
Bedspread weight size 10
   crochet thread
   70 yds White

Note: *Photographed model made with J&P Coats® Opera® #500 White*

Stitch marker or safety pin

Four size 3 (3.25 mm) double-point knitting needles (or size required for gauge)

24" Size 3 (3.25 mm) circular knitting needle

Note: *Begin doily with double point needles and switch to circular needle when the number of sts increases.*

GAUGE
16 sts = 2" in circular stock st (knit each row)

INSTRUCTIONS

Note: *Mark the start of each rnd by with a stitch marker or small safety pin.*

CO 9 sts onto one double-point needle. Divide the sts onto three needles; join, being careful not to twist sts.

Rnds 1 and 2: Knit.

Rnd 3: *YO, K1; rep from * around: 18 sts.

Rnds 4 through 6: Knit.

Rnd 7: Rep Rnd 3: 36 sts.

Rnds 8 through 10: Knit.

Rnd 11: K1; *YO, K1, YO, K3; rep from * around, ending last rep with K2: 54 sts.

Rnd 12 through 14: Knit.

Rnd 15: P1; *(YO, K1) 3 times, YRN, P3; rep from * around, ending last rep with P2: 90 sts.

Rnds 16 through 18: Knit.

Rnd 19: *P1, P2tog, (YO, K1) 3 times, YRN, (P2tog) twice; rep from * around: 99 sts.

Rnds 20 through 22: Knit.

Rnd 23: *(P2tog) twice, (YO, K1) 3 times; YRN, (P2tog) twice; rep from * around: 99 sts.

Rnds 24 through 26: Knit.

Rnd 27: Rep Rnd 23.

Rnds 28 through 30: Knit.

Rnd 31: Rep Rnd 23.

Rnds 32 through 34: Knit.

Rnd 35: *P2tog, P1, (YO, K1) 5 times, YRN, P1, P2tog; rep from * around: 135 sts.

Rnds 36 through 38: Knit.

Rnd 39: *P2, (YO, K1) 11 times, YRN, P2; rep from * around: 243sts.

Rnds 40 through 42: Knit.

Rnd 43 (edging): K1; *K2tog, YO, K2tog; turn, P1, M5, P1, sl 1, turn; BO 7 sts (one st remains on right needle); rep from * around to last 2 sts on left needle, K1, YO, K1; turn; P1, M5, P1, sl 1; turn, BO rem sts.

Finishing

Weave in all ends. Carefully block doily.

#4749 BOLDLY STRIPED

Designed by Patons Design Staff

114

SIZE

Hat
  Fits up to 21" head

Scarf
  Approx 8 ½" x 130" not including fringe

Mittens
  Fit average lady

MATERIALS

Worsted weight yarn

Hat
  7 oz black

Scarf
  10 ½ oz black
  10 ½ oz taupe

Mittens
  1 ¾ oz black
  1 ¾ oz taupe

Note: Photographed model made with Patons® Décor #1603 Black and #1631 Taupe

14" Size 7 (4.5 mm) knitting needles (or size required for gauge) for hat and scarf

Four Size 6 (4 mm) double-point knitting needles (or size required for gauge) for mittens

2 Safety pins or small stitch holders

Stitch marker

GAUGE

For hat: 19 sts and 38 rows = 4" in patt

For scarf: 20 sts and 26 rows = 4" in stock st (knit 1 row, purl 1 row)

For mittens: 21 sts and 28 rows = 4" in stock st

HAT

INSTRUCTIONS

Starting at bottom of hat, CO 89 sts with black.

Row 1 (right side): Knit.

Row 2: K1; *K1B, P1; rep from * to last 2 sts, K1B, K1.

Rep Rows 1 and 2 until work measures 10 ½", ending by working a wrong-side row.

Shape Top

Row 1: K8; *sl 1, K2tog, PSSO, K11; rep from * 4 more times, sl 1, K2tog, PSSO, K8: 77 sts.

Row 2 and all even rows: K1; *K1, P1; rep from * to last 2 sts, K2.

Row 3: K7; *sl 1, K2tog, PSSO, K9; rep from * 4 more times, sl 1, K2tog, PSSO, K7: 65 sts.

Row 5: K6; *sl 1, K2 tog, PSSO, K7; rep from * 4 more times, sl 1, K2tog, PSSO, K6: 53 sts.

Row 7: K5; *sl 1, K2 tog, PSSO, K5; rep from * 4 more times, sl 1, K2tog, PSSO, K5: 41 sts.

Row 9: K4; *sl 1, K2tog, PSSO, K3; rep from * 4 more times, sl 1, K2tog, PSSO, K4: 29 sts.

Row 11: K3; *sl 1, K2 tog, PSSO, K1; rep from * 4 more times, sl 1, K2tog, PSSO, K3: 17 sts.

Instructions continue on next page. →

Cut yarn leaving a long end. Thread into a yarn needle and draw through rem sts, pull up and fasten securely. Sew center back seam, reversing seam in cuff area for turn-back.

SCARF

INSTRUCTIONS

Starting at bottom of scarf, CO 48 sts with black.

Row 1 (right side): K2, *P2, K4; rep from * to last 4 sts, P2, K2.

Row 2: P2, *K2, P4; rep from * to last 4 sts, K2, P2.

Rows 3 through 6: Rep Rows 1 and 2. At end of Row 6, cut black and attach taupe.

**With taupe, rep Rows 1 and 2 twenty-six times (52 rows) ending by working Row 2. Cut taupe and attach black.

With black, rep Rows 1 and 2 twenty-six times (52 rows), ending by working Row 2. Cut black and attach taupe.**

Rep from ** to ** until work from beg measures approx 129" working last 52 rows with taupe.

With black, rep Rows 1 through 6. CO in patt.

Fringe

Following fringe instructions on page 251, cut 12" strands of black and work Single Knot Fringe, using 4 strands in each knot approx ½" apart along top and lower edges of scarf.

MITTENS

INSTRUCTIONS

Right Mitten

With black, CO 40 sts onto one double-point needle. Divide sts on 3 needles (14, 14, 12) sts. Join, being careful not to twist stitches. Mark first st with st marker. Replace the marker at the start of every rnd.

Ribbing

Rnd 1: *K2, P2; rep from * around. This rnd forms (K2, P2) ribbing.

Rnds 2 through 21: Rep Rnd 1, inc 2 sts evenly across last rnd: 42 sts.

Knit 10 rnds.

Thumb Gusset

Rnd 1: K21, inc 1 st in each of next 2 sts, knit to end of rnd: 44 sts.

Rnd 2 and all even rnds: Knit.

Rnd 3: K21, inc 1 st in next st, K2, inc 1 st in next st, knit to end of rnd: 46 sts.

Rnd 5: K21, inc 1 st in next st, K4, inc 1 st in next st, knit to end of rnd: 48 sts.

Rnd 7: K21, inc 1 st in next st, K6, inc 1 st in next st, knit to end of rnd: 50 sts.

Rnd 9: K21, inc 1 st in next st, K8, inc 1 st in next st, knit to end of rnd: 52 sts.

Rnd 11: K21, inc 1 st in next st, K10, inc 1 st in next st, knit to end of rnd: 54 sts.

Rnd 12: Knit.

Rnd 13: K35, slip last 14 sts just worked onto safety pin (thumb opening); turn, CO 2 sts over slipped sts, turn, knit to end of rnd: 42 sts.

***Knit in rnds until work measures 6 ins from ribbing.

Rearrange sts as follows: 21 sts on 1st needle. 10 sts on 2nd needle. 11 sts on 3rd needle.

Shape Top

Rnd 1: First needle: K1, sl 1, K1, PSSO, knit to last 3 sts, K2tog, K1. Second needle: K1, sl 1, K1, PSSO, knit to end of needle. Third needle: knit to last 3 sts, K2tog, K1: 38 sts.

Rnds 2 through 9: Rep Rnd 1. At end of Rnd 9: 6 sts. Cut yarn and thread end through rem 6 sts. Draw up and fasten securely.

Thumb

K14 from safety pin. Pick up and knit 2 sts at base of thumb. Divide these 16 sts onto 3 needles.

Rnds 1 through 18: Knit.

Rnd 19: (K2, K2tog) 4 times: 12 sts.

Rnd 20: (K1, K2tog) 4 times: 8 sts.

Rnnd 21: (K2tog) 4 times: 4 sts.

Cut yarn. And thread end through rem 4 sts. Draw up and fasten securely. ***

Left Mitten

With Taupe, CO 40 sts onto one double-point needle. Work same as for Right Mitten to Thumb Gusset: 42 sts.

Thumb Gusset

Rnd 1: K19, Inc 1 st in each of next 2 sts, knit to end of rnd: 44 sts.

Rnd 2 and all even rnds: Knit.

Rnd 3: K19, inc 1 st in next st, K2, inc 1 st in next st, knit to end of rnd: 46 sts.

Rnd 5: K19, inc 1 st in next st, K4, inc 1 st in next st, knit to end of rnd: 48 sts.

Rnd 7: K19, inc 1 st in next st, K6, inc 1 st in next st, knit to end of rnd: 50 sts.

Rnd 9: K19, inc 1 st in next st, K8, inc 1 st in next st, knit to end of rnd: 52 sts.

Rnd 11: K21, inc 1 st in next st, K10, inc 1 st in next st, knit to end of rnd: 54 sts.

Rnd 12: Knit.

Rnd 13: K33, slip last 14 sts just worked onto safety pin (thumb opening); turn, CO 2 sts over slipped sts, turn, knit to end of rnd: 42 sts.

Work from *** to *** as given for Right Mitten.

#50 CABLE YOKE PULLOVER

Designed by Donna Druchunas

Note: *Instructions are written for size Small; changes for sizes Medium and Large are in parentheses. When only one number is listed, it applies to all sizes.*

SIZES	Small	Medium	Large
Body Bust Measurements	32"	36"	40"
Finished Bust Measurements	36"	40"	44"

MATERIALS

Worsted weight yarn
  1020 (1210, 1400) yards off white

Note: *Photographed model made with Plymouth Galaway Worsted #01 Off White*

Cable needle

8 stitch markers

Tapestry needle

20" Size 6 (4 mm) circular knitting needles

Three 20" Size 8 (5 mm) circular knitting needle (or size required for gauge)

16" Size 4 (3 mm) circular knitting needles

Size 6 double point needles (dpn)

Size 8 (5 mm) double point needles (dpn)

GAUGE

20 st = 4" with largest needles in circular stock st (knit all rnds)

INSTRUCTIONS

Back

Starting at lower edge with size 6 (4 mm) circular needle, CO 180 (200, 220) sts; join, being careful not to twist sts; place marker to indicate beg of rnds.

On first round, place a second marker halfway around: after 90 (100, 110) sts.

Body

Work in K1, P1 ribbing until piece measures 1".

Change to one of the Size 8 (5 mm) circular needle and work in stock st until body measures 14" (14 1/2", 16").

On last rnd, end 5 sts before first marker.

Divide for Front and Back

BO 10 sts; knit to 5 sts before next marker: 80 (90, 100) sts on front; BO 10 sts, knit to end of round: 80 (90, 100) sts on back.

Leave work on needle; set aside and work sleeves.

Sleeves (make 2)

Starting at cuff, with size 6 (4 mm) dpn, CO 46 (46, 50) sts; join, being careful not to twist sts; place marker to indicate beg of rnds.

Work in K1, P1 rib until cuff measures 1".

Change to size 8 (5 mm) dpn and work in stock st (knit every rnd), inc one st before and after marker every 8 rnds 10 (11, 11) times: 66 (68, 72) sts.

Note: Change to size 8 (5 mm) circular needle when you have too many sts to fit comfortably on the dpn.

Work even until sleeve measures 16 3/4" (17 3/4", 19").

On last round, end 5 sts before marker.

BO 10 sts, knit to end of round: 56 (58, 62) sts. Leave one sleeve on second circular needle.

Join Sleeves and Body

With right side facing and size 8 (5 mm) circular needle, knit across left sleeve sts, place marker, knit across front sts, place marker, knit across right sleeve sts, place marker, knit across back sts, place marker: 272 (296, 324) sts.

Yoke

On next rnd, dec 2 (6, 9) sts evenly spaced: 270 (290, 315) sts. Knit until yoke measures 2" (2 1/4", 2 1/2").

Decrease Rnd 1: *K3, K2tog; rep from * around : 216 (232, 252) sts.

Decrease Rnd 2: Dec 6 (8, 0) sts evenly spaced: 210 (224, 252) sts.

Cable Pattern

Rnds 1, 3, 5, 7, 9 and 11: Knit.

Rnd 2: *K4; (sl one st to cable needle and hold in back, K2, K1 from cable needle); (sl 2 sts to cable needle and hold in front, K1, K2 from cable needle), K4; rep from * around.

Rnd 4: *K3; (sl one st to cable needle and hold in back, K2, K1 from cable needle), K2; (sl 2 sts to cable needle and hold in front, K1, K2 from cable needle), K3; rep from * around.

Rnd 6: *K3; (sl 2 sts to cable needle and hold in front, K1, K2 from cable needle), K2; (sl 1 st to cable needle and hold in back, K2, K1 from cable needle), K3; rep from * around.

Rnd 8: *K4; (sl 2 sts to cable needle and hold in front, K1, K2 from cable needle); (sl 1 st to cable needle and hold in back, K2, K1 from cable needle), K4; rep from * around.

Rnd 10: *K5; sl 2 sts to cable needle and hold in back, K2, K2 from cable needle, K5; rep from * around.

Rnd 12: *K4; sl one st to cable needle and hold in back, K2, K1 from cable needle, sl 2 sts to cable needle and hold in front, P1, K2 from cable needle, K4; rep from * around

Rnd 13: *K7, P1, K6; rep from * around.

Rnd 14: *K3; sl one st to cable needle and hold in back, K2, P1 from cable needle, K1, P1; sl 2 sts to cable needle and hold in front, K1, K2 from cable needle, K3; rep from * around.

Rnd 15: *K5, (P1, K1) twice, K5; rep from * around.

Rnd 16: *K2, sl one st to cable needle and hold in back, K2, K1 from cable needle; (P1, K1) twice; sl 2 sts to cable needle and hold in front, P1, K2 from cable needle, K2; rep from * around.

Rnd 17: *K5; (P1, K1) 3 times, K3; rep from * around.

Rnd 18: *K1, sl one st to cable needle and hold in back, K2, P1 from cable needle; (K1, P1) 3 times, sl 2 sts to cable needle and hold in front, K1, K2 from cable needle, K1; rep from * around.

Rnd 19: *K3; (P1, K1) 4 times, K3; rep from * around.

Rnd 20: *Sl one st to cable needle and hold in back; K2, K1 from cable needle, (P1, K1) 4 times, sl 2 sts to cable needle and hold in front; P1, K2 from cable needle; rep from * around.

Rnd 21: *K3; (P1, K1) 5 times, K1; rep from * around.

Rnd 22: *P2tog; (K1, P1) 5 times, ssk; rep from * around: 180 (192, 216)

Rnds 23 and 24: *P1, K1; rep from * around.

Change to size 6 circular needles.

Continue in K1, P1 ribbing as established until yoke measures 6" (6 1/2", 6 3/4").

Change to size 4 circular needles.

Continue in K1, P1 ribbing until yoke measures 8" (8 1/2", 9").

Neckband

Dec Row: *SSK, P2tog; repeat from * to end of round: 90 (96, 108) sts.

Continue in K1, P1 ribbing until neck measures 1".

BO loosely.

Finishing

Sew underarm seams.

Weave in ends and block.

#5 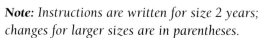HOODED ROBE

Designed by Patons Design Staff

Note: *Instructions are written for size 2 years; changes for larger sizes are in parentheses.*

SIZES	2 years	4 years	6 years
Body Chest Measurements	22"	24"	28"
Garment Chest Measurements	32"	36"	40"

MATERIALS

Super Bulky weight yarn
 17 1/2 (21, 24 1/2) oz yellow

Note: *Photographed model made with Patons® Melody #09622 Sunny Yellow*

29" Size 13 (9 mm) circular needle (or size required for gauge)

10" Size 13 (9 mm) straight knitting needles

3 stitch holders

GAUGE

9 sts and 15 rows = 4" in patt

Row 1 (right side): *K1, P1; rep from * across.

Row 2 (wrong side): Rep Row 1.

Row 3: *P1, K1; rep from * across.

Row 4: Rep Row 3.

INSTRUCTIONS

Note: Body is worked in one piece to arm-holes.

Starting at lower edge with circular needle, CO 72 (82, 90) sts.

Work back and forth in rows in patt until piece from beg measures 11 1/2" (13", 16"), ending by working a wrong-side row.

Divide for Right Front

With straight needles, work in patt across 21 (23, 25) sts, turn. Leave rem sts on circular needle and cont in patt on straight needles until work measures 14 3/4" (17", 20 3/4") from CO edge, ending by working a wrong-side row.

Neck Shaping

Row 1: BO 5 sts. Work in patt across next 3 sts and slip these 3 sts onto st holder (neck edge). Cont in patt across: 13 (15, 17) sts.

Next 3 rows: Dec 1 st at neck edge: 10 (12, 14) sts.

Work even in patt until work measures 17" (19 1/2", 23 1/4") from CO edge, ending by working a wrong-side row. BO.

Divide for Back

With right side of work facing and straight needles, join yarn to rem sts and work in patt across 30 (36, 40) sts; turn. Leave rem sts on circular needle and cont in patt on straight needles until work measures 17" (19 1/2", 23 1/4") from CO edge, ending by working a wrong-side row.

Next Row: BO 10 (12, 14) sts. Work in patt across next 10 (12, 12) sts. Sl these sts onto st holder. BO rem 10 (12, 14) sts.

Left Front

With right side of work facing and straight needles, join yarn to rem 21 (23, 25) sts and work in patt across. Work even in patt until piece on straight needles measures 14 3/4" (17", 20 3/4") from CO edge, ending by working a right-side row.

Neck Shaping

Row 1: BO 5 sts. Work in patt across next 3 sts and sl these 3 sts onto st holder (neck edge). Cont in patt across: 13 (15, 17) sts.

Next 3 rows: Dec 1 st at neck edge: 10 (12, 14) sts.

Work even in patt until piece measures 17" (19 1/2", 23 1/4") from CO edge, ending by working a wrong- side row. BO.

Sleeve (make 2)

Starting at lower edge with straight needles, CO 16 (18, 20) sts.

Row 1: Work Row 1 of Irish Moss st pattern.

Row 2: Inc, work Row 2 of Irish Moss st pattern, inc: 18 (20, 22) sts.

Instructions continue on next page. →

Cont in patt, inc one st at beg and end of every 6th row until there are 26 (30, 34) sts. Work even in patt until sleeve measures 9 1/2" (11", 12 1/2") from CO edge, ending by working a wrong-side row. BO.

Finishing

Sew shoulder and sleeve seams. Sew in sleeves.

Hood

With right side of work facing and straight needles, join yarn and knit across 3 sts from right front stitch holder. Pick up and knit 9 (10, 12) sts up right front neck edge. Knit across 10 (12, 12) sts from back neck edge stitch holder, at same time increasing 8 sts evenly across back neck edge as you knit. Pick up and knit 9 (10, 12) sts down left front neck edge. Knit across 3 sts from left front edge stitch holder: 42 (46, 50) sts. Starting with Row 2 of Irish Moss patt, work in patt as given for body until hood from picked-up sts measures 8" (8 1/2", 9 1/2"), end by working a wrong-side row. BO. Sew center top bound-off rows tog.

Twisted Cord (make 2)

Cut 2 strands of yarn 10" long. With both strands held tog, secure one end to a doorknob or other stationary object and twist strands to the right as they begin to curl. Fold the 2 ends tog and tie in a knot so they will not unravel. The strands will now twist themselves tog. Adjust length if necessary.

Sew one twisted cord to each side of robe for belt lp.

Tie Belt

With straight needles, CO 6 sts. Work in patt until piece measures 33" (35", 37") from CO edge. BO.

#52 MOCK CABLES

MATERIALS

Sport or DK weight yarn
  800 (850, 900, 900, 950) g white

Note: Photographed model made with Twilleys Freedom Cotton #2 Old White

3 stitch holders

Size 5 (3.75 mm) knitting needles

Size 6 (4 mm) knitting needles (or
  size required for gauge)

GAUGE

29 sts and 26 rows = 4" with larger
  needles in patt st

STITCH GUIDE

Twist Two Purl (T2P): Insert needle into back of first st on left needle from behind the work, from left to right, and purl it; rep for second st: T2P made.

Twist Two Knit (T2K): Insert needle into back of first st on left needle from right to left, and knit it; rep for second st: T2K made.

PATTERN STITCH

(multiple of 9 + 2)

Row 1 (wrong side): P2; * K2, T2P, P1, K2, P2; rep from * across.

Row 2: *K2, P2, T2K, K1, P2; rep from * to last 2 sts, K2.

Rep Rows 1 and 2 for patt.

Note: Instructions are written for size X-Small; changes for Small, Medium, Large and X-Large are in parentheses.

SIZES	X-Small	Small	Medium	Large	X-Large
Body Bust Meaurements	32"	34"	36"	38"	40"
Finished Bust Measurements	34 1/2"	37"	39 1/2"	42"	44 1/2"

Instructions continue on next page. →

INSTRUCTIONS

Back

With smaller needles CO 114 (122, 130, 138, 146) sts.

Row 1 (right side): * K2, P2; rep from * to last 2 sts, K2.

Row 2: * P2, K2; rep from * to last 2 sts, P2.

Rep Rows 1 and 2 until piece measures 2", ending by working a Row 2.

Increase Row: * K2, P2, K1, M1, K1, P2; rep from * to last 2 sts, K2: 128 (137, 146, 155, 164) sts.

Body

Change to larger needles. Work in Pattern Stitch (see Stitch Guide) until piece measures 17 1/4" (17 1/2", 18", 18 1/2", 18 1/2") from CO edge, ending by working a wrong-side row.

Shape Armhole

Keeping patt as established, CO 4 sts at beg of each of next 2 rows; then dec one st at each end of next 6 rows.

Then dec 1 st at each end of every other row six times: 96 (105, 114, 123, 132) sts.

Work even in patt as established until armhole measures 7 1/4" (8", 8 1/2", 9", 9 1/2"), ending by working a wrong-side row.

Shape Shoulders

Row 1: BO 12 (14, 16, 18, 20) sts, work in patt across.

Rows 2 and 3: Rep Row 1.

Row 4: BO 12 (14, 16, 18, 20) sts, work in patt to last 0 (2, 0, 2, 0) sts, work last 2 sts tog.

Place rem 48 (48, 50, 50, 52) sts on a st holder for neck back.

Front

Work same as Back until Front measures 21 1/2" (22", 22 3/4", 23 1/2", 24") from cast-on edge, ending by working a wrong-side row.

Shape Left Neck

Row 1 (right side): Keeping patt as established, work 47 (52, 56, 60, 64) sts; place rem sts on a st holder for Left Neck to be worked later.

Rows 2 through 18: Work in patt, dec one st at neck (inner) edge of each row.

Row 19: Work even in patt.

Row 20: Dec one st at neck edge.

Row 21: Work even.

Rep Rows 20 and 21 three (4, 4, 4, 4) times.

Work even in patt until armhole measures same as back, ending by working a wrong-side row.

Shape Left Shoulder

Row 1: BO 12 (14, 16, 18, 20) sts, work in patt across.

Row 2: Work even.

Row 3: BO 14 (16, 18, 20, 22) sts.

Shape Right Neck

Row 1: With right side facing, return to Row 1 of Left Neck; leaving center 2 (1, 2, 3, 4) sts on holder, join yarn and work in patt as established across rem sts.

Rows 2 through 18: Work in patt, dec one st at neck (inner) edge.

Row 19: Work even in patt.

Row 20: Work even in patt; dec one st at neck edge.

Row 21: Work even.

Rep Rows 20 and 21 three (4, 4, 4, 4) times.

Work even in patt until armhole measures same as Back Armhole, end by working a right-side row.

Shape Right Shoulder
Row 1: BO 12 (14, 16, 18, 20) sts, work even across.

Row 2: Work even.

Row 3: BO 14 (16, 18, 20, 22) sts.

Sleeve (make 2)
With smaller needles, CO 64 (64, 64, 72, 72) sts.

Row 1: *K2, P2; rep from * across.

Rep Row 1 until piece measures 2".

Increase Row (right side): *K2, P2, K1, M1, K1, P2; rep from * across: 72 (72, 72, 81, 81) sts.

Change to larger needles. Inc 1 st at each side of next row as you work Row 1 of patt across. Continue in patt and inc every following 6th row until there are 98 (98, 98, 99, 99) sts, keeping patt as est.

Work even in patt until sleeve measures 19" or desired length, ending by working a wrong-side row.

Shape Sleeve Cap
Rows 1 and 2: BO 4 sts, work in patt across.

Rows 3 through 7: Dec 1 st at each end of row. At end of Row 7: 80 (80, 80, 81, 81) sts.

Row 8: Dec 1 st at each end of row.

Row 9: Work even.

Rep Rows 8 and 9 six more times. At end of final Row 9: 66 (66, 66, 67, 67) sts.

Work 2 (4, 6, 8, 10) rows even.

Dec one st at each end of next 6 rows: 54 (54, 54, 55, 55) sts.

BO 4 sts at beg of next 4 rows.

BO rem 38 (38, 38, 39, 39) sts in patt.

V-Neck Ribbing
Sew right shoulder seam.

Row 1: With right side facing and with smaller needles, pick up and knit 30 sts down left front; from center holder, for size X-Small, K2; for size Small, K1; for size Medium, K2; for size Large, K1, K2 tog; and for size X-Large, (K2tog) twice; pick up and knit 30 (31, 30, 30, 30) sts up right front and knit 48 (48, 50, 50, 52) sts from holder at center back: 110 (110, 112, 112, 114)sts

Row 2: K2 (2, 0, 0, 2), [P2, K2] across.

Row 3: Work in patt across 28 sts, P2tog, K2, P2tog, work in patt across.

Row 4: Work in patt across 74 (74, 76, 76, 78) sts, P1, P2tog, P2, P2tog, P1, work in patt to end.

Row 5: Work in patt across 26 sts, K2tog tbl, K2, K2tog, work in patt to end.

Row 6: Work in patt across 72 (72, 74, 74, 76) sts; K1, K2 tog, P2, K2 tog, K1; work in patt to end.

BO in patt.

Finishing
Sew left shoulder seam. Sew in sleeves, matching center of sleeve cap to shoulder seams. Sew side and sleeve seams.

#53 CELEBRATION SHRUG

Designed by Patons Design Staff

MATERIALS

Eyelash yarn
  7 (7, 7, 8 3/4, 8 3/4) oz variegated

Note: *Photographed model made with Patons® Cha Cha #2003 Be Bop*

Size 11 (8 mm) knitting needles
  (or size required for gauge)

Two stitch markers

GAUGE

11 sts and 16 rows = 4" in stock st
  (knit 1 row, purl 1 row)

Note: *Instructions are written for size X-Small; changes for sizes Small, Medium, Large and X-Large are in parentheses.*

SIZES	X-Small	Small	Medium	Large	X-Large
Body Bust Measurements	30"	32" - 34"	36" - 38"	40"	42"

INSTRUCTIONS

Right Side

Starting at wrist edge of right sleeve, CO 24 sts.

Rows 1 through 6: Knit.

Row 7: Inc in first st, knit to last st, inc in last st: 26 sts.

Row 8: Knit.

Row 9: Purl.

Rows 10 and 11: Rep Rows 8 and 9.

Row 12: Rep Row 8.

Row 13: Rep row 7: 28 sts.

Rep Rows 8 through 13 until there are 42 (44, 46, 52, 54) sts.

Work even in stock st until piece measures 18" (19", 19 1/2", 19 1/2", 20") from CO edge, ending by working a purl row.

Next row: BO 4 sts, place marker, knit to end of row, place marker: 38 (40, 42, 48, 50) sts.

Work 3 rows even in stock st.

Back Shaping

Row 1 (right side): Knit to last 2 sts, inc in next st, K1: 39 (41, 43, 49, 51) sts.

Row 2: Knit.

Rows 3 through 12: Rep Rows 1 and 2. At end of last row: 44 (46, 48, 54, 56) sts.

Rep Row 2 until work measures 25 1/2" (26 1/2", 27", 28", 28 1/2") from CO edge, ending by working a wrong-side row. BO.

Left Side

Starting at wrist edge of Left Sleeve, work same as Right side to Back Shaping.

Back Shaping

Row 1 (right side): K1, inc 1 st in next st, knit to end of row: 39 (41, 43, 49, 51) sts.

Row 2: Knit.

Rows 3 through 12: Rep Rows 1 and 2. At end of last row: 44 (46, 48, 54, 56) sts.

Rep Row 2 until work measures 25 1/2" (26 1/2", 27", 28", 28 1/2") from CO edge, ending by working a wrong-side row. BO.

Finishing

Sew center back BO edges. Sew sleeve seams between CO edge and markers.

#54 SASSY STOLE

Designed by Marlaine DesChamps

SIZE
24" x 66" (without fringe)

MATERIALS
Bulky weight mohair blend yarn
21 oz

Note: *Photographed model made with Patons® Divine #6006 Icicle White.*

Size 8 (5 mm) 14" straight knitting needles, or size required for gauge

GAUGE
12 sts and 18 rows = 4" in double moss stitch

INSTRUCTIONS

CO 72 sts.

Eyelet Edging

Row 1: Knit.

Row 2: *K2 tog, YO, K1, rep from * across.

Rows 3 and 4: Knit.

Continue in Double Moss Stitch until piece measures 65" from CO edge.

Eyelet Edging

Rows 1 and 2: Knit.

Row 3: *K2 tog, YO, K1; rep from * across.

Row 4: Knit.

BO loosely.

Finishing

Block stole if necessary.

Weave in all loose ends.

Fringe

Following fringe instructions on page 251, cut strands of yarn 17" long. Knot 4 strands folded in half in each eyelet hole at ends of stole. Trim ends of fringe evenly.

#55 FURRY FUN

Designed by Patons Design Staff

MATERIALS

Eyelash yarn
14 (14, 15 3/4, 17 1/2, 19 1/4) oz variegated

Note: *Photographed model made with Patons® Cha Cha #02002 Vegas*

Size 11 (8 mm) knitting needles (or size required for gauge)

4 Stitch markers

GAUGE

11 sts and 16 rows = 4" in stock st (knit 1 row, purl 1 row)

Note: *Instructions are written for size X-Small; changes for larger sizes are in parentheses.*

SIZES	X-Small	Small	Medium	Large	X-Large
Body Bust Measurements	30"	32" - 34"	36" - 38"	40"	42"
Garment Bust Measurements	34"	35 1/2"	40"	44"	46"

INSTRUCTIONS

Back

CO 43 (45, 50, 56, 58) sts loosely.

Knit 7 rows, inc 4 (4, 5, 5, 5) sts evenly across last row: 47 (49, 55, 61, 63) sts.

Row 1: Knit.

Row 2: Purl.

Rep Rows 1 and 2 until piece measures 24" (24 1/2", 25", 25", 25 1/2") from CO row.

BO loosely.

Place markers 4" (4 1/2", 5 1/2", 6 1/2", 7") in from both side edges for shoulders.

Front

Work same as back.

Sleeve (make two)

CO 23 sts for all sizes.

Knit 7 rows, inc 3 sts evenly across last row: 26 sts.

Row 1: Knit.

Row 2: Purl.

Row 3: Inc, knit to last st, inc: 28 sts.

Row 4: Purl.

Row 5: Knit.

Row 6: Purl.

Row 7: Rep Row 3: 30 sts.

Rep Rows 4 through 7 until there are 50 (52, 56, 56, 58) sts.

Rep Rows 1 and 2 until piece measures 18" (19", 19 1/2", 19 1/2", 20") from CO row. BO.

Finishing

Sew shoulder seams to markers. Place markers 9" (9 1/2", 10", 10", 10 1/2") down from shoulders on Front and Back side edges. Sew in sleeves between markers. Sew side and sleeve seams.

#56 CARDIGAN CHIC

MATERIALS

Eyelash type yarn
14 ½ (14 ½, 16 ½) oz black (MC)

Ribbon yarn
2 oz black and white variegated (CC)

Note: Photographed model made with S.R. Kertzer Limited Molash #1006 Charcoal (MC) and Sari #10 Charcoal Mix (CC)

Size 10 ½ (6.5 mm) straight knitting needles (or size required for gauge)

Size J (6 mm) crochet hook

GAUGE

12 sts and 18 rows = 4" in stock stitch (knit 1 row, purl 1 row

Note: Instructions are written for size Small; changes for sizes Medium and Large are in parentheses.

SIZES	Small	Medium	Large
Body Bust Measurements	34"	36"	40"
Finished Bust Measurements	37"	40"	44"

INSTRUCTIONS

Back

With MC, CO 56 (60, 66) sts.

Row 1: Knit.

Row 2: Knit.

Row 3 (right side): Purl.

Rep Rows 2 and 3, working in reverse stock st, until piece measures 12", ending by working a wrong-side row.

Armhole Shaping

BO 3 sts at beg of next 2 rows: 50 (54, 60) sts. Then every other row dec one st each side 5 (5, 6) times: 40 (44, 48) sts.

Work even in reverse stock st until armhole measures 7", ending by working a wrong-side row.

Neck shaping

Row 1 (right side): P14 (16, 18), BO 12 sts; join second ball of yarn and purl across, working both shoulders at same time with separate balls of yarn.

Row 2 (wrong side): Knit, BO 3 sts at each neck edge: 11 (13, 15) sts on each shoulder.

Row 3: Purl, BO 2 sts at each neck edge: 9 (11, 13) sts on each shoulder.

Work even until piece measures 19 1/2".

BO rem sts on each side of shoulder.

Left Front

With MC, CO 28 (30, 33) sts.

Row 1: Knit.

Row 2: Knit.

Row 3 (right side): Purl.

Rep Rows 2 and 3 until piece measures 12", ending by working a wrong-side row.

Armhole and Neck Shaping

Row 1 (right side): BO 3 sts, purl to end: 25 (27, 30) sts.

Row 2: Knit.

Row 3: Dec one st, purl across: 24 (26, 29) sts.

Row 4: BO 5 sts, knit across: 19 (21, 24) sts.

Row 5: Dec one st, purl across: 18 (20, 23) sts.

Row 6: BO 3 sts, knit across: 15 (17, 20) sts.

Row 7: Dec one st, purl across: 14 (16, 19) sts.

Row 8: BO 2 sts, knit across: 12 (14, 17) sts.

Row 9: Dec one st, purl across: 11 (13, 16) sts.

Row 10: BO one st, knit across: 10 (12, 15) sts.

Row 11: Dec one st, purl across: 9 (11, 14) sts.

Instructions continue on next page. →

For Size Large Only

Row 12: Knit.

Row 13: Dec one st, purl across: 13 sts.

Work even until piece measures 19 $\frac{1}{2}$".

BO rem sts.

Right Front

Work as for Left Front to Armhole and Neck Shaping, ending by working a right-side row.

Armhole and Neck Shaping

Row 1 (wrong side): BO 3 sts, knit across: 25 (27, 30) sts.

Row 2: Purl.

Row 3: Dec one st, knit across: 24 (26, 29) sts.

Row 4: BO 5 sts, purl across: 19 (21, 24) sts.

Row 5: Dec one st, knit across: 18 (20, 23) sts.

Row 6: BO 3 sts, purl across: 15 (17, 20) sts.

Row 7: Dec one st, knit across: 14 (16, 19) sts.

Row 8: BO 2 sts, purl across: 12 (14, 17) sts.

Row 9: Dec one st, knit across: 11 (13, 16) sts.

Row 10: BO one st, purl across: 10 (12, 15) sts.

Row 11: Dec one st, knit across: 9 (11, 14) sts.

For Size Large Only

Row 12: Purl.

Row 13: Dec one st, knit across: 13 sts.

Work even until piece measures 19 $\frac{1}{2}$".

BO rem stitches.

Sleeve (make 2)

With MC, cast on 38 sts.

Row 1 (right side): Knit.

Row 2: Knit.

Row 3 (right side): Purl.

Row 4: Knit.

Row 5: Purl, dec one st at each end.

Rows 6 through 17: Rep Rows 2 through 5 until 30 sts remain.

Rows 18 through 26: Work even in reverse stock st.

Row 27: Purl, inc one st at each end of row: 32 sts.

Continue in reverse stock st, inc one st at each end of every 8th row 6 times: 44 sts.

Work even until piece measures 18", ending by working a wrong-side row.

Sleeve Cap Shaping

Row 1 (right side): BO 2 sts, purl across.

Row 2: BO 2 sts, knit across.

Rows 3 through 6: Rep Rows 1 and 2: 32 sts.

Row 7: Dec one st, purl to last 2 sts, dec one st: 30 sts.

Row 8: Knit.

Row 9: Dec one st, purl to last 2 sts, dec one st.

Rows 10 through 19: Rep Rows 8 and 9: 18 sts.

Row 20: BO 2 sts, knit across.

Row 21: BO 2 sts, purl across.

Rows 22 through 25: Rep Rows 20 and 21: 6 sts.

BO.

Finishing

Sew shoulder, side and sleeve seams.

Set in sleeves.

With crochet hook and CC, work one row of single crochet evenly along front edge and neck edges. Do not turn.

Work one row of reverse single crochet (rev sc).

Ties (make 2)

With CC, ch 46.

Row 1: Sl st in 2nd ch from hook and in each rem ch; finish off.

Sew to fronts at neck as shown in photo.

#57 A CABLE LOVER'S FAVORITE

Designed by Patons Design Studio

MATERIALS

Bulky weight yarn
  38 1/2 (42, 45 1/2, 49) oz blue.

Note: Photographed model was made with Patons® Shetland Chunky #3105 Steel Blue

14" Size 10 (6 mm) knitting needles

14" Size 10 1/2 (6.5 mm) knitting needles (or size required for gauge)

2 st holders

Cable needle

GAUGE

13 sts and 18 rows = 4" with larger needles in stock st (knit 1 row, purl 1 row)

Note: Instructions are written for size X-Small; changes for Small, Medium and Large are in parentheses.

SIZES	X-Small	Small	Medium	Large
Body Bust Measurements	32"	34"	36"	38"
Finished Bust Measurements	38"	40"	42"	43 1/2"

STITCH GUIDE

C5F: Slip next 3 sts onto a cable needle and leave at front of work, K2, then K3 from cable needle.

C5B: Slip next 2 sts onto a cable needle and leave at back of work, K3, then K2 from cable needle.

C6F: Slip next 3 sts onto a cable needle and leave at front of work, K3, then K3 from cable needle.

C6B: Slip next 3 sts onto a cable needle and leave at back of work, K3, then K3 from cable needle.

Increase (inc): Knit or purl into front and back of st: inc made

PANEL PATT
(24 row rep, worked over 51 sts)

Row 1 (right side): P2, K6, (P1, K1) 3 times, K2, P6, K3, P1, K3, P6, K3, (P1, K1) 3 times, K5, P2.

Row 2: K2, P7, (K1, P1) twice, P3, K6, P3, K1, P3, K6, P4, (K1, P1) twice, P6, K2.

Row 3: Rep Row 1.

Row 4: Rep Row 2.

Row 5: P2, C6B, (P1, K1) twice, P1, C5F, P4, K3, P1, K3, P4, C5B, (P1, K1) twice, P1, C6F, P2.

Row 6: K2, P7, (K1, P1) 3 times, P3, K4, P3, K1, P3, K4, P4, (K1, P1) 3 times, P6, K2.

Row 7: P2, K3, C5F, (P1, K1) twice, P1, C5F, P2, K3, P1, K3, P2, C5B, (P1, K1) twice, P1, C5B, K3, P2.

Row 8: K2, P3, K2, P4, (K1, P1) 3 times, P3, K2, P3, K1, P3, K2, P4, (K1, P1) 3 times, (P3, K2) twice.

Row 9: P2, K3, P2, C5F, (P1, K1) twice, P1, C5F, K3, P1, K3, C5B, (P1, K1) twice, P1, C5B, P2, K3, P2.

Row 10: K2, P3, K4, P4, (K1, P1) 3 times, P6, K1, P7, (K1, P1) 3 times, P3, K4, P3, K2.

Row 11: P2, K3, P4, C5F, (P1, K1) twice, P1, C6F, P1, C6B, (P1, K1) twice, P1, C5B, P4, K3, P2.

Row 12: K2, P3, K6, P4, (K1, P1) twice, P6, K1, P7, (K1, P1) twice, P3, K6, P3, K2.

Row 13: P2, K3, P6, K3, (P1, K1) 3 times, K5, P1, K6, (P1, K1) 3 times, K2, P6, K3, P2.

Row 14: Rep Row 12.

Row 15: Rep Row 13.

Row 16: Rep Row 12.

Row 17: P2, K3, P4, C5B, (P1, K1) twice, P1, C6F, P1, C6B, (P1, K1) twice, P1, C5F, P4, K3, P2.

Row 18: Rep Row 10.

Row 19: P2, K3, P2, C5B, (P1, K1) twice, P1, C5B, K3, P1, K3, C5F, (P1, K1) twice, P1, C5F, P2, K3, P2.

Row 20: Rep row 8.

Row 21: P2, K3, C5B, (P1, K1) twice, P1, C5B, P2, K3, P1, K3, P2, C5F, (P1, K1) twice, P1, C5F, K3, P2.

Row 22: Rep Row 6.

Row 23: P2, C6B, (P1, K1) twice, P1, C5B, P4, K3, P1, K3, P4, C5F, (P1, K1) twice, P1, C6F, P2.

Row 24: Rep Row 2.

RIBBING PATT

Row 1 (right side): K2; *P2, K2; rep from * to end of row.

Row 2: P2; *K2, P2; rep from * to end of row.

Rep Rows 1 and 2 for pattern.

Instructions continue on next page. →

INSTRUCTIONS

Back
Bottom Border
With smaller needles, CO 62 (62, 66, 70) sts.

Row 1 (right side): K2; *P2, K2; rep from * across.

Row 2: P2; *K2, P2; rep from * across.

Rows 3 through 8: Rep Rows 1 and 2.

Row 9: Rep Row 1.

Row 10: Rep Row 2, inc 1 (3, 3, 1) st(s) evenly across row: 63 (65, 69, 71) sts.

Body
Change to larger needles and and work in stock st until piece measures 17" (17 1/2", 17 1/2", 18") from CO edge, ending by working a wrong-side row.

Armhole Shaping
BO 5 sts at beg of next 2 rows: 53 (55, 59, 61) sts.

Work even until armhole measures 9" (9 1/2", 9 1/2", 10"), ending by working a wrong-side row.

Shoulder Shaping
BO 8 (8, 9, 9) sts at beg of next 4 rows.

Place rem 21 (23, 23, 25) sts on a st holder.

Front
Bottom Border
Work as for Back Bottom Border through Row 9.

Row 10: Rep Row 2, inc 15 (17, 17, 17) sts evenly across row: 77 (79, 83, 87) sts.

Body
Change to larger needles.

Row 1: K13 (14, 16, 18), work Row 1 of Panel Patt, K13 (14, 16, 18).

Row 2: P13 (14, 16, 18), work Row 2 of Panel Patt, P13 (14, 16, 18).

Panel Patt is now in position.

Cont in patt as established, working corresponding rows of Panel Patt until work measures 17" (17 1/2", 17", 18") from CO edge, ending by working a wrong-side row.

Armhole Shaping
BO 5 sts at beg of next 2 rows: 67 (69, 73, 77) sts.

Work even in patt until armhole measures 6 1/2" (7", 7", 7 1/2") ending by working a wrong-side row.

Neck Shaping
Row 1: Work in patt over 21 (21, 23, 23) sts, K2tog; place rem sts on a st holder.

Dec 1 st at neck edge on next 2 rows, then every other row 3 times: 17 (17, 19, 19) sts.

Work even in patt until work measures same length as Back to beg of shoulder shaping, ending by working a wrong-side row.

Shoulder Shaping
Row 1: BO 8 (8, 9, 9) sts, work in patt across.

Row 2: Work even. BO rem 9 (9, 10, 10) sts.

With right side of work facing, sl next 21 (23, 23, 27) sts onto a st holder. Join yarn to rem 23 (23, 25, 25) sts and proceed as follows:

Row 1: Sl 1, K1, PSSO, work in patt across.

Dec 1 st at neck edge on next 2 rows, then every other row 3 times: 17 (17, 19, 19) sts.

Work even in patt until work measures same length as Back to beg of shoulder shaping, ending by working a right-side row.

Shoulder Shaping
BO 8 (8, 9, 9) sts beg next row. Work one row even. BO rem 9 (9, 10, 10) sts.

Sleeve (make 2)
With smaller needles, CO 30 (30, 34, 34) sts.

Rows 1 through 10: Work in (K2, P2) ribbing as given for Back, ending by working a wrong-side row.

Change to larger needles and proceed in stock st.

Row 11 (right side): Knit.

Row 12: Purl.

Inc 1 st each end of needle on 5th row and then every 6 rows until there are 48 (50, 50, 54) sts.

Work even until piece measures 20" (21", 21 1/2", 22") from CO edge, ending by working a wrong-side row.

Sleeve Cap Shaping
BO off 3 sts beg next 8 rows. BO rem 24 (26, 26, 30) sts.

Finishing
Block garment pieces if needed.

Sew right shoulder seam.

Collar
With right side of work facing and smaller needles, pick up and knit 12 sts down left front neck edge. K21 (23, 23, 27) from front st holder while dec 4 (4, 4, 6) sts evenly across. Pick up and knit 12 sts up right front neck edge, K21 (23, 23, 25) sts from back st holder: 62 (66, 66, 70) sts.

Work in (K2, P2) ribbing as given for Back until Collar measures 2" from beg.

Change to larger needles and continue in (K2, P2) ribbing until Collar measures 7" from beg, ending by working a wrong-side row.

BO in ribbing.

Sew left shoulder and Collar seam, reversing seam fold-back.

Place markers 1 3/4" down from BO edge at each side of sleeve.

Sew in sleeves, placing rows above markers along BO sts at front and back armholes to form square armholes.

Sew side and sleeve seams.

#58 FRINGE BENEFIT

Designed by Laura Gebhardt

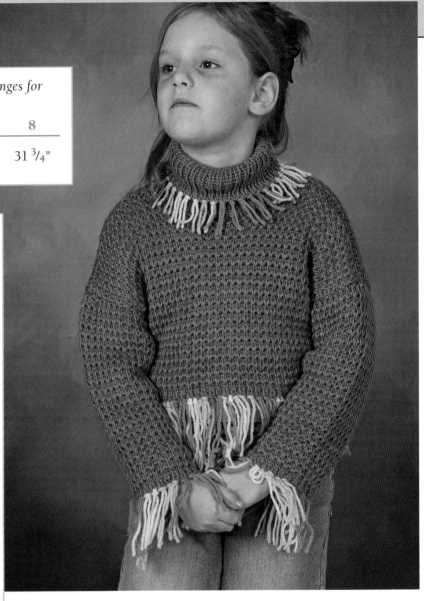

Note: *Instructions are written for size 2; changes for sizes 4, 6 and 8 are in parentheses.*

SIZES	2	4	6	8
Garment Chest Measurements	25"	27 $^1/_4$"	29 $^1/_2$"	31 $^3/_4$"

MATERIALS

DK or sport weight yarn
  14 oz pink (MC)
  2.8 oz variegated pink (A)

Note: *Photographed model made with Bernat® Satin #4732 Maitai (MC) and #5733 Bermuda (A)*

14" Size 8 (5 mm) knitting needles
  (or size required for gauge)

Set of 4 size 7 (4.5 mm) double-point
  knitting needles

Set of 4 size 8 (5 mm) double-point
  knitting needles

2 stitch holders

Stitch markers

Tapestry needle

GAUGE

22 sts and 34 rows = 4" in patt with
  larger needles

INSTRUCTIONS

Back

With 14" needles and MC, CO 69 (75, 81, 87) sts.

Work even in patt until piece measures 9" (10", 10 $^1/_2$", 11") from CO row, ending by working a wrong- side row.

Shape Neck and Shoulders

Next Row: Work in patt, BO 5 (6, 7, 7) sts at beg next 4 (6, 4, 4) rows, then 6 (7, 7, 8) sts at beg of next 4 (2, 4, 4) rows; place rem 25 (25, 25, 27) sts on holder.

PATTERN

Row 1 (right side): Knit.

Row 2: Purl.

Row 3: K1; *sl 1 as to purl, K1, rep from * across.

Row 4: K1; *sl one with yarn in front, K1, rep from * across

Front

Work same as back until piece measures 7 1/2" (8 1/2", 9", 9 1/2") from CO row.

Shape Neck and Shoulders

Work even in patt across 30 (33, 36, 38) sts; sl next 9 (9, 9, 11) sts onto st holder; join separate ball of yarn and work in patt across last 30 (33, 36, 38) sts.

Working both shoulders at the same time, dec 1 st at neck edge every row 8 times. Work in patt on rem 22 (25, 28, 30) sts until work measures same as back to beg of shoulder shaping. At each arm edge, BO 5 (6, 7, 7) sts every other row 2 (3, 2, 2) times, then 6 (7, 7, 8) sts every other row 2 (1, 2, 2) times.

Sleeve (make 2)

With 14" knitting needles and MC, CO 41 (45, 47, 49) sts.

Work in patt as given for back and keeping continuity of patt, inc one st each side on 5th row then every 6 rows to 57 (65, 73, 73) sts. Work even in patt until sleeve measures 9" (10 1/2", 11", 12") from CO row. BO.

Block pieces. Sew shoulder seams.

Collar

Using smaller double pointed needles, pick up and knit 25 (25, 25, 27) sts from back holder, 15 sts down left front neck, 9 (9, 9, 11) sts from holder and pick up and knit 15 sts up right front shoulder: 64, (64, 64, 68) sts. Join and work in rnds. Place marker on first st; move marker up as you work.

Rnd 1: *K1, P1; rep from * across.

Rnd 2: *K1, P1; rep from * across

Rep Rnds 1 and 2 for 3". Change to larger double-point needles and rep Rnds 1 and 2 for another 3". BO loosely in patt. Fold collar over to form turtleneck.

Finishing

Measure down front at armhole edges 5 1/4" (6", 6 1/2", 6 1/2") from shoulder seam and place markers. Rep on back. Sew sleeves in place between markers having center of sleeve at shoulder seam. Join sleeve and side seams.

Fringe

Following fringe instructions on page 251, cut 8" lengths of A and and knot across CO row of front and back. Rep with 6" lengths for bottom of sleeves. Knot 4" pieces to BO sts of collar. Trim ends evenly to desired length.

#59 KIDDIE CABLES

Designed by Marlaine DesChamps

MATERIALS
Worsted weight yarn
  9 (9, 12) oz natural heather

Note: Photographed model made with Lion Brand® Wool-Ease® #98 Natural Heather

Cable needle

6 stitch holders

Size 5 (3.75 mm) knitting needles (or size required for gauge)

14" Size 7 (4.50 mm) knitting needles

10" Size 5 (3.75 mm) double-point knitting needles (dpn)

GAUGE
18 sts and 30 rows = 4" on larger needles in moss stitch

Note: Instructions are written for size 2; changes for sizes 4 and 6 are in parentheses.

SIZE	2	4	6
Body chest Measurement	22"	24"	26"
Finished Chest Measurement	24"	26"	28"

INSTRUCTIONS

Back
Starting at lower edge with smaller straight needles, CO 62 (66, 70) sts.

Ribbing
Rows 1 through 6: * K1, P1; rep from * across row.

Body
Change to larger needles and work patt as follows:

Row 1: (K1, P1) 6 (7, 8) times; K3, P3, K3, P1; K4, P1, K8, P1, K4, P1; K3, P3, K3, P1; (K1, P1) 5 (6, 7) times, K1.

Row 2: (K1, P1) 5 (6, 7) times; K2, P3, K3, P3; K1, P4, K10, P4, K1; P3, K3, P3, K2; (P1, K1) 5 (6, 7) times.

Row 3: Rep Row 1.

Row 4: (K1, P1) 5 (6, 7) times; K5, P3, K4; P4, K1, P8, K1, P4; K4, P3, K5; (P1, K1) 5 (6, 7) times.

Row 5: (K1, P1) 6 (7, 8) times; P3, K3, P4; slip next 2 sts to cable needle, hold at back of work, knit next 2 sts, knit 2 sts from cable needle; P1, K8, P1; slip next 2 sts to cable needle, hold at front of work, knit next 2 sts, knit 2 sts from cable needle; P4, K3, P4; (K1, P1) 5 (6, 7) times; K1.

Row 6: Rep Row 4.

Rep Rows 1 through 6 for patt until piece measures 8" (9", 10") from beg.

Shape Armhole

Continuing in patt as established, BO 5 (6, 7) sts at beg of the next 2 rows: 52 (54, 56) sts.

Work even in patt as established until armhole measures 5 1/2" (6 1/4", 7").

Shoulders and Back Neck

Last Row: BO first 15 sts for shoulder, finish off. Place next 22 (24, 26) sts on a st holder for back neck; rejoin yarn and BO rem 15 (15, 15) sts.

Front

Work same as back until armhole measures 3" (3 1/2", 4").

Shape Neck

Work in patt as established over first 17 (18, 19) sts, place next 18 (18, 18) sts on a holder for front of neck, attach another ball of yarn, work in patt as established over rem 17 (18, 19) sts.

Working on both sides at once, dec 1 st at neck edge of every other row 2 (3, 4) times: 15 (15, 15) sts.

Work even until armhole measures same as back. BO 15 sts on each side.

Join Shoulders

With right sides tog, sew front and back shoulder seams.

Neckband

With right side facing and using dpn, pick up and K64 (68, 72) sts around neck edge including sts on holders. Mark beg of rnd.

Rnd 1: * K1, P1; rep from * around.

Rep Rnd 1 until neckband measures 1" (all sizes). BO loosely.

Sleeve (make 2)

With right side facing and with larger needles, pick up and K58 (64, 70) sts at armhole edge. Work in moss stitch for 1" (all sizes). Continuing in patt as established, dec 1 st each end of every 3rd (4th, 4th) row 14 (16, 18) times: 30 (32, 34) sts.

Work even, if necessary, until sleeve measures 7 1/2" (9 1/2", 11 1/2") from armhole. Change to smaller straight needles. Work in ribbing as for back for 1" (all sizes). BO all sts.

Sew sleeve and underarm seams. Sew sleeves into armholes.

Weave in loose ends.

#60 CLASSIC FISHERMAN

#60 CLASSIC FISHERMAN

SIZE	One size fits most
Finished Bust Measurement	47"

MATERIALS

Worsted weight yarn
  24 oz natural

Note: *Photographed model made with Lion Brand® Wool-Ease® #099 Fisherman*

Size 7 (4.5 mm) knitting needles

Size 8 (5 mm) knitting needles (or size required for gauge)

16" size 7 (4.5 mm) circular needle

Cable needle

4 stitch markers

GAUGE

25 ½ sts = 4" with larger needles in Cable patt

INSTRUCTIONS

Back

With smaller needles, CO 150 sts. Work in Rib patt for 2 ½", ending by working a Row 2. Change to larger needles. Rep Rows 1 through 12 of Cable patt until Back measures 27" from beg. BO in patt.

Front

Work same as Back until piece measures 25" from beg.

Shape Neck

Keeping continuity of patt, work 59 sts, join a second ball of yarn, work center 32 sts and place on holder, work rem 59 sts. Working both sides at once, with separate balls of yarn, BO 3 sts at each neck edge every other row twice: 53 sts each side.

Then BO 2 sts at each neck edge every other row twice: 49 sts each side.

Work even in Cable patt until front measures same as back to shoulder. BO rem sts on each side.

Sleeve (make 2)

With smaller needles, CO 42 sts.

Ribbing

Work in Rib patt for 2 1/2", ending by working a right-side row.

Arm

Row 1 (wrong side): P1; *P1, inc in next st; rep from * across to last st, P1: 62 sts.

Row 2: K1; *K1, inc in next st, K2, inc in next st; rep from * across to last st, K1: 86 sts.

Change to larger needles.

Row 3: Work Row 3 of Cable patt.

Keeping continuity of Cable patt, inc 1 st at each end of every 3rd row 21 times, working added sts into Cable patt: 128 sts.

Work even in Cable patt until sleeve measures 18 1/2" from beg or desired length. BO all sts.

PATTERN STITCHES

RIB PATTERN

(multiple of 4 sts + 2)

Row 1 (wrong side): K2; *P2, K2; rep from * across.

Row 2: P2; *T2, P2; rep from * across.

Repeat Rows 1 and 2 for Rib patt.

CABLE PATTERN

(multiple of 16 sts + 6)

Row 1 (wrong side): *K2, P2, K2, P10; rep from * across to last 6 sts, K2, P2, K2.

Rows 2, 4, 6, 8, and 10: *P2, T2, P2, K10; rep from * across to last 6 sts, P2, T2, P2.

Rows 3, 5, 7, 9, and 11: Rep Row 1.

Row 12 (cable row): *P2, T2, P2, C5; rep from * across to last 6 sts, P2, T2, P2.

Repeat Rows 1 through 12 for Cable patt.

Finishing

Sew shoulder seams.

Neckband

With right side facing and circular needle, pick up and knit 88 sts evenly around neck edge, including sts on front holder. Join and work around as follows, marking beg of rnd.

Rnd 1 (right side): *T2, P2; rep from * around.

Rnd 2: *K2, P2; rep from * around.

Rep Rnds 1 and 2 for 2". BO in patt.

Place markers 10 1/2" down from shoulder seam on front and back. Sew sleeve in place between markers. Sew side and sleeve seams.

#61 TINY TOT'S KIMONO

Designed by Theresa Belville for Little Turtle Knits

Note: *Instructions are written for size 6 months; changes for sizes 18 months and 36 months are in parentheses.*

SIZES	6 months	18 months	36 months
Body Chest Measurement	17 - 18"	19 - 20"	21 - 22"
Finished Chest Measurements	20"	22"	24"

MATERIALS

Sport weight yarn
4 1/2 (5 1/2, 6 1/2) oz lavender

Note: *Photographed model made with Lion Brand® Microspun #143 Lavender*

Glass Rochaille "E" beads: 648 (738, 828)

Sewing needle and thread

Small hook and eye fastener

Size F (3.75 mm) crochet hook

14" size 5 (3.75 mm) knitting needles (or size required for gauge)

GAUGE

20 1/2 sts and 28 rows = 4 in stock st (knit 1 row, purl 1 row)

INSTRUCTIONS

Left Front

String 126 (144, 162) beads.

Row 1: CO 3, b6, (CO 2, b6) 6 (7, 8) times, CO 1.

Row 2: P1, (b5, P1, M1, P1) 7 (8, 9) times, P1.

Row 3: K4, b4, (K3, b4) 6 (7, 8) times, K1.

Row 4: P1, (b3, P3) 7 (8, 9) times, P1.

Row 5: K4, M2, (K3, M2) 6 (7, 8) times, K1: 37 (42, 47) sts.

Work even in stock st until piece measures 3" (4", 5") measured from Row 5, ending by working a wrong-side row.

Left Front Shaping

Row 1: Knit to last 5 sts, K2tog, K3.

Row 2: Sl 3, purl to end.

Rep Row 1 and 2 for 3": 27 (32, 37) sts.

Armhole Shaping

Row 1: BO 5 sts for underarm, knit to last 5 sts, K2tog, K3.

Row 2: Sl 3, purl across.

Row 3: Knit to last 5 sts, K2tog, K3.

Rep Rows 2 and 3 until armhole measures 3½" (4", 5"): 14 (17, 19) sts. BO.

Right Front

Work same as Left Front to Left Front Shaping.

Right Front Shaping

Row 1: K2, SSK, knit across.

Row 2: Purl to last 3 sts, sl 3.

Rep Rows 1 and 2 for 3": 27 (32, 37) sts.

Armhole Shaping

Row 1: K2, SSK, knit to end.

Row 2: BO 5 sts for undrarm, purl to last 3 sts, sl 3.

Row 3: K2, SSK, knit to end.

Row 4: Purl to last 3 sts, sl 3.

Rep Rows 2 through 3 until armhole measures 3½" (4", 5"): 10 (13, 14) sts. BO.

Back

String 180 (198, 216) beads.

Row 1: CO 3, b6, (CO 2, b6) 9 (10, 11) times, CO 1.

Row 2: P1, (b5, P1, M1, P1) 10 (11, 12) times, P1.

Instructions continue on next page. →

Row 3: K4, b4, (K3, b4) 9 (10, 11) times, K1.

Row 4: P1, (b3, P3) 10 (11, 12) times, P1.

Row 5: K4, M2, (K3, M2) 9 (10, 11) times, K1: 52 (57, 62) sts.

Work in stock st until piece measures 6" (7" 8") measured from Row 5, ending by working a wrong-side row.

Armhole Shaping

Continuing in stock st, BO 5 sts at beg of next 2 rows for underarms: 42 (47, 52) sts.

Work even in stock st until armholes measures same as Front. BO.

Sleeve (make 2)

String 108 (126, 144) beads.

Row 1: CO 3, b6, (CO 2, b6) 5 (6, 7) times, CO 1.

Row 2: P1, (b5, P1, M1, P1) 6 (7, 8) times, P1.

Row 3: K4, b4, (K3, b4) 5 (6, 7) times, K1.

Row 4: P1, (b3, P3) 6 (7, 8) times, P1.

Row 5: K4, M2, (K3, M2) 5 (6, 7) times, K1: 32 (37, 42) sts.

Work stock st, increasing one st at each end of 6th (8th, 10th) and every foll 6th (8th, 10th) row until piece measures 6" (8", 10"). (Do not work increases on the last row): 44 (49, 54) sts. BO loosely.

Finishing

Sew shoulders. Sew sleeves into armholes. Sew sleeve and side seams.

Front Ties

Hold piece with wrong side facing. Join yarn at bottom of left front opening; work single crochet in sides of rows to where the front shaping decs began. Ch 40 to make tie. Finish off.

Place left front over right front Make separate chain the same length and sew in place on right front, adjacent to where left tie is.

Sew hook and eye to inside of front, where the point of the left front meets the right front. Tie a bow.

Neck Finishing

Hold piece with right side of back facing. With crochet hook, join yarn in first bound-off st at right shoulder seam. Work sc across back of neck to stop work from rolling outward.

#62 DIVINE IN DENIM

Instructions continue on next page. →

MATERIALS

DK cotton lightweight yarn
7 1/4 (7 1/4, 9, 9, 10 3/4, 12 1/2) oz light denim

Note: *Photographed model made with Twilleys of Stamford Freedom Denim #102 Light Denim.*

Size 6 (4 mm) knitting needles (or size required for gauge)

Size 8 (5 mm) knitting needles (or size required for gauge)

Stitch holder

GAUGE

11 sts and 25 rows = 4" with larger needles in pattern

20 1/2 sts and 27 rows = 4" with smaller needles in stock st (knit 1 row, purl 1 row)

PATTERN

Row 1: K1, *YO, sl 1, K1, PSSO; rep from * to last st, K1.

Rep Row 1 for patt

Note: *Instructions are written for size X-Small; changes for Small, Medium, Large, X-Large and XX-Large in parentheses.*

SIZE	X-Small	Small	Medium	Large	X-Large	XX-Large
Body bust Measurememts	32"	34"	36"	38"	40"	42"
Finished Bust Measurements	33"	36"	39"	41"	44"	47"
Length	20 3/4"	21 1/4"	21 1/2"	22'	22 1/2"	22 3/4"

INSTRUCTIONS

Back

With smaller needles, CO 88 (95, 102, 109, 116, 123) sts.

Rows 1 through 3: Knit.

Row 4 (right Side): K2tog twice; *K1, K2tog 3 times; rep from * across: 50 (54, 58, 62, 66, 70) sts.

Change to larger needles.

Work in patt until Back measures 13 1/4" (13 3/4", 13 3/4", 14", 14", 14 1/2"), ending by working a wrong-side row.

Shape Armholes

Rows 1 and 2: BO 2 (3, 3, 4, 4, 5) sts loosely; K1, work in patt across to last st, K1.

Rows 3 through 5 (5, 7, 7, 9, 9): K2tog, work in patt across to last 2 sts, K2tog: 40 (42, 42, 44, 44, 46) sts.

Row 6 (6, 8, 8, 10, 10): Work in patt.

Row 7 (7, 9, 9, 11, 11): K2tog, work in patt across to last 2 sts, K2tog: 38 (40, 40, 42, 42, 44) sts.

Work even in patt until armholes measure 5 1/2" (5 1/2", 6", 6", 6 1/4", 6 1/4") ending by working a wrong-side row.

Shape Right Neck and Shoulder

Next Row (right side): Work 12 sts in patt, place rem sts on a holder.

Working on these 12 sts only, dec 1 st at neck edge of next 4 rows: 8 sts.

Work even in patt until armholes measure 7 1/2" (7 1/2", 7 3/4", 7 3/4", 8 1/4", 8 1/2"), ending by working a wrong-side row. BO rem 8 sts loosely.

With right side facing, join yarn to rem 26 (28, 28, 30, 30, 32) sts, BO center 14 (16, 16, 18, 18, 20) sts loosely, work in patt to end.

Dec 1 st at neck edge of next 4 rows: 8 sts.

Continue even in patt until armholes measure 7 1/2" (7 1/2", 7 3/4", 7 3/4", 8 1/4", 8 1/2"), ending by working a wrong-side row. 80 rem sts.

Front

Work same as Back through Row 2 of Armhole Shaping.

Divide for Front Opening

Next Row (right side): K2tog, work 19 (20, 22, 23, 25, 26) sts in patt, K2tog, place rem sts on a holder.

Work on these 21 (22, 24, 25, 27, 28) sts only for first side.

Dec 1 st at armhole edge of next 2 (2, 4, 4, 6, 6) rows: 19 (20, 20, 21, 21, 22) sts.

Work even in patt for one row.

Dec 1 st at armhole edge of next row: 18 (19, 19, 20, 20, 21) sts.

Work even in pattern until armhole measures 2 3/4" (2 3/4", 3 1/4", 3 1/4", 3 1/2", 3 1/2") , ending at front opening edge.

Shape Left Neck and Shoulder

Continuing in patt, BO 6 (7, 7, 8, 8, 9) sts loosely at beg of next row: 12 sts.

Dec 1 st at neck edge of next 4 rows: 8 sts.

Work even in patt until Front matches Back to shoulder bind-off, ending by working a wrong-side row. BO rem 8 sts loosely.

Second Side

With right side facing, rejoin yarn to rem 23 (24, 26, 27, 29, 30) sts, K2tog, work in patt across to last 2 sts, K2tog: 21 (22, 24, 25, 27, 28) sts.

Dec 1 st at armhole edge of next 2 (2, 4, 4, 6, 6) rows: 19 (20, 20, 21, 21, 22) sts.

Work even in patt for one row.

Dec 1 st at armhole edge of next row: 18 (19, 19, 20, 20, 21) sts

Work even in patt until armhole measures 2 3/4" (2 3/4", 3 1/4", 3 1/4", 3 1/2", 3 1/2"), ending at front opening edge.

Continuing in patt, BO 6 (7, 7, 8, 8, 9) sts loosely at beg of next row: 12 sts.

Dec 1 st at neck edge of next 4 rows: 8 sts.

Work even in patt until Front matches Back to shoulder bind-off, ending by working a wrong-side row. BO rem 8 sts loosely.

Finishing

Front Opening Edging

With smaller needles and with right side facing, pick up and knit 15 sts down left side of front opening, then pick up and knit 15 sts up right side of front opening: 30 sts.

BO loosely as to knit. Sew shoulder seams.

Neck Edging

With smaller needles and with right side facing, starting and ending at bound-off edge of Front Opening Border, pick up and knit 12 (14, 14, 15, 15, 17) sts from right front BO edge, 34 sts up right side of front neck, 15 sts down right side of back neck, 25 (28, 28, 32, 32, 35) sts from back, 15 sts up left side of back neck, 34 sts down left side of front neck, then 12 (14, 14, 15, 15, 17) sts from left front BO edge: 147 (154, 154, 160, 160, 167) sts. BO loosely as to knit.

Armhole Edging

For each armhole, with smaller needles and with right side facing, pick up and knit 92 (96, 101, 103, 107, 111) sts. BO loosely as to knit.

Sew side and armhole edging seams.

#6 CELTIC CABLES

Designed by Patons Design Staff

MATERIALS

DK or sport weight yarn
24 1/2 (26 1/4, 28, 29 3/4) oz red

Note: Photographed model made with Patons® Grace #60705 Cardinal

Cable needle

Size G (4 mm) crochet hook

14" Size 8 (5 mm) knitting needles
  (or size required for gauge)

One 14" Size 8 (5 mm) spare knitting needle

GAUGE

20 sts and 26 rows = 4" in rib patt
  with 2 strands of yarn

Note: Instructions are written for size Small; changes for sizes Medium, Large and X-Large are in parentheses.

SIZES	Small	Medium	Large	X-Large
Body Bust Measurements	30" - 32"	34" - 36"	38" - 40"	42" - 44"
Finished Bust Measurements	37 1/2"	40"	42"	47"

STITCH GUIDE

C6B: Sl next 3 sts onto cable needle and hold at back of work; K3, then K3 from cable needle.

C6F: Sl next 3 sts onto cable needle and hold at front of work; K3, then K3 from cable needle.

T5B: Sl next 2 sts onto cable needle and hold at back of work; K3, then P2 from cable needle.

T5F: Sl next 3 sts onto cable needle and hold at front of work; P2, then K3 from cable needle.

T4B: Sl next st onto cable needle and hold at back of work; K3, then P1 from cable needle.

PANEL PATTERNS
(8 row pattern rep worked over 31 sts)

Row 1 (right side): P3, K3, (P4, C6F) twice; P5.

Row 2: K5, (P6, K4) twice; P3, K3.

Row 3: P3, (T5F, T5B) twice; T5F, P3.

Row 4: K3, P3, (K4, P6) twice; K5.

Row 5: P5, (C6B, P4) twice; K3, P3.

Row 6: Rep Row 4.

Row 7: P3, (T5B, T5F) twice; T5B, P3.

Row 8: Rep Row 2.

(K3, P3) Ribbing

Row 1: *K3, P3; rep from * across.

Row 2: *P3, K3; rep from * across.

INSTRUCTIONS

Front

Bottom Border

With 2 strands of yarn held tog, CO 97 (103, 109, 121) sts.

Row 1: *K1, P1; rep from * to last st, K1.

Row 2: Rep Row 1.

Row 3 (right side): K1, P1, K1 (4, 1, 1); (P3, K3) 6 (6, 7, 8) times; (P4, K6) twice; P5, (K3, P3) 5 (5, 6, 7) times; K1 (4, 1, 1), P1, K1.

Row 4: K1, P1, K4 (1, 4, 4); (P3, K3) 4 (5, 5, 6) times; P3, K5, (P6, K4) twice; (P3, K3) 6 (6, 7, 8) times; purl 0 (3, 0, 0), K1, P1, K1.

Establish Center Panel Patt

Row 1 (right side): K1, P1, K1 (4, 1, 1); (P3, K3) 5 (5, 6, 7) times; Work Row 1 of Panel Patt; (K3, P3) 5 (5, 6, 7) times; K1 (4, 1, 1), P1, K1.

Row 2: K1, P1, K4 (1, 4, 4); (P3, K3) 4 (5, 5, 6) times; P3, Work row 2 of Panel Patt, (P3, K3) 5 (5, 6, 7) times; purl 0 (3, 0, 0), K1, P1, K1.

Panel Patt is now established.

Work in patt as established, working corresponding row of Panel Patt, until work measures 2 1/2" from CO edge.

Body

Row 1 (right side): K3 (0, 3, 3); (P3, K3) 5 (6, 6, 7) times; work next row of Panel Patt, (K3, P3) 5 (6, 6, 7) times, K3 (0, 3, 3).

Row 2: P3 (0, 3, 3); (K3, P3) 5 (6, 6, 7) times; work next row of Panel Patt, (P3, K3) 5 (6, 6, 7) times, P3 (0, 3, 3).

Rep Rows 1 and 2 until piece measures about 16" from CO edge, ending by working a Row 2 of Panel Patt.

Shape Armholes

Row 1: BO 7 (4, 7, 7) sts, work across in patt: 90 (99, 102, 114) sts.

Row 2: BO 7 (4, 7, 7) sts, work across in patt: 83 (95, 95, 107) sts.

Row 3: Dec 1 st, work across in patt to last 2 sts, dec 1 st.

Rows 4 through 6: Rep Row 3: 75 (87, 87, 99) sts.

Rows 7 through 8: Work even in patt.

Instructions continue on next page. →

Row 9: Work patt over 22 (28, 28, 34) sts, P3, K3, P3, T4B, K3, P3, T4B, T5F, P3, work across in patt.

Row 10: Work patt over 22 (28, 28, 34) sts; (K3, P3) twice, K7, (P3, K3) twice, work across in patt.

Left Front Opening

Row 1 (right side): Work in (K3, P3) rib patt across 36 (42, 42, 48) sts, P2tog, turn; leave rem 37 (43, 43, 49) sts on needle; continue with spare needle.

Rows 2 through 6: Work even in (K3, P3) rib patt.

Row 7: Work in patt to last 3 sts, YO, P2tog, P1.

Rows 8 through 14: Work even.

Row 15: Rep Row 7.

Rows 16 through 19: Work even.

Neck Shaping

Row 1 (wrong side): BO 10 (12, 12, 12) sts; work in patt across.

Continue in pattern, decreasing one st at neck edge on next 6 (6, 6, 10) rows: 21 (25, 25, 27) sts.

Work even until armhole measures 6 ½" (7", 8", 8 ½"), ending by working a right-side row.

Shoulder Shaping

Row 1: BO 10 (12, 12, 13) sts, work even across.

Row 2: Work even.

Row 3: BO rem 11 (13, 13, 14) sts.

Right Side Front Opening

Join yarn to rem sts on spare needle.

Rows 1 through 6: Work even in rib patt.

Row 7 (right side): P1, P2tog, YO, work in patt across

Rows 8 through 14: Work even.

Row 15: Rep Row 7.

Rows 16 through 19: Work even.

Neck shaping

Row 1 (right side): BO 10 (12, 12, 12) sts. Work in patt across. Continue in pattern, decreasing one st at neck edge on next 6 (6, 6, 10) rows: 21 (25, 25, 27) sts.

Work even until armhole measures same as opposite side; ending by working a right-side row.

Shoulder Shaping

Row 1: BO 10 (12, 12, 13) sts; work even across.

Row 2: Work even.

Row 3: BO rem 11 (13, 13, 14) sts.

Back

With 2 strands of yarn, cast on 93 (99, 105, 117) sts.

Row 1 (right side): *K1, P1; rep from * to last st, K1.

Row 2: Rep Row 1.

Row 3 (right side): K1, P1, K1 (4, 1, 1); *P3, K3, rep from * to last 6 (3, 6, 6) sts, P3 (0, 3, 3), K1, P1, K1.

Row 4: K1, P1, K4 (1, 4, 4); *P3, K3, rep from * to last 3 (6, 3, 3) sts, purl 0 (3, 0, 0), K1, P1, K1.

Rep Rows 3 and 4, until work measures 2 ½" from CO edge.

Body

Row 1 (right side): K3 (0, 3, 3), *P3, K3; rep from * to last 0 (3, 0, 0) sts, purl 0 (3, 0, 0).

Row 2: K0 (3, 0, 0); *P3, K3, rep from * to last 3 (0, 3, 3) sts, P3 (0, 3, 3).

Rep Rows 1 and 2, until work from CO edge measures same length as Front to beg of armhole shaping, ending by working a wrong-side row.

Shape Armholes

Row 1: BO 7 (4, 7, 7) sts, work in patt across.

Row 2: BO 7 (4, 7, 7) sts, work in patt across: 79 (91, 91, 103) sts.

Dec 1 st at each end of needle on next 4 rows: 71 (83, 83, 95) sts.

Work even in patt until armhole measures 6 ½" (7", 8", 8 ½"), ending by working a wrong-side row.

Row 1: BO 10 (12, 12, 13) sts; work in patt across.

Row 2: Rep Row 1.

Row 3: BO 11 (13, 13, 14) sts; work in patt across..

Row 4: Rep Row 3. At end of Row 4, BO rem 29 (33, 33, 41) sts.

Sleeves (make 2)

With 2 strands of yarn, CO 60 (66, 72, 72) sts.

Row 1 (right side): *K1, P1, rep from * across.

Row 2: *P1, K1, rep from * across.

Row 3: *K3, P3, rep from * to end of row.

This row establishes (K3, P3) ribbing patt.

Row 4: Work even in est patt.

Row 5: Inc 1 st, work even in patt to last st, inc 1 st.

Note: Work inc sts into rib patt.

Rows 6 through 10: Work even in est patt.

Row 11: Rep row 5: 64 (70, 76, 76) sts.

Work 11 rows even.

Shape Cap

Row 1: BO 4 sts; work in patt across.

Row 2: Rep Row 1.

Rows 3 through 12: Dec 1, work in patt to last two sts, dec 1.

Row 13: BO 3 sts, work in patt across.

Row 14: Rep row 13.

Bind off rem 30 (36, 42, 42) sts.

Finishing

Pin garment pieces to measurements and cover with a damp cloth; allow cloth to dry.

Sew shoulder seams.

With right side of work facing, with crochet hook and 2 strands of yarn, work 1 row of single crochet around neck edge and front opening.

With 2 strands of yarn, crochet a chain 36" long. Finish off. Thread through YO eyelet holes at front opening as shown in photo. Knot ends.

Sew in sleeves.

Leaving 2 ½" open at bottom of side seams, sew side and sleeve seams.

Weave in ends.

VICTORIA'S LITTLE RED COAT AND HAT

Designed by Sheila Jones

SIZES	3-4 yrs	5-6 yrs	7-8 yrs
Body Chest Measurements	24"	26"	28"
Finished Chest Measurements	32"	34 ½"	37 ½"

COAT

MATERIALS

Worsted weight yarn
  950 (1036, 1122) yds red (MC)
  320 (380, 440) yds black (A)

Bulky weight eyelash yarn
  120 (140, 160) yds black (B)

Note: *Photographed model made with Brown Sheep Lamb's Pride Worsted #M81 Red Baron (MC) Brown Sheep Lamb's Pride Worsted #M05 Black Onyx (A) and Gedifra Techno Hair Lungo #9714 Black (B)*

4 stitch holders

5 red 1" diameter shank buttons

Sewing needle and red sewing thread

Size 11 (8 mm) knitting needles (or size required for gauge)

GAUGE

12 sts = 4" with 2 strands of MC held tog in stock st (knit 1 row, purl 1 row)

INSTRUCTIONS

Back
Border

Starting at bottom border with 2 strands of A and one strand of B held tog, CO 47 (51, 55) sts.

Work in garter st (knit every row) until piece measures 2".

Finish off A and B.

PATTERN NOTES

Body is worked in stock st (knit one row, purl one row) with 2 strands of MC held tog throughout.

Bottom borders of body, sleeves, and collar are worked in garter stitch (knit every row) with 2 strands of A and one strand of B held tog.

Front center borders are worked in garter stitch with 2 strands of A held tog.

When changing yarn colors, twist yarns around each other to prevent holes; always pick up the new color from underneath the previous color.

Body

Join 2 strands of MC.

Row 1 (right side): Knit.

Row 2: Purl.

Rep Rows 1 and 2 until piece measures 12" (13", 15") from CO edge, ending by working a purl row.

Shape Armholes

Row 1: BO 5 sts, K42 (46, 50) sts.

Row 2: BO 5 sts, P37 (41, 45) sts.

Work even in stock st until armhole measures 7 ½" (8", 8 ½"); ending by working a purl row.

Neckline and Shoulder Shaping

Row 1: BO 12 (13, 14) sts and mark these for Right Shoulder; BO 13 (15, 17) sts for center back neck; BO rem 12 (13, 14) sts and mark for Left Shoulder.

Left Front

Starting at bottom border, with 2 strands of A and 1 strand of B, CO 27 (29, 31) sts. Work in garter st for 2".

Cut Colors A and B. Using two strands of the MC for body, and two strands of A for front center border, begin body.

Instructions continue on next page. →

Body

Row 1 (right side): With MC, K22 (24, 26) sts; with A, K5 for front border.

Row 2: With A, K5; With MC. P22 (24, 26) sts.

Keeping 5 sts of front border in Color A and garter stitch, work even in patt as established until piece measures 12" (13", 15") from CO edge; ending by working a wrong-side row.

Shape Armhole

Row 1 (right side): BO 5 sts, work in patt as established across 22 (24, 26) sts.

Row 2: K5, P17 (19, 21) sts.

Work even until armhole measures, 6" (6 1/4", 6 1/2"); ending by working a right-side row.

Shoulder and Neck Shaping

Row 1 (wrong side): BO 6 sts, P16 (18, 20).

Dec 1 st at neck edge on next 3 (4, 5) rows and then BO one st on the next alternate row once. BO rem 12 (13, 14) sts.

Mark center front border for button spacing. Place top button 1/2" down from top of border, and bottom button 9" (10 1/2", 12 1/2") up from bottom border.

Right Front

Work as for Left Front to start of Body.

Body

Work with 2 strands of MC for body, and 2 strands of A for front border.

Row 1 (right side): With A, K5 for front border; with MC, K22 (24, 26).

Row 2: With MC, P22 (24, 26) sts; with A, K5.

Keeping 5 sts of front border in A and garter stitch, work even until piece measures 9" (10 1/2", 13"), ending by working a wrong-side row.

Buttonhole Rows

Row 1 (right side): With A, K2, YO, K2tog, K1; with MC, K22 (24, 26).

Row 2: With MC, P22 (24, 26); with A, K2, knit the YO, K2: buttonhole made.

Work even in patt as established, working buttonholes as before opposite marked button placement on Left front, until piece measures 12" (13", 15") from CO edge, ending by working a right-side row.

Shape Armhole

Row 1 (wrong side): BO 5 sts, P17 (19, 21), K5.

Row 2: K5, K17 (19, 21) sts,

Work even until armhole measures, 6" (6 1/4", 6 1/2"); ending by working a wrong-side row.

Shoulder and Neck Shaping

Row 1 (right side): BO 6 sts, K16, (18, 20) sts.

Dec one st at the neck edge on the next 3 (4, 5) rows, and then one st on the next alternate row once. BO rem 12, (13, 14) sts.

Sleeve (make 2)

Starting at bottom border with 2 strands of A and one strand of B, CO 31 (33, 35) sts

Work in garter st for 2". Cut Colors A and B. With 2 strands of MC, start sleeve body.

Sleeve Body

Row 1 (right side): K2, inc, knit to last 2 sts, inc, K2: 33 (35, 37) sts.

Work in stock st, inc at each end of every 4th row 4 times, and then every 6th row until there are 49 (51, 53) sts.

Work even until sleeve measures 12" (13", 14 1/2") from CO edge. BO.

STITCH GUIDE

SSK (sl, sl, knit): Sl next two sts one at a time to right needle, then knit these 2 sts tog.

Finishing

Sew shoulder seams.

Collar

With 2 strands of A and one strand of B, hold piece with right side facing. Pick up and knit 14 (14, 15) sts on right front neckline, 13 (15, 17) sts on center back, and 14 (14, 15) sts on left front neckline: 41 (43, 47) sts.

Knit 14 rows; BO.

Sew in sleeves, and then sew side seams. Sew on buttons opposite buttonholes.

HAT

INSTRUCTIONS

Starting at bottom border with 2 strands of Color A and one strand of Color B held tog, CO 50 (55) sts; place marker to indicate beg of rnd. Join, being careful not to twist sts.

Rnd 1: Knit.

Rnd 2: Purl.

Rep Rnds 1 and 2 until border measures 2" from the CO edge. Finish off Colors A and B. Attach 2 strands of MC.

Body

With 2 strands of MC, knit even (this creates stock st) until piece measures 3 1/2" (4") from CO edge.

Drop MC but do not finish off.

SIZES

Small
  Fits 18"to 19 1/2" head
Medium
  Fits 20"to 22 1/2" head

Note: Instructions are written for smaller size with changes for larger size in parentheses

MATERIALS

Worsted weight yarn
  110 (120) yards red (MC)
  75 (85) yards black (A)

Bulky weight eyelash yarn
  35 (40) yards black (B)

Note: Photographed model made with Brown Sheep Lamb's Pride Worsted #M81 Red Baron (MC) Brown Sheep Lamb's Pride Worsted #M05 Black Onyx (A) and Gedifra Techno Hair Lungo #9714 Black (B).

One red 1" diameter shank button

Sewing needle and red thread

1 stitch marker

16" Size 10 1/2 (6.5 mm) circular knitting needle (or size required for gauge)

4 Size 10 1/2 double-point knitting needles

GAUGE

12 sts = 4" with 2 strands of MC held tog in stock st (knit every rnd on circular needle)

Ridge

Join 2 strands of A and purl 3 rows.

Drop Color A, do not finish off. Pick up MC and with right side facing, * pick up the back lp of the next st in the last knit rnd (directly below the next st) and sl this st to left needle; knit the lifted st tog with the next st; rep from * around. Finish off A: 50 (55) sts.

With MC, knit 3 (5) rnds even.

Instructions continue on next page. ➜

Shape Top

Note: Change to double point needles when necessary.

Rnd 1: *K3, K2tog; rep from * around: 40 (44) sts.

Rnds 2 and 3: Knit.

Rnd 4: *K2, SSK; rep from * around: 30 (33) sts.

Rnds 5 and 6: Knit.

Rnd 7: *K1, K2 tog; rep from * around: 20 (22) sts.

Rnd 8: *SSK; rep from * around: 10 (11) sts.

For Small Size Only

Rnd 9: K2tog to end of rnd: 5 sts.

For Medium Size Only

Rnd 9: *K2tog; rep from * 4 times more, K1: 6 sts.

Finish off, leaving a long yarn end. Thread end into a yarn needle and draw through rem sts; draw up tightly and secure. Fasten off and weave in ends.

Flower

With one strand of A, CO 53 sts. Do not join; work back and forth in rows.

Row 1: *P1, P2tog; rep from * across to last 2 sts, P2: 36 sts.

Row 2: *K3tog; rep from * across: 24 sts.

Row 3: *P3tog, rep from * across: 8 sts.

Row 4: (K2tog) 4 times: 4 sts.

Row 5: P2tog twice: 2 sts.

BO, leaving a long yarn end.

Thread yarn into a needle and draw yarn through rem sts; draw up and fasten securely. Sew short edges of flower tog. Sew flower to hat. Sew button to center of flower.

#66 TRIPLET POT HOLDERS

Designed by Rita Weiss

SIZE
6" x 6"

MATERIALS
Worsted weight cotton yarn
- 1 oz blue variegated
- 1 oz blue
- 1 oz white

Note: Photographed models made with Lily® Sugar'n Cream® #00181 Faded Denim Ombre, #00026 Light Blue and #00001 White

Size 7 (4.5 mm) straight knitting needles (or size required for gauge)

Two size 7 double-point knitting needles

GAUGE
15 sts = 2" in patt

Note: The pot holders are made by a process called double knitting which produces a tubular piece that is the same on both sides and joined at the bottom cast-on edge. The stitch can be used to create a double thickness for a flat piece for which extra insulation is desired, such as these pot holders.

INSTRUCTIONS
(make one of each color)

Note: Slip all sts as to purl.

Starting at bottom, CO 44 sts.

Rows 1 and 2: *K1, sl 1, P1, sl 1; rep from * across.

Rows 3 and 4: *P1, sl 1, K1, sl 1; rep from * across.

Rep Rows 1 through 4 until pot holder measures 6". BO, working 2 sts tog each time, until 2 sts rem on needle. Place 2 sts on double point needle and work I-cord (see page 252) for approx 3". BO. Sew loose end of I-cord to pot holder to make lp.

#67 SWEATER DRAMA

MATERIALS

Bulky weight mohair blend yarn
  350 (400, 450) g multicolor (MC)

Silk-like ribbon yarn
  150 (200, 200) g multicolor (A)

Note: *Photographed model made with S.R. Kertzer Molash #1001 (MC) and S.R. Kertzer Sari #51 (A)*

Size 9 (5.5 mm) knitting needles

Size 10 (6 mm) knitting needles (or size required for gauge)

GAUGE

12 $^1/_2$ sts and 23 rows = 4" with larger needles in pattern stitch

Note: *Instructions are written for size Small with changes for larger sizes in parentheses.*

SIZES	Small	Medium	Large
Body Bust Measurements	36" - 38"	40" - 42"	44" - 46"
Finished Bust Measurements	40"	43 $^1/_2$"	47"

INSTRUCTIONS

Back

With larger needles and MC, CO 62 (68, 74) sts. Work in patt until piece measures 15 1/2" from beg.

Armhole Shaping

Dec 1 st at each end of next and then every other row 5 times: 50 (56, 62) sts.

Work even in patt until armhole measures 8" (8 1/2", 9"). BO.

Front

Work as for Back until piece measures 20 1/2" (21", 21 1/2") from beg.

Divide for Neck

Row 1 (right side): Work 20 (22, 24) sts, join 2nd ball of yarn and BO center 10 (12, 14) sts, work across.

Working both sides at once, BO from each neck edge 2 sts twice, then dec one st every other row twice. Work even until same length as back. BO rem 14 (16, 18) sts each side for shoulder.

Sleeve (make 2)

With MC, cast on 30 (32, 32) sts. Work in pattern st and at the same time, inc 1 st at each end of the 7th row, then every following 6th row after previous inc 2 (0, 0) times, then every following 8th row 7 (10, 11) times: 50 (54, 56) sts.

Work even in patt until piece from beg measures 18" (18 1/2", 19").

Cap Shaping

Dec one st each side on next row, then every other row 5 times more. BO.

Finishing

Sew right shoulder seam.

With smaller needles and MC, pick up and knit 72 (76, 76) sts evenly around neck edge.

Neck Ribbing

Row 1: P2, *K2, P2; rep from * across.

Row 2: K2, *P2, K2; rep from * across.

Continue in K2, P2 rib for 3". BO in rib.

Finishing

Sew left shoulder and neck seam. Sew in sleeves. Sew side and sleeve seams.

TWEED JACKET

Note: *Instructions are written for size Small; changes for sizes Medium and Large are in parentheses.*

SIZES	Small	Medium	Large
Body Bust Measurements	30" - 32"	34" - 36"	38" - 40"
Finished Bust Measurements	36 ³/₄"	40 ¹/₂"	44"

MATERIALS

Chunky weight yarn
   28 (28, 31 ¹/₂) oz dark grey
   28 (28, 31 ¹/₂) oz cream

Note: *Photographed model made with Patons® Shetland Chunky #3042 Charcoal and #3008 Aran*

2 stitch holders

18" separating zipper

14" Size 15 (10 mm) knitting needles (or size required for gauge)

One 14" Size 15 (10 mm) spare knitting needle

GAUGE

9 sts and 13 rows = 4" with 2 strands of yarn held tog, in stock st (knit 1 row, purl 1 row)

INSTRUCTIONS

Back

Starting at bottom of ribbing with one strand of each color held tog, CO 42 (46, 50) sts.

Row 1 (right side): K2; *P2, K2; rep from * across.

Row 2: P2; *K2, P2; rep from * across.

Rows 3 through 11: Work in ribbing as established, ending by working a right-side row.

Row 12: P2, (K2, P2) 4 (5, 5) times; K2 (0, 2), dec 1 st, work even in (K2, P2) ribbing as established: 41 (45, 49) sts.

Work even in stock st, beg with a knit row, until work from beg measures 11 ¹/₂" (11 ¹/₂", 12"), ending by working a wrong-side row.

Armhole Shaping

Row 1: BO 3 sts, knit across: 38 (42, 46) sts.

Row 2: BO 3 sts, purl across: 35 (39, 43) sts.

Row 3: K2, K2tog, knit to last 4 sts, sl 1, K1, PSSO, K2.

Rows 4 through 6: Work even in stock st.

Rep Rows 3 through 6, 2 (2, 3) times more: 29 (33, 35) sts.

167

Instructions continue on next page. →

Work even in stock st until armhole measures 8 1/2" (8 3/4", 9"), ending by working a wrong-side row.

Shoulder Shaping

Row 1: BO 8 (9, 10) sts, knit across.

Row 2: BO 8 (9, 10) sts, purl across.

Place rem 13 (15, 15) sts on spare needle.

Left Front

Beg at bottom of ribbing with one strand of each color held tog, CO 22 (22, 26) sts.

Row 1 (right side): K2; *P2, K2; rep from * across.

Row 2: P2; *K2, P2; rep from * to across.

Rows 3 through 11: Rep last 2 rows, end by working a right-side row.

Row 12: P2 (K2, P2) 4 (5, 5) times; K2 (0, 2), dec 1 (inc 1, dec 1) st, work even in (K2, P2) ribbing across: 21 (23, 25) sts.

Work even in stock st until piece measures 11 1/2" (11 1/2," 12") from CO row, ending by working a wrong-side row.

Armhole Shaping

Row 1: BO 3 sts, knit across: 18 (20, 22) sts.

Row 2: Purl.

Row 3: K2, K2tog, knit across.

Rows 4 through 6: Work even in stock st.

Rep Rows 3 through 6 two (2, 3) times more: 15 (17, 18) sts.

Work even in stock st until armhole measures 6" (6 1/4", 6 1/2") ending by working a wrong-side row.

Neck Shaping

Row 1: Knit to last 5 sts, turn, sl these 5 sts on a st holder.

Row 2: Purl: 10 (12, 13) sts.

Row 3: Knit to last 4 sts, sl 1, K1, PSSO, K2.

Row 4: Purl.

Rep Rows three and four 1 (2, 2) time(s) more: 8 (9, 10) sts.

Work even in stock st until armhole measures same length as Back, ending by working a wrong-side row. BO all sts.

Right Front

Work same as Left Front to armhole shaping, ending by working a right-side row.

Armhole Shaping

Row 1: BO 3 sts: 18 (20, 22) sts.

Row 2: Knit to last 4 sts, sl 1, K1, PSSO, K2.

Rows 3 through 5: Work even in stock st.

Rep Rows 2 through 5 two (2, 3) times more: 15 (17, 18) sts.

Work even in stock st until armhole measures 6" (6 1/4", 6 1/2") ending by working a right-side row.

Neck Shaping

Row 1: Purl to last 5 sts, turn; sl these 5 sts on a st holder: 10 (12, 13) sts.

Row 2: K2, K2tog, knit across.

Row 3: Purl.

Rep Rows two and three 1 (2, 2) time(s) more: 8 (9, 10) sts.

Work even in stock st until armhole measures same length as Back, ending by working a right-side row. BO all sts.

Sleeves (make 2)

Starting at bottom of cuff ribbing, with with one strand of each color, CO 26 sts.

Rows 1 through 11: Work in K2, P2 ribbing, ending by working a right-side row.

Row 12: K13, inc, K12: 27 sts.

Sleeve Body

Row 1 (right side): Knit.

Rows 2 through 8: Work even in stock st.

Row 9: Inc, knit to last st, inc: 29 sts.

Rows 10 through 18: Work even in stock st.

Row 19: Inc, knit to last st, inc.

Rep Rows 10 through 19, until there are 31 (33, 35) sts.

Work even in stock st until piece measures 18 ½" (19 ½", 20") from CO row, ending by working a wrong-side row.

Shape Sleeve Cap

Row 1: BO 3 sts, knit to end.

Row 2: BO 3 sts, purl to end: 25 (27, 29) sts.

Row 3: K2, K2tog, knit to last 4 sts, sl 1, K1, PSSO, K2.

Rows 4 through 6: Work even in stock st.

Rep Rows three through six 1 (2, 2) time(s) more: 21 (21, 23) sts.

Upper Sleeve Cap

Row 1: K2, K2tog, knit to last 4 sts, sl 1, K1, PSSO, K2.

Row 2: Purl.

Row 3 through 6: Rep Rows 1 and 2: 15 (15, 17) sts.

Row 7: BO 3 sts, knit across: 12 (12, 14) sts.

Row 8: BO 3 sts, purl across: 9 (9, 11) sts.

BO rem 9 (9, 11) sts.

Sew shoulder seams.

Collar

With right side of work facing and one strand of each color, K5 from right st holder, pick up and knit 10 (11, 11) sts up Right Front neck edge; K13 (15, 15) from back spare needle and dec 1 st at center; pick up and knit 10 (11, 11) sts down Left Front neck edge; K5 from left st holder: 42 (46, 46) sts.

Work in K2, P2 ribbing until Collar measures 5".

BO in ribbing.

Finishing

Weave in all yarn ends.

Sew side and sleeve seams. Sew in sleeves. Sew zipper in place.

Instructions continue on next page. →

TURTLENECK PULLOVER

Note: *Instructions are written for size Small; changes for sizes Medium and Large are in parentheses.*

SIZES	Small	Medium	Large
Body Bust Measurements	30" - 32"	34" - 36"	38" - 40"
Finished Bust Measurement	36 $^1/_2$"	40"	43 $^1/_2$"

MATERIALS

Chunky weight yarn
   28 (31 $^1/_2$, 35) oz dark grey
   28 (31 $^1/_2$, 35) oz dark red

Note: *Photographed Model made with Patons® Shetland Chunky #3042 Charcoal and #3532 Deep Red*

2 stitch holders

14" Size 15 (10 mm) knitting needles (or size required for gauge)

One 14" Size 15 (10 mm) spare knitting needle

GAUGE

9 sts and 13 rows = 4" with 2 strands of yarn held tog, in stock st (knit 1 row, purl 1 row)

STITCH GUIDE

Increase (inc): Knit into front and back of stitch: inc made.

INSTRUCTIONS

Back

Starting at bottom with one strand of each color held tog, CO 42 (46, 50) sts.

Row 1 (right side): K2; *P2, K2; rep from * across.

Row 2: P2; *K2, P2; rep from * to across.

Rows 3 through 11: Rep Rows 1 and 2, ending by working a right-side row.

Row 12: P2, (K2, P2) 4 (5, 5) times; K2 (0, 2), dec 1 st, work even in (K2, P2) ribbing as established to end of row: 41 (45, 49) sts.

Work even in stock st until piece measures 11 $^1/_2$" (11 $^1/_2$", 12") from CO edge, ending by working a wrong-side row.

Armhole Shaping

Row 1: BO 3 sts, knit across: 38 (42, 46) sts.

Row 2: BO 3 sts, purl across: 35 (39, 43) sts.

Row 3: K2, K2tog, knit to last 4 sts, sl 1, K1, PSSO, K2.

Rows 4 through 6: Work 3 rows even in stock st.

Rep Rows 3 through six 2 (2, 3) times more: 29 (33, 35) sts.

Work even in stock st until armhole measures 8 1/2" (8 3/4," 9"), ending by working a wrong-side row.

Shoulder Shaping

Row 1: BO 8 (9, 10) sts, knit across.

Row 2: BO 8 (9, 10) sts, purl across.

Place rem 13 (15, 15) sts on a spare needle.

Front

Work same as back to armhole shaping.

Armhole Shaping

Row 1: BO 3 sts, knit across: 38 (42, 46) sts.

Row 2: BO 3 sts, purl across: 35 (39, 43) sts.

Row 3: K2, K2tog, knit to last 4 sts, sl 1, K1, PSSO, K2.

Rows 4 through 6: Work 3 rows even in stock st.

Rep Rows 3 through six 2 (2, 3) times more: 29 (33, 35) sts.

Work even in stock st until armhole measures 6" (6 1/4", 6 1/2"), ending by working a wrong-side row.

Neck Shaping

Row 1: K11 (12, 13) (neck edge), turn; place rem sts on a spare needle.

Row 2: Purl.

Row 3: Knit to last 4 sts, sl 1, K1, PSSO, K2.

Rep last 2 rows twice more: 8 (9, 10) sts.

Work even in stock st until armhole measures same length as back, ending by working a wrong-side row.

BO all sts.

With right side of work facing, sl next 7 (9, 9) sts from spare needle onto a st holder.

Row 1: Join yarn to rem 11 (12, 13) sts and knit to end of row.

Row 2: Purl.

Row 3: K2, K2tog, knit to end of row.

Rep last 2 rows twice more: 8 (9, 10) sts.

Work even in stock st until armhole measures same length as back, ending by working a wrong-side row.

BO all sts.

Sleeves (make 2)
Cuff

With one strand of each color held tog, CO 26 sts.

Rows 1 through 11: Work in (K2, P2) ribbing, ending by working a right-side row.

Row 12: Continuing in K2, P2 ribbing, inc one st in center of row: 27 sts.

Instructions continue on next page. →

Sleeve Body

Row 1 (right side): Knit

Rows 2 through 8: Work even in stock st.

Row 9: Inc, knit to last st, inc: 29 sts.

Rows 10 through 18: Work even in stock st.

Row 19: Inc, knit to last st, inc.

Rep Rows 10 through 19, until there are 31 (33, 35) sts.

Work even in stock st until work measures 18 ½" (19 ½", 20") from beg, or desired length, ending by working a wrong-side row.

Shape Sleeve Cap

Row 1: BO 3 sts, knit across.

Row 2: BO 3 sts, purl across: 25 (27, 29) sts.

Row 3: K2, K2tog, knit to last 4 sts, sl 1, K1, PSSO, K2.

Rows 4 through 6: Work even in stock st.

Rep Rows 3 through six 1 (2, 2) time(s) more: 21 (21, 23) sts.

Upper Sleeve Cap

Row 1: K2, K2tog, knit to last 4 sts, sl 1, K1, PSSO, K2.

Row 2: Purl.

Rows 3 through 6: Rep Rows 1 and 2: 15 (15, 17) sts.

Row 7: BO 3 sts, knit across: 12 (12, 14) sts.

Row 8: BO 3 sts, purl across: 9 (9, 11) sts. BO all sts.

Collar

Sew right shoulder seam.

With right side of work facing and one strand of each color held tog, pick up and knit 11 sts down Left Front neck edge. K7 (9, 9) from front st holder. Pick up and knit 11 sts up Right Front neck edge. K13 (15, 15) from Back spare needle: 42 (46, 46) sts.

Work in K2, P2 ribbing until Collar measures 8". BO in ribbing.

Finishing

Sew left shoulder and Collar seams, reversing seam for Collar turnback.

Sew side and sleeve seams. Sew in Sleeves. Weave in all ends.

#76 TWO SIDES TO EVERY STORY

Designed by Suzanne Atkinson

SIZE
6" x 60"

MATERIALS
Worsted weight brushed
  mohair type yarn
  3 oz black (MC)

Eyelash yarn
  4 oz raspberry (CC)

*Note: Photographed model made
with Classic Elite LaGran
Mohair #6513 Black (MC) and
Sandnesgarn Funny Eyelash
#4517 Raspberry (CC)*

16" Size 10 (6 mm) circular
  knitting needle

GAUGE
22 sts = 4" in Pattern Stitch

STITCH GUIDE
yif: yarn in front (on side of work facing you)

yib: yarn in back (on side of work away from you).

Note: All sts are slipped as to purl

PATTERN STITCH
Row 1: With CC, K1, *sl 1 with yif, K5; rep from * 5
times more, sl 1 with yif, K1; turn.

Row 2: With CC, P1; *sl 1 with yib, P5; rep from * 5
times more, sl 1 with yib, P1. Do not turn work; slide
sts to opposite end of needle.

Row 3: With MC, K4; *sl 1 with yif, K5; rep from * 5
times more, sl 1 with yif, K4; turn.

Row 4: With MC, P4; *sl 1 with yib, P5, rep from * 5
times more, sl 1 with yib, P4. Do not turn work; slide
sts to opposite end of needle.

INSTRUCTIONS

With MC, CO 33 sts. Do not turn,
slide sts to opposite end of circular
needle and join CC.

Rep Rows 1 through 4 of Pattern
Stitch until scarf measures 60". With
MC, BO as to knit. Weave in ends.

#71 SHAKER RIB TUNIC

Designed by Patons Design Staff

MATERIALS

Super bulky weight yarn
  28 (31 $\frac{1}{2}$, 35, 38 $\frac{1}{2}$) oz white

Note: Photogaphed model made with Patons® Melody #00901 White

29" Size 15 (10 mm) circular knitting needle (or size required for gauge)

Size 15 (10 mm) straight knitting needles

Three stitch holders

Four stitch markers

GAUGE

8 $\frac{1}{2}$ sts and 18 rows = 4" in Shaker rib patt

Note: Instructions are written for size Small; changes for sizes Medium, Large and X-Large are in parentheses.

SIZES	Small	Medium	Large	X-Large
Body Bust Measurements	30" - 32"	34" - 36"	38" - 40"	42" - 44"
Garment Bust Measurements	40"	43"	46 $\frac{1}{2}$"	50"

INSTRUCTIONS

Front

Starting at lower edge with circular needles, CO 43 (45, 49, 53) sts. Do not join. Work back and forth in rows.

Work in Shaker Rib patt until piece measures 23" (23 $\frac{1}{2}$", 23 $\frac{1}{2}$", 24") from CO edge, end by working a wrong-side row.

Neck Shaping (First Half)

Row 1: With straight needles, work in patt across 18 (19, 21, 22) sts (neck edge); turn, leaving rem sts on circular needle and work in patt across with circular needle.

Row 2 (right side): Working with straight needles, dec 1 st at neck edge, cont in patt across rem 17 (18, 20, 21) sts.

Row 3: Work across in patt.

Row 4: Dec 1 st at neck edge, cont in patt across rem sts : (16, 17, 19, 20) sts.

Rows 5 through 8: Rep Rows 3 and 4. At end of row 4: 14 (15, 17, 18) sts.

Work 3 (3, 5, 5) rows in patt. BO.

With right side of work facing slip next 7 (7, 7, 9) sts from circular needle onto a stitch holder. Join yarn to rem sts and with straight needles, work in patt across rem 18 (19, 21, 22) sts.

Rep Rows 2 through 8.

Work 3 (3, 5, 5) rows even in patt. BO.

Back

Work as for Front until piece measures same length as Front to Neck Shaping, ending by working a wrong-side row. Then work even in patt for 11 (11, 13, 13) more rows.

Next row: BO 14 (15, 17, 18) sts. Sl next 15 (15, 15, 17) sts onto a stitch holder. BO rem 14 (15, 17, 18) sts.

Sleeve (make 2)

Starting at lower edge with straight needles, CO 21 (21, 23, 23) sts.

Rows 1 through 4: Work in Shaker Rib patt.

Row 5: Inc, work in patt to last st, inc: 23 (23, 25, 25) sts

Row 6: Inc, work in patt to last st, inc: 25 (25, 27, 27) sts.

Rep Rows 1 through 6 until there are 41 (43, 33, 39) sts.

For Sizes Large and X-Large Only

Inc 1 st at beg and end of every 8th row until there are (43, 45) sts.

For All Sizes

Cont in patt until sleeve measures 17 1/2" (18", 18 1/2", 18 1/2") from CO edge, ending by working a wrong-side row. BO.

Finishing
Collar

Sew right shoulder seam. With right side of work facing, pick up and knit 8 (8, 9, 9) sts down left front neck edge. Knit across 7 (7, 7, 9) sts from stitch holder. Pick up and knit 8 (8, 9, 9) sts up right front edge. Knit across 15 (15, 15, 17) sts from back stitch holder, increasing 1 st at center: 39 (39, 41, 45) sts.

Next Row (wrong side): Purl.

Work in patt until collar measures 6 1/2" from pick-up row, end by working a wrong-side row. BO as to knit.

Sew left shoulder and collar seam.

With right side facing, place markers 9 1/2" (10", 10", 10 1/2") down from shoulder seams on front and back side edges. Sew in sleeves between markers.

Sew side and sleeve seams.

#72 MERRY CHRISTMAS SWEATER

Designed by Donna Druchunas

MATERIALS

Worsted-weight yarn
   440 (560, 670) yds green
   15 yards white (for bobbles)
   15 yards red (for bobbles)

Note: Photographed model made with Plymouth Galway Worsted #82 Green, #01 Off White and #44 Red

Tapestry needle

8 markers

Cable needle

16" Size 4 (3.5 mm) circular knitting needle

20" Size 6 (4 mm) circular knitting needle

Two 20" Size 8 (5 mm) circular knitting needles (or size required for gauge)

Size 6 (4 mm) double-point knitting needles (dpn)

Two sets Size 8 (5 mm) double-point knitting needles (dpn)

GAUGE

20 sts = 4" in circular stock st (knit all rounds) on largest circular needles

Note: Instructions are written for size 4; changes for sizes 6 and 8 are in parentheses. When only one number is listed, it applies to all sizes.

SIZES	4	6	8
Body Chest Measurements	22"	24"	26"
Finished Chest Measurements	26"	28"	30"

INSTRUCTIONS

Starting at lower edge with Size 6 circular needle and green, CO 130 (140, 150) sts; join, being careful not to twist sts. Place marker to indicate beg of rnds.

Rnd 1: K65 (70, 75), place a marker; knit around.

Knit even until piece measures 1 1/2".

Change to one of the Size 8 circular needles and continue to knit until piece measures 8 1/2" (9 1/2", 11").

On last rnd, end 4 sts before first marker.

Divide for Front and Back

BO 8 sts; knit to 4 sts before next marker: 56 (62, 66) sts on front. BO 8 sts, knit to end of round: 56 (62, 66) sts on back.

Leave work on circular needle; set aside and work sleeves.

Sleeve (make 2)

Starting at lower edge with green and smaller dpn, CO 30 (32, 36) sts. Place marker and join to work in rounds, being careful not to twist sts.

Knit until sleeve measures 1 1/2".

Change to larger dpn and knit, inc one st before and after marker every 6 rnds, 9 (10, 9) times: 48 (52, 54) sts.

Work even until sleeve measures 11 1/2" (12", 13 1/2"). On last rnd, end 4 sts before marker. BO 8 sts, knit to end of round: 40 (44, 46) sts. Leave one sleeve on dpn and work second sleeve with second set of dpn.

Join Sleeves and Body

With right side facing, knit across left sleeve sts, place marker, knit across front sts, place marker, knit across right sleeve sts, place marker, knit across back sts, place marker: 194 (212, 226) sts.

Yoke

On next rnd, dec 4 (2, 6) sts evenly spaced: 190 (210, 220) sts. Work even until yoke measures 1 1/2" (1 3/4", 2").

Dec Round: *K3, K2tog; rep from * around: 152 (168, 176) sts.

Cable Pattern

On next rnd, inc 2 (0, 6) sts evenly spaced: 154 (168, 182) sts.

Rnd 1: Knit.

Rnd 2: *K4, sl one st to cable needle and hold in back, K2, K1 from cable needle; sl 2 sts to cable needle and hold in front, P1, K2 from cable needle, K4; rep from * around.

Rnd 3: *K7, P1, K6; rep from * around.

Rnd 4: *K3, sl one st to cable needle and hold in back, K2, P1 from cable needle, K1, P1; sl 2 sts to cable needle and hold in front, K1, K2 from cable needle, K3; rep from * around.

177

Instructions continue on next page. →

Rnd 5: *K5, (P1, K1) twice, K5; rep from * around.

Rnd 6: *K2, sl one st to cable needle and hold in back, K2, K1 from cable needle; (P1, K1) twice; sl 2 sts to cable needle and hold in front, P1, K2 from cable needle, K2; rep from * around.

Rnd 7: *K5; (P1, K1) 3 times, K3; rep from * around.

Rnd 8: *K1, sl one st to cable needle and hold in back, K2, P1 from cable needle; (K1, P1) 3 times; sl 2 sts to cable needle and hold in front, K1, K2 from cable needle, K1; rep from * around.

Rnd 9: *K3; (P1, K1) 4 times, K3; rep from * around.

Rnd 10: *Sl one st to cable needle and hold in back; K2, K1 from cable needle; (P1, K1) 4 times; sl 2 sts to cable needle and hold in front, P1, K2 from cable needle; rep from * around.

Rnd 11: *K3; (P1, K1) 5 times, K1; rep from * around.

Rnd 12: *P2 tog; (K1, P1) 5 times, SSK; rep from * around: 132 (144, 156) sts.

Rnds 13 and 14: *P1, K1; rep from * around.

Change to Size 6 Circular Needle
Continue in K1, P1 ribbing as established until yoke measures 4" (4 3/4", 5 1/4").

Change to Smallest Circular Needle
Continue in K1, P1 ribbing until yoke measures 5 1/4" (6 1/4", 6 3/4").

Neckband
Dec Row: *SSK, P2tog; rep from * to end of round: 66 (72, 78) sts.

Continue in K1, P1 ribbing until neckband measures 1".

BO loosely.

Bobbles
Make 11 (12, 13) in an assortment of red and white.

With largest needle, CO 1 st.

Row 1: (K1, P1, K1, P1) all in same st.

Row 2: Purl.

Row 3: Knit.

Row 4: Purl.

Row 5: Sl 2, K2tog, PSSO. Finish off.

Finishing
Sew bobbles to bottom points of cables as shown in photo. Sew underarm seams. Weave in ends.

#73 CUTE CAMISOLE

MATERIALS

DK cotton light weight yarn
   250 (300, 300, 350, 400, 400) g
   light denim

Note: Photographed model made with Twilleys of Stamford Freedom Denim #102 Light Denim

Size 6 (4 mm) knitting needles
   (or size required for gauge)

Size 3 (3.25 mm) knitting needles

Stitch holder

Stitch markers

GAUGE

21 sts and 32 rows = 4" with sport
   weight yarn and larger needles in
   stock st (knit 1 row, purl 1 row)

Note: Instructions are written for size X-Small; changes for Small, Medium, Large, X-Large and XX-Large are in parentheses.

SIZES	X-Small	Small	Medium	Large	X-Large	XX-Large
Body Bust Measurements	32"	34"	36"	38"	40"	42"
Finished Bust Measurements	31"	34"	36"	38"	40"	43"

INSTRUCTIONS

Back

Upper Section

Starting at bottom edge with larger needles, CO 77 (83, 89, 95, 101, 107) sts.

Row 1 (right side): Knit.

Row 2: Purl

Rows 3 through 6: Rep Rows 1 and 2.

Row 7: Inc in first st, knit to last st, inc in last st.

Continue in stock st, increasing one st at each end of needle every 6 rows until there are 85 (91, 97, 105, 111, 117) sts.

Work 5 more rows even, ending by working a purl row.

Top Edging

Change to smaller needles.

Rows 1 through 3: Knit.

Row 4: P2; * YO, P2tog; rep from * to last st, P1.

Rows 5 through 8: Rep Rows 1 through 4.

Row 9: Knit.

BO as to knit.

Midriff Section

Hold Upper Section upside down with right side facing. With smaller needles pick up and knit 77 (83, 89, 95, 101, 107) sts from cast-on edge of Upper Section.

Rows 1 and 2: Knit.

Row 3: P2, *YO, P2tog; rep from * to last st, P1.

Rows 4 and 5: Knit.

Begin Diamond Pattern

Row 1 (right side): K2 (0, 0, 3, 1, 1); [K2tog, YO, K3] 0 (1, 0, 0, 1, 0) times; *K3, K2tog, YO, K3; rep from * to last 3 (6, 1, 4, 7, 2) sts, [K3, K2tog, YO] 0 (1, 0, 0, 1, 0) times, K3 (1, 1, 4, 2, 2).

Row 2 and all following even-numbered rows: Purl.

Row 3: K2 (2, 0, 3, 0, 1); [K2tog, YO, K1] 0 (0, 0, 0, 1, 0) times; [YO, sl 1, K1, PSSO, K1] 0 (1, 0, 0, 1, 0) times; *K2, K2tog, YO, K1, YO, sl 1, K1, PSSO, K1; rep from * to last 3 (6, 1, 4, 7, 2) sts, [K2, K2tog, YO] 0 (1, 0, 0, 1, 0) times; [K1, YO, sl 1, K1, PSSO] 0 (0, 0, 0, 1, 0) times, K3 (2, 1, 4, 0, 2).

Row 5: K2 (3, 0, 1, 4, 1); [YO, sl 1, K1, PSSO] 0 (1, 0, 1, 1, 0) times; *K1, K2tog, YO, K3, YO, sl 1, K1, PSSO; rep from * to last 3 (6, 1, 4, 7, 2) sts, [K1, K2tog, YO] 0 (1, 0, 1, 1, 0) times, K3 (3, 1, 1, 4, 2).

Row 7: K1 (4, 0, 2, 5, 1); [sl 1, K1, PSSO, YO, K5] 0 (0, 1, 0, 0, 1) times; *YO, sl 1, K2tog, PSSO, YO, K5; rep from * to last 4 (7, 2, 5, 0, 3) sts; [YO, sl 1, K2tog, PSSO, YO] 1 (1, 0, 1, 0, 0) times, [YO, sl 1, K1, PSSO] 0 (0, 1, 0, 0, 1) times; K1 (4, 0, 2, 0, 1).

Row 9: K1 (4, 7, 2, 5, 0); *K1, YO, sl 1, K1, PSSO, K5, rep from * to last 4 (7, 2, 5, 0, 3) sts, [K1, YO, sl 1, K1, PSSO] 1 (1, 0, 1, 0, 1) times, K1 (4, 2, 2, 0, 0).

Row 11: K0 (3, 0, 1, 4, 1); [K2tog, YO] 1 (1, 0, 1, 1, 0) times, *K1, YO, sl 1, K1, PSSO, K3, K2tog, YO; rep from * to last 3 (6, 1, 4, 7, 2) sts, [K1, YO, sl 1, K1, PSSO] 1 (1, 0, 1, 1, 0) times, K0 (3, 1, 1, 4, 2).

Row 13: K2 (2, 0, 0, 3, 1); [K2tog, YO, K1] 0 (1, 0, 1, 1, 0) times; *K2, YO, sl 1, K1, PSSO, K1, K2tog, YO, K1; rep from * to last 3 (6, 1, 4, 7, 2) sts, [K2, YO, sl 1, K1, PSSO] 0 (1, 0, 1, 1, 0) times, K3 (2, 1, 0, 3, 2).

Row 15: K2 (1, 0, 3, 1, 1); [K2tog, YO, K2] 0 (1, 0, 0, 0, 0) times; [YO, K3tog, YO, K2] 0 (0, 0, 0, 1, 0) times; *K3, YO, K3tog, YO, K2; rep from * to last 3 (6, 1, 4, 7, 2) sts, [K3, YO, K3tog, YO] 0 (0, 0, 0, 1, 0) times; [K3, YO, K2tog] 0 (1, 0, 0, 0, 0) times, K3 (1, 1, 4, 1, 2).

Row 16: Purl.

These 16 rows form diamond patt.

Cont in diamond patt, shaping sides by inc one st at each end of next and every following 6th row until there are 85 (91, 97, 105, 111, 117) sts, taking inc sts into patt.

Work even until Back measures 14" (14 1/2", 14 1/2", 15", 15", 15 1/2"), ending after a patt Row 2 or 10.

Change to smaller needles.

Rows 1 through 3: Knit.

Row 4 (wrong side): P2; *YO, P2tog, rep from * to last st, P1.

Rows 5 through 8: Rep Rows 1 through 4.

Row 9: Knit.

Work picot BO as follows: BO2 sts; *sl the rem st now on right needle back onto left needle, CO 2 sts, BO 5 sts; rep from * across.

Front
Upper Section

With larger needles, CO 3 sts.

Row 1 (right side): K3.

Row 2: P3.

Row 3: Inc in first st, M1, K1 and mark this st, M1, inc in last st: 7 sts.

Row 4: Purl.

Row 5: Inc in first st, K to marked st, M1, K marked st, M1, K to last st, inc in last st.

Row 6: Knit.

Row 7: Rep Row 5.

Row 8: Purl.

Row 9: Rep Row 5.

Row 10: Purl.

Rep Rows 5 through 10 twice more, then rep Rows 5 through 8 once more, ending by working a wrong-side row: 51 sts. Place sts on a holder.

Finish off.

Work Upper Section once more, but at end of last row, do not finish off.

Instructions continue on next page. →

First Joining Row (right side)

CO and knit 2 (5, 8, 11, 14, 17) sts, mark last st; K2tog, knit to next marked st, M1, knit marked st, M1, knit to last 2 sts of this piece, sl 1, K1, PSSO, turn and CO one st, mark this st. Working across sts of first piece on holder, K2tog, knit to marked st, M1, knit marked st, M1, knit to last 2 sts, sl 1, K1, PSSO.

Second Joining Row

CO and purl 2 (5, 8, 11, 14, 17) sts, mark last st, purl across: 107 (113, 119, 125, 131, 137) sts.

Top Shaping Pattern

Row 1 (right side): Knit to first marked st, K2tog, knit to next marked st, M1, knit marked st, M1, knit to within 2 sts of next marked st, sl 1, K1, PSSO, K marked st, K2tog, knit to next marked st, M1, knit marked st, M1, knit to within 2 sts of next marker, sl 1, K1, PSSO, knit to end.

Row 2: Knit.

Row 3: Rep Row l.

Row 4: Purl.

Row 5: Rep Row 1.

Row 6: Purl.

These 6 rows form Top Shaping Pattern.

Keeping shaping at markers as est, cont in upper patt, inc one st at each end of next and every 6th row until there are 115 (121, 127, 133, 139, 145) sts.

Work 5 more rows, ending by working a wrong-side row. Finish off.

Place first and last 28 (31, 34, 37, 40, 43) sts onto holders.

With smaller needles and right side facing, join yarn to center 59 sts.

Row 1: Knit to within 2 sts of marked st, sl 1, K1, PSSO, knit marked st, K2tog, knit across.

Row 2: Knit.

Row 3: Rep Row 1.

Row 4: P2; *YO, P2tog; rep from * to last st, P1.

Rep last 4 rows once more.

Row 9: Rep Row 1. CO as to knit.

Midriff Section

Work as for Midriff of Back through Row 16. Work even until Midriff of Front matches Midriff of Back, ending by working a wrong-side row.

Left Shoulder Strap and Upper Edging

With smaller needles and right side facing, knit across 28 (31, 34, 37, 40, 43) sts left front holder, pick up and knit 6 sts from row end edge of upper edging, then turn and CO 55 (56, 59, 60, 63, 64) sts: 89 (93, 99, 103, 109, 113) sts.

Rows 1 and 2: Knit.

Row 3: P2; *YO, P2tog; rep from * to last st, P1.

Row 4: Knit.

Rep last 4 rows once more. BO as to knit.

Right Shoulder Strap and Upper Edging

With smaller needles, CO 55 (56, 59, 60, 63, 64) sts. With right side facing, pick up and knit 6 sts from row end edge of upper edging, and knit across 28 (31, 34, 37, 40, 43) sts on right front holder: 89 (93, 99, 103, 109, 113) sts.

Rows 1 and 2: Knit.

Row 3: P21 *YO, P2tog; rep from * to last st, P1.

Row 4: Knit.

Rep last 4 rows once more. BO as to knit.

Finishing

Join side seams. Sew free end of straps to upper edge of back, adjusting length to fit.

COAT

Note: *Instructions are written for size Small; changes for sizes Medium and Large are in parentheses.*

SIZES	Small	Medium	Large
Body Bust Measurements	30" - 32"	34" - 36"	38" - 40"
Finished Bust Measurements	41 1/4"	44 1/4"	46 3/4"

MATERIALS

Chunky weight yarn
   63 (66 1/2, 70) oz cream

Note: *Photographed model made with Patons® Shetland Chunky #3024 Biscuit*

2 small stitch holders

1 large stitch holder

6 buttons to fit buttonholes

14" Size 10 1/2 (6.5 mm) knitting needles (or size required for gauge)

14" Size 10 (6 mm knitting needles)

GAUGE

13 sts and 18 rows = 4" with larger needles in stock st (knit 1 row, purl 1 row)

INSTRUCTIONS

Back
Bottom Border

With smaller needles, CO 67 (71, 77) sts.

Row 1 (right side): K1; *P1, K1; rep from * across.

Rep Row 1 (Seed st) until piece measures 3" from CO row, ending by working a wrong-side row, and inc 1 st at each end of last row: 69 (73, 79) sts.

Coat Body

Change to larger needles and work in stock st, dec 1 st at each end of row on 17th and every following 30th row until 61 (65, 71) sts rem.

Work even in stock st until piece measures 30" from CO row, ending by working a wrong-side row.

Shape Armhole

Row 1: BO 4 sts, knit across.

Row 2: BO 4 sts, purl across: 53 (57, 63) sts.

Row 3: K2, K2tog, knit to last 4 sts, sl 1, K1, PSSO, K2.

Row 4: Purl.

Rep Rows 3 and four 3 (4, 6) more times: 45 (47, 49) sts.

Work even until armhole measures 8" (8 1/2", 9 1/4"), ending by working wrong-side row.

Instructions continue on next page. →

Shape Shoulders
BO 12 sts at beg of next 2 rows; place rem 21 (23, 25) sts on a large st holder.

Left Front
Bottom Border
With smaller needles, CO 43 (45, 47) sts.

Work in Seed st for 3", ending by working a right-side row. Work one more row, inc 1 st at each end of row: 45 (47, 49) sts.

Coat Body
Change to larger needles.

Row 1 (right side): Knit to last 9 sts, work last 9 sts in Seed st for Center Front Border.

Row 2: Work 9 sts in Seed st, purl across.

Rep Rows 1 and 2, at same time, dec one st at armhole edge on 15th and every following 30th row until 41 (43, 45) sts rem.

Work even until piece measures same as Back to Shape Armhole, ending by working a wrong-side row.

Shape Armhole
Row 1: BO 4 sts, work in patt across: 37 (39, 41) sts.

Row 2: Work even.

Row 3: K2, K2tog, work in patt across.

Row 4: Work even.

Rep Rows 3 and four 3 (4, 6) times more: 33 (34, 34) sts.

Work even in patt until armhole measures 4 1/2 (5, 5 3/4)", ending by working wrong-side row.

Shape Neck
Row 1: Knit to last 14 sts, turn; sl rem 14 sts to a small st holder: 19 (20, 20) sts.

Row 2: P2, P2tog, purl to end of row.

Row 3: Knit to last 4 sts, K2tog, K2.

Row 4: Rep Row 2.

Row 5: Rep Row 3: 15 (16, 16) sts.

Row 6: Purl.

Row 7: Knit to last 4 sts, K2 tog, K2.

Rep Rows 6 and seven 2 (3, 3) times more: 12 sts.

Work even in Stock st until armhole measures same length as Back, ending by working a wrong-side row; BO rem 12 sts.

Mark positions for 6 buttons on Left Front. Place first button 3/4" down from top neck edge, and last button 9" up from CO edge. Evenly space rem 4 buttons between top and bottom buttons.

Right Front
Note: As you work Right Front, work buttonholes in center front border to correspond to button markers on Left Front.

To Work a Buttonhole
Row 1 (right side): (K1, P1) twice, BO 2 sts, work in patt across.

Row 2: Work in pattern across, CO 2 sts over bound-off sts.

With smaller needles, CO 43 (45, 47) sts.

Work in Seed st pattern for 3". Work one more row, inc 1 st at each side of row: 45 (47, 49) sts.

Body
Change to larger needles.

Row 1: Work Seed st over 9 sts for center front border, knit across.

Row 2: Purl to last 9 sts, work last 9 sts in seed st.

Rep Rows 1 and 2, and at same time dec one st at armhole edge on 15th and every following 30th row until 41 (43, 45) sts rem.

Work even until piece measures same as Back to armhole shaping (working buttonholes as noted), ending by working a right-side row.

Shape Armhole

Row 1: BO 4 sts, work in pattern across: 37 (39, 41) sts.

Row 2: Work to last 4 sts, sl 1, K1, PSSO, K2.

Row 3: Work even.

Rep Rows 2 and three 3 (4, 6) times more: 33 (34, 34) sts.

Work even until armhole measures 4 ½ (5, 5 ¾)", ending by working a right-side row.

Shape Neck

Row 1: Purl to last 14 sts, turn; place rem 14 sts on a small st holder: 19 (20, 20)sts.

Row 2: K2, sl 1, K1, PSSO, knit across.

Row 3: Purl to last 4 sts, P2tog through back lps, P2.

Row 4: Rep Row 2.

Row 5: Rep Row 3: 15 (16, 16) sts.

Row 6: K2, sl 1, K1, PSSO, knit across.

Row 7: Purl.

Rep last 2 rows 2 (3, 3) times more: 12 sts.

Work even in Stock St until armhole measures same as Back, ending by working a right-side row. BO rem 12 sts.

Sleeve (make 2)

Starting at cuff with smaller needles, CO 33 (33, 35) sts.

Work in Seed st for 20 rows, at same time dec 1 st at each side on the 9th and 17th rows: 29 (29, 31) sts. Mark last row.

Sleeve Body

Change to larger needles.

Row 1 (right side): Knit, inc 1 st at each side: 31 (31, 33) sts.

Continue in Stock st, inc one st at each side on 4th and every following 6th row, until there are 33 (37, 37) sts; then inc 1 st at each side every following 8th row until there are 47 (49, 51) sts. Work even until sleeve measures 18" (18", 18 ½") from marked row, ending by working wrong-side row.

Shape Sleeve Cap

Row 1: BO 3 sts, knit across.

Row 2: BO 3 sts, purl across: 41 (43, 45) sts.

Row 3: K2, K2tog, knit to last 4 sts, sl 1, K1, PSSO, K2.

Row 4: Purl.

Rows 5 through 16: Rep Rows 3 and 4 in sequence: 27 (29, 31) sts.

Row 17: K2, K2tog, knit to last 4 sts, sl 1, K1, PSSO, K2.

Row 18: P2, P2tog tbl, purl to last 4 sts, P2tog, P2.

Rep last 2 rows 0 (1, 1) time more: 23 (21, 23) sts.

BO 5 (4, 5) sts at beg of next 2 rows; BO rem 13 sts.

Instructions continue on next page. →

Weave in ends.

Sew shoulder seams.

Collar

With right side of work facing and smaller needles, work 14 sts from Right Front st holder in Seed st. Pick up and knit 12 sts up right front neck edge. K21 (23, 25) from back st holder. Pick up and knit 12 sts down left front neck edge. Work 14 sts from Left Front stitch holder in Seed st: 73 (75, 77) sts.

Work even in Seed st until Collar measures 7", ending by working a wrong-side row. BO in patt.

Assembly

Weave in all ends. Sew in sleeves. Sew side and sleeve seams. Sew on buttons to correspond to buttonholes. Try on garment and mark positions for pockets.

Pocket (make 2)

With smaller needles, CO 25 sts. Work 14 rows in Seed st, inc 1 st in center of last row: 26 sts. Work in Stock st until pocket measures 7", ending by working a wrong-side row. BO. Sew pockets to fronts of coat where marked.

SCARF

SCARF SIZE
38" long x 7 1/2" wide.

MATERIALS
Chunky weight yarn
   10 1/2 oz light blue
*Note: Photographed model made with Patons®
Shetland Chunky #3105 Ice Blue*
14" Size 10 (6 mm) knitting needles
Stitch holder

INSTRUCTIONS

CO 23 sts.

Row 1 (right side): K1, *P1, K1; rep from * across.

Rep Row 1 (Seed st) until piece measures 27", ending by working a wrong-side row.

Dividing Row: Work in pattern across 11 sts, turn, place rem 12 sts on a st holder.

Continue in Seed st across 11 sts for 2", ending by working a right-side row. Cut yarn, leaving 11 sts on needle.

Join yarn and work 12 sts from st holder in Seed st as established until piece measures 2" from Dividing Row, ending by working a right-side row; do not cut yarn.

Joining Row

With wrong side facing, work in Seed st across first 12 sts, then across the rem 11 sts. Continue in patt for 9 1/2" more, ending by working a wrong-side row. Finish off; weave in ends.

#76 COMFY SWEATER

MATERIALS

Chunky weight yarn
   18 (25, 28, 32) oz olive

Note: Photographed model made with Stylecraft® Braemar Chunky #3439 Kinross

Size 11 (8 mm) knitting needles
   (or size required for gauge)

Size 10 (6 mm) knitting needles

4 stitch holders

GAUGE

11 sts and 14 rows = 4" with
   larger needles in stock st (knit
   1 row, purl 1 row)

Note: Instructions are written for X-Small; changes for Small, Medium and Large are in parentheses.

SIZE	X-Small	Small	Medium	Large
Body Bust Measurements	28" - 30"	32" - 34"	36" - 38"	40" - 42"
Garment Bust Measurements	35 1/2"	40"	45"	48"

STITCH GUIDE

Make 1 stitch (M1): Pick up horizontal bar between next 2 sts with left needle and knit into back of the stitch: inc made.

INSTRUCTIONS

Note: Always slip the st as if to knit.

Front

Starting at bottom with smaller needles, CO 45 (51, 57, 61) sts.

Ribbing

Row 1 (right side): *K1, P1; rep from * to last st, K1.

Row 2: *P1, K1; rep from * to last st, P1.

Rep Rows 1 and 2 until piece measures 5", ending by working a wrong-side row.

Body
Change to larger needles.

Row 1 (right side): Knit.

Row 2: Purl.

Rep Rows 1 and 2 until piece measures 20" from cast-on row, ending by working a wrong-side row.

Shape Raglan
Row 1 (right side): BO 2 sts, knit across row: 43 (49, 55, 59) sts.

Row 2: BO 2 sts, purl across row: 41 (47, 53, 57) sts.

Row 3: K2, sl 1, K1, PSSO, knit to last 4 sts, K2tog, K2: 39 (45, 51, 55) sts.

Row 4: Purl.

Rep Rows 3 and 4 eight (10, 12, 13) times in sequence: 23 (25, 27, 29) sts.

Shape Neck
First Side
Row 1: K2, sl 1, K1, PSSO, K3, turn; place rem 16 (18, 20, 22) sts on stitch holder and work on 6 sts only.

Row 2: Purl.

Row 3: K2, sl 1, K1, PSSO, K2tog: 4 sts.

Row 4: Purl.

Row 5: (K2tog) twice.

Row 6: P2tog. Finish off.

Second Side
Row 1 (right side): Working on rem 16 (18, 20, 22) sts, sl 9 (11, 13, 15) sts onto stitch holder. Attach yarn to rem 7 sts and K3, K2tog, K2: 6 sts.

Row 2: Purl.

Row 3: (K2tog) twice, K2: 4 sts.

Row 4: Purl.

Row 5: (K2tog) twice: 2 sts.

Row 6: P2tog. Finish off.

Back
Work as for Front to Shape Raglan

Shape Raglan
Row 1 (right side): BO 2 sts, knit across row: 43 (49, 55, 59) sts.

Row 2: BO 2 sts, purl across row: 41 (47, 53, 57) sts.

Row 3: K2, sl 1, K1, PSSO, knit to last 4 sts, K2tog, K2: 39 (45, 51, 55) sts.

Row 4: Purl.

Rep Row 3 and 4 eleven (13, 15, 16) times in sequence: 17 (19, 21, 23) sts. Place these 17 (19, 21, 23) sts on stitch holder.

Sleeves (make 2)
Starting at bottom with smaller needles, CO 23 (25, 27, 29) sts.

Ribbing

Row 1 (right side): *K1, P1; rep from * to last st, K1.

Row 2: *P1, K1; rep from * to last st, P1.

Rep Rows 1 and 2 until piece measures 5", ending by working a right-side row.

Body

For Size X-Small Only
Row 1: P1, K1, P1, M1, [(K1, P1) 3 times, M1] 3 times, K1, P1: 27 sts.

For Size Small Only
Row 1: P1, K1, P1, M1, [(K1, P1) 3 times, M1] 3 times, (K1, P1) twice: 29 sts.

For Size Medium Only
Row 1: (P1, K1) twice, P1, M1, [(K1, P1) 3 times, M1] 3 times, (K1, P1) twice: 31 sts.

For Size Large Only
Row 1: (P1, K1) three times, M1, [(K1, P1) 3 times, M1] 3 times, (K1, P1) twice, K1: 33 sts.

For All Sizes
Change to larger needles.

Row 1 (right side): Knit.

Row 2: Purl.

Rows 3 and 4: Rep Rows 1 and 2.

Row 5: Inc, knit to last st, inc: 29 (31, 33, 35) sts.

Rows 6 through 35 (41, 43, 47): Continue in stock st and inc 1 st at beg and end of every 6th row 5 (6, 3, 7) times, then every 5th row 0 (0, 4, 0) times: 39 (43, 47, 49) sts.

Work even until sleeve measures 16" (17", 18", 19"), ending by working a wrong-side row.

Shape Raglan

Row 1: BO 2sts, knit to end of row: 37 (41, 45, 47) sts.

Row 2: BO 2 sts, purl to end of row: 35 (39, 43, 45) sts.

Row 3: K2, sl 1, K1, PSSO, knit to last 4 sts, K2tog, K2: 33 (37, 41, 43) sts.

Row 4: Purl.

Rep last 2 rows 11 (13, 15, 16) times: 11 sts.

Place rem 11 sts on stitch holder.

Neckband

Sew raglan seams, leaving left back raglan open.

With right side facing, with smaller needles pick up and knit 11 sts from stitch holder for left sleeve, 4 sts evenly along left side of neck, 9 (11, 13, 15) sts from st holder at front of neck, 4 sts evenly along right side of neck, 11 sts from st holder for right sleeve, and 17 (19, 21, 23) sts from st holder for back of neck: 56 (60, 64, 68) sts.

Row 1: Knit.

Row 2: Purl.

Rep Rows 1 and 2 until neckband measures 4", ending by working a purl row. BO loosely.

Finishing

Sew left back raglan and neckband seams reversing seams for turn back. Sew side and sleeve seams. Weave in all ends.

LITTLE DARLING'S SWEATER AND HAT

Designed by Sheila Jones

MATERIALS

Chunky weight yarn
   Hat
   2 1/2 oz pink (MC)
   Sweater
   12 1/2 (14 3/4, 17 1/2) oz pink (MC)

Worsted Weight yarn
   Hat
   1/4 oz multicolor (A)
   Sweater
   1 3/4 (2, 2 1/4) oz (A)

Note: *Photographed model made with Stylecraft Charleston #5194 Pink (MC) and Berroco® Cotton Twist™ #8446 Rosbush (A)*

Size 8 (5 mm) knitting needles (for hat)

Size 9 (5.5 mm) knitting needles (for sweater)

Size 10 (6 mm) knitting needles (or size required for gauge)

4 stitch holders

12 (13, 15) half-inch buttons

Sewing needle and matching thread

GAUGE

16 sts = 4" with larger needles in stock st (knit 1 row, purl 1 row)

SIZES

HAT

Fits 19 1/2" to 21 1/2" head

Note: *Instructions are written for size 3-4 years, changes for larger sizes are in parentheses.*

SWEATER	3-4 years	5-6 years	7-8 years
Body Chest Measurements	24"	26"	28"
Finished Garment Chest Measurement	28"	29 1/2"	31"

SWEATER

INSTRUCTIONS

Pocket Lining (make 2)

With MC and larger needles CO 11 sts.

Row 1: Knit.

Row 2: Purl.

Work even in stock st for 12 (14, 16) more rows. Place all sts on holder to use later for pockets.

Back
Bottom Border

With smaller needles and A, CO 54 (56, 58) sts.

Rows 1 (right side) through 6: Work 6 rows in Seed st. Finish off A.

Body

Change to larger needles and MC.

Row 1 (right side): Knit.

Row 2: Purl.

Work even in Stock st until piece measures 9" (10", 11 1/2") from CO edge.

Underarm Shaping

Row 1 (right side): BO 4 sts, K50 (52, 54).

Row 2: BO 4 sts, P46 (48, 50).

Work even until armhole measures, 7 1/2" (8", 8 1/2") end by working a wrong-side row.

Back Neckline and Shoulder Shaping

Rows 1 through 4: BO 6 sts at beg of the next 4 rows. Place rem 22 (24, 26) sts on stitch holder for center back neck.

Left Front
Bottom Border

With smaller needles and A, CO 32 (34, 36).

Rows 1 (right side) through 6: Work 6 rows of Seed st patt. Finish off A.

Body

Change to larger needles and MC.

Row 1 (right side): K27 (29, 31), place rem 5 sts on holder for front border.

Row 2: P27 (29, 31).

Work even for 14 (16, 18) rows above seed st border, end by working a wrong-side row.

Instructions continue on next page. →

Place Pocket

Row 1 (right side): K7 (8, 9) sts, place next 11 sts on a holder; then knit across the 11 sts of a pocket lining from holder, K9 (10, 11) sts.

Work even until piece measures 9" (10", 11 ½") from CO edge, ending by working a wrong-side row.

Underarm Shaping

Row 1 (right side): BO 4 sts, K23 (25, 27).

Row 2: Purl.

Work even until piece measures 8 (10, 12) rows less than back. End by working a right-side row.

Front Neckline and Shoulder Shaping

Row 1 (wrong side): BO 6 sts, P17 (19, 21).

Row 2: Knit.

Row 3: BO 4 sts, P13 (15, 17).

Row 4: Knit.

Then BO one st on the next and every other row until 12 sts rem, ending by working a wrong-side row.

Shoulder

Row 1: BO 6 sts, K6.

Row 2: Purl.

BO rem 6 sts.

Left Center Front Border

Using smaller needles, attach A and pick up 5 sts for front border from holder.

Work in Seed st patt, slightly stretching to match front edge and mark for 12 (13, 15) buttons. Place first button 3 rows down from top edge and last one 5 rows up from CO edge.

When front band matches left front edge, BO 5 sts.

Sew in place.

Right Front Border

Work as for Left Front. Finish off A.

Body

Row 1 (right side): Place 5 sts on holder for front border, changing to larger needles and MC, K27 (29, 31).

Row 2: P27 (29, 31).

Work even for 14 (16, 18) rows above Seed st border, ending by working a wrong-side row.

Place Pocket

Row 1 (right side): K9 (10, 11) sts, place next 11 sts on a holder; then knit across the 11 sts of a pocket lining from holder, K7 (8, 9) sts.

Work even until piece measures 9" (10", 11 ½") from CO edge. End by working a right-side row.

Underarm Shaping

Row 1 (wrong side): BO 4 sts, P23 (25, 27).

Row 2: Knit.

Work even until piece measures 8 (10, 12) rows fewer than back ending by working a wrong-side row.

Front Neckline and Shoulder Shaping

Row 1 (right side): BO 6 sts, K17 (19, 21).

Row 2: Purl.

Row 3: BO 4 sts, K13 (15, 17).

Row 4: Purl.

Then BO one st on the next and then every other row until 12 sts rem ending by working a right-side row.

Shoulder

Row 1: BO 6 sts, P6.

Row 2: Knit.

Row 3: BO rem 6 sts.

Right Center Front Border

Using smaller needles, attach Color A and pick up 5 sts for front border from holder. Work in Seed st patt, slightly stretching to match front edge and making buttonholes opposite markers on left front as follows:

Buttonhole Row (right side): K1, P1, YO, P2tog, K1.

Repeat buttonholes to match placement of buttons on left center front border. When center front band matches right front edge, BO 5 sts. Sew in place.

Sleeve (make 2)

With smaller needles and A, CO 26 (28, 30).

Rows 1 (right side) through 6: Work 6 rows of Seed st patt.

Change to larger needles and Main Color.

Rows 7 through 10: Work Stock st patt for 4 rows.

Row 11 (increase row): K2, M1, knit across to last two sts, M1, K2.

Repeat Row 11 every 4th row to 46 (50, 52) sts.

Then, repeat Row 11 every alternate row to 54 (58, 60) sts.

Work even until sleeve measures 12" (13", 14½")

BO 54 (58, 60) sts.

Finishing

Sew shoulder seams.

Collar

With smaller needles and A, with right side facing pick up 27 (28, 29) sts from right front, 22 (24, 26) sts from back neck stitch holder, and 27 (28, 29) sts from left front. Work Seed st for 5 rows. BO 76 (80, 84) sts knitwise.

Sew in sleeves, and then side seams. Weave in ends. Sew on buttons.

Instructions continue on next page. →

HAT

INSTRUCTIONS

Using smaller needles CO 72 sts. Work in Seed st patt for 5 rows. Finish off Color A.

Change to larger needles and MC.

Row 1 (right side): Knit.

Row 2: Purl.

Continue in Stock st until piece measures 4 ½" or desired length from CO edge.

Shape Top

Row 1: K6, K2tog; *K5, K2tog; rep from * to last st, K1: 62 sts.

Row 2 and all even rows through Row 26: Purl.

Row 3: K5, K2tog; *K4, K2tog; rep from * to last st, K1: 52 sts.

Row 5: K4, K2tog; *K3, K2tog; rep from * to last st, K1: 42 sts.

Row 7: K3, K2tog; *K2, K2tog; rep from * to last st, K1: 32 sts.

Row 9: Knit.

Row 11: K2; *K2tog, K1; rep from * across: 22 sts.

Row 13: Knit.

Row 15: K1; *K2tog; rep from * to last st, K1: 12 sts.

Row 17: *K2tog; rep from * to end of row: 6 sts.

Row 19: Knit.

Row 21: *K2 tog; rep from * to end of row: 3 sts.

Row 23: Knit.

Row 25: K2tog, K1: 2 sts.

Row 27: K2tog; finish off.

Finishing

Sew back seam and weave in ends.

#79 & 80 MOMMY AND ME PONCHOS

Designed by Patons Design Staff

SIZE

Mommy's version fits women
   32" through 38" bust

Child's version fits children 4 to
   8 years

MATERIALS

Bulky weight yarn

Mommy's version
   17 ½ oz grey

Child's version
   14 oz grey

Note: *Both photographed models
made with Patons® Shetland
Chunky #3046 Oxford Grey*

Size 10 (6 mm) knitting
   needles (or size required
   for gauge)

Cable needle

Stitch marker or small safety pin

2 Stitch holders

Tapestry needle or yarn needle

4 ½" wide piece of cardboard

GAUGE

15 sts and 20 rows = 4" in stock
   st (knit 1 row, purl 1 row)

Instructions continue on next page. →

STITCH GUIDE

C3Bdec: Sl next 2 sts onto cable needle and leave at back of work, K1, K2tog from cable needle: C3Bdec made.

C3Fdec: Sl next st onto cable needle and leave at front of work, K2tog, K1 from cable needle: C3Fdec made.

Hint: To avoid a hole when purling or knitting a previously slipped st, pick up the st below the slipped st and slip it onto left-hand neede. Knit or purl this st tog with slipped st above.

MOMMY'S VERSION

INSTRUCTIONS

Note: Poncho is worked in two pieces which are sewn tog at center back and center front.

Right Side

Starting at bottom, CO 106 sts.

Seed Stitch Border:

Row 1: *K1, P1; rep from * to end of row.

Row 2: *P1, K1; rep from * to end of row.

Rows 3 through 6: Rep Rows 1 and 2.

Body

Row 1 (right side): K2, C3Bdec, knit to last 5 sts, C3Fdec, K2: 104 sts.

Row 2: Purl.

Row 3: Knit.

Row 4: Purl.

Rep last 4 rows 12 times more. At end of last row: 80 sts.

Shoulder Shaping

Row 1: K2, C3Bdec, K31, C3Fdec, K1, place marker between sts, K1, C3Bdec, K31, C3Fdec, K2: 76 sts.

Row 2: Purl.

Row 3: Knit.

Row 4: Purl.

Row 5: K2, C3Bdec, K29, C3Fdec, K2, C3Bdec, K29, C3Fdec, K2: 72 sts.

Rows 6 through 8: Rep Rows 2 through 4.

Row 9: K2, C3Bdec, K27, C3Fdec, K2, C3Bdec, K27, C3Fdec, K2: 68 sts.

Rows 10 through 12: Rep Rows 2 through 4.

Row 13: K2, C3Bdec, K25, C3Fdec, K2, C3Bdec, K25, C3Fdec, K2: 64 sts.

Rows 14 through 16: Rep Rows 2 through 4.

Row 17: K2, C3Bdec, K23, C3Fdec, K2, C3Bdec, K23, C3Fdec, K2: 60 sts.

Row 18: Purl.

Neck Shaping

Row 1: Knit.

Row 2: P52, turn, leaving rem sts unworked on needle.

Row 3: Sl 1 as to knit, knit to last 4 sts before marker, C3Fdec, K2, C3Bdec, knit to last 5 sts, C3Fdec, K2: 57 sts on needle.

Row 4: P46, turn, leaving rem sts unworked on needle.

Row 5: Sl 1 as to knit, knit to 4 sts before marker, C3Fdec, K2, C3Bdec, knit to end of row: 55 sts.

Row 6: P42, turn, leaving rem sts unworked on needle.

Row 7: Sl 1 as to knit, knit to last 4 sts before marker, C3Fdec, K2, C3Bdec, knit to last 5 sts, C3Fdec, K2: 52 sts.

Row 8: P38, turn, leaving rem sts unworked on needle.

Row 9: Sl 1 as to knit, knit to 4 sts before marker, C3Fdec, K2, C3Bdec, knit to end of row: 50 sts.

Row 10: P35, turn, leaving rem sts unworked on needle.

Row 11: Sl 1 as to knit, knit to 4 sts before marker, C3Fdec, K2, C3Bdec, knit to last 5 sts, C3Fdec, K2: 47 sts.

Row 12: Purl all sts.

Row 13: Knit, dec 9 sts evenly spaced across; place rem 38 sts on st holder.

Left Side
Rep Edging, Body and Shoulder Shaping as given for right side: 60 sts.

Neck Shaping
Row 1: Purl.

Row 2: K2, C3Bdec, K21, C3Fdec, K2, C3Bdec, K18, turn, leaving rem sts unworked on needle: 57 sts.

Row 3: Sl 1 as to purl, purl to end of row.

Row 4: Knit to 4 sts before marker, C3Fdec, K2, C3Bdec, K14, turn, leaving rem sts unworked on needle: 55 sts.

Row 5: Sl 1 as to purl, purl to end of row.

Row 6: K2, C3Bdec, knit to 4 sts before marker, C3Fdec, K2, C3Bdec, K11, turn, leaving rem sts unworked on needle: 52 sts.

Row 7: Sl 1 as to purl, purl to end of row.

Row 8: Knit to 4 sts before marker, C3Fdec, K2, C3Bdec, K7, turn, leaving rem sts unworked on needle: 50 sts.

Row 9: Sl 1 as to purl, purl to end of row.

Row 10: K2, C3Bdec, knit to 4 sts before marker, C3Fdec, K2, C3Bdec, K7, turn, leaving rem sts unworked on needle: 47 sts.

Row 11: Sl 1 as to purl, purl to end of row.

Row 12: Knit to end of row, dec 9 sts evenly spaced across: 38 sts. Place rem sts on st holder.

Finishing
Sew center back seam, carefully matching rows.

Hood
With right side of work facing, K38 sts from right st holder and then 38 sts from left st holder: 76 sts.

Row 1 (wrong side): K1, (P1, K1) twice, purl to last 5 sts, K1, (P1, K1) twice.

Row 2: P1, (K1, P1) twice, knit to last 5 sts, P1, (K1, P1) twice.

Rep Rows 1 and 2 until Hood measures 12" ending by working a wrong-side row. BO. Cut yarn, leaving a long end for sewing Fold hood in half and sew center top seam.

Sew center front seam of Poncho, carefully matching rows.

Tassels (make 21)
Wind yarn around 4 1/2" piece of cardboard 15 times. Cut yarn, leaving a long end and thread end through needle. Slip needle through all lps and tie tightly. Remove cardboard and wind yarn tightly around lps 3/4" below fold. Fasten securely. Cut through rem lps and trim ends evenly. Attach 20 tassels to poncho along CO edge, evenly spaced. Attach 1 tassel to top of Hood.

199

Instructions continue on next page. →

CHILD'S VERSION

INSTRUCTIONS

Note: *Poncho is worked in two pieces which are sewn tog at center back and center front.*

Right Side

Starting at bottom, CO 98 sts.

Seed Stitch Border:

Row 1: *K1, P1; rep from * to end of row.

Row 2: *P1, K1; rep from * to end of row.

Rows 3 and 4: Rep Rows 1 and 2.

Body

Row 1 (right side): K2, C3Bdec, knit to last 5 sts, C3Fdec, K2: 96 sts.

Row 2: Purl.

Rep last 2 rows 21 times more in sequence. At end of last rep: 54 sts.

Shoulder Shaping

Row 1: K2, C3Bdec, K18, C3Fdec, K1, place marker between sts, K1, C3Bdec, K18, C3Fdec, K2: 50 sts.

Row 2 and all even rows: Purl.

Row 3: Knit to 4 sts before marker, C3Fdec, F2, C3Bdec, knit to end of row: 48 sts.

Row 5: K2, C3Bdec, knit to 4 sts before marker, C3Fdec, K2, C3Bdec, knit to last 5 sts, C3Fdec, K2: 44 sts.

Rows 6 through 9: Rep Rows 2 through 5 in sequence. At end of Row 9: 38 sts.

Row 10 and 11: Rep Row 2 and 3: 36 sts.

Neck Shaping

Row 1: P33, turn, leaving rem sts unworked on needle.

Row 2: Sl 1 as to knit, knit to last 4 sts before marker, C3Fdec, K2, C3Bdec, knit to last 5 sts, C3Fdec, K2: 33 sts.

Row 3: P27, turn, leaving rem sts unworked on needle.

Row 4: Sl 1 as to knit, knit to 4 sts before marker, C3Fdec, K2, C3Bdec, knit to end of row: 31 sts.

Row 5: P21, turn, leaving rem sts unworked on needle.

Row 6: Sl 1 as to knit, knit to last 4 sts before marker, C3Fdec, K2, C3Bdec, knit to last 5 sts, C3Fdec, K2: 28 sts.

Row 7: Purl.

Row 8: Knit. Place rem 28 sts on st holder.

Left Side

Rep Seed Stitch Border, Body and Shoulder Shaping as given for Right Side: 36 sts.

Neck Shaping

Row 1: Purl

Row 2: K2, C3Bdec, K9, C3Fdec, K2, C3Bdec, K11, turn, leaving rem sts unworked on needle: 33 sts.

Row 3: Sl 1 as to purl, purl to end of row.

Row 4: Knit to 4 sts before marker, C3Fdec, K2, C3Bdec, K7, turn, leaving rem sts unworked on needle: 31 sts.

Row 5: Sl 1 as to purl, purl to end of row.

Row 6: K2, C3Bdec, knit to 4 sts before marker, C3Fdec, K2, C3Bdec, K3, turn, leaving rem sts unworked on needle: 28 sts.

Row 7: Sl 1 as to purl, purl to end of row.

Row 8: Knit. Place rem 28 sts on st holder.

Finishing

Sew center back seam, carefully matching rows.

Hood

With right side of work facing, K28 sts from right st holder and then 28 sts from left st holder: 56 sts.

Row 1 (wrong side): K1, (P1, K1) twice, purl to last 5 sts, K1, (P1, K1) twice.

Row 2: P1, (K1, P1) twice, knit to last 5 sts, P1, (K1, P1) twice.

Rep Rows 1 and 2 until Hood measures 11", ending by working a wrong-side row. Cut yarn, leaving a long end. Fold hood in half and sew center top seam.

Sew front seam of Poncho, carefully matching rows.

Tassels (make 21)

Make and attach as for Mommy's Version.

SIZE

Adult
   About 24" long x 10 3/4" around thigh

MATERIALS

Worsted weight yarn
   1 1/2 oz red
   1 1/2 oz green
   1 1/2 oz blue
   1 1/2 oz yellow

Note: Photographed model made with Red Heart® Kids™ #2390 Red, #2652 Lime, #2845 Blue and #2230 Yellow

Four size 7 (4.5 mm) double-point knitting needles (or size required for gauge)

Four size 8 (5 mm) double-point knitting needles (or size required for gauge)

Four size 9 (5.5 mm) double-point knitting needles (or size required for gauge)

Four size 10 (6 mm) double-point knitting needles (or size required for gauge)

Four size 10 1/2 (6.5 mm) double-point knitting needles (or size required for gauge)

GAUGE

20 sts = 4" in stock st (knit one row purl one row) with size 7 needles

18 sts = 4" in stock st with size 8 needles

16 sts = 4" in stock st with size 10 needles

15 sts = 4" in stock st with size 10 1/2 needles

INSTRUCTIONS (make 2)

Starting at ankle with red, CO 40 sts onto one double-point size 7 needle. Divide sts on 3 needles as follows: 13, 14, 13. Join, being careful not to twist sts. Place a marker to indicate start of rnd.

Work in K1, P1 ribbing for 3". Cut red and attach green.

Knit 3" with green. Cut green and attach blue.

Change to size 8 needles and work 3" with blue. Cut blue and attach yellow. Knit 2" with yellow.

Change to size 10 needles and knit 1" more with yellow. Cut yellow and attach red. Knit 3" with red. Cut red and attach green. Knit 2" with green.

Change to size 10 1/2 needles and knit 1" more with green. Cut green and attach blue. Knit 3" with blue. Cut blue and attach yellow.

With yellow, work K1, P1 ribbing for 3". BO loosely in ribbing. Weave in all ends.

#82 PRETTY PETAL TOP

Designed by Marnie MacLean

MATERIALS

Worsted weight yarn
   100 (120) yards blue

Note: *Photographed model made with Artfiber Paco #2 Blue Marble*

Four Size 9 (5.5 mm) double
   point knitting needles

Stitch marker

GAUGE

37 sts = 8"

Note: *Instructions are written for size Small/Medium; changes for size Medium/Large are in parentheses.*

SIZES	Small/Medium	Medium/Large
Head Circumference	19" - 21"	22"
Finished Hat Circumference	19"	22 $^1/_2$"

STITCH GUIDE

Slip, slip, knit (SSK): Sl 2 sts as if to knit, one at a time to right-hand needle. Insert tip of left-hand needle into fronts of these 2 sts and knit them together: SSK made, decreasing 1 st.

Inrease (Inc): Knit into front and back of stitch: increase made.

Ktbl: Knit through back lp.

INSTRUCTIONS

CO 8 sts on one double-point needle. Divide sts on 3 needles: 3 each on first and second needle and 2 on third needle. Join and work in rnds. Place marker on first st, move marker up as you work.

Rnds 1 and 2: Knit.

Rnd 3: Inc in each st: 16 sts.

Rnd 4: Knit

Rnd 5: *K2, (YO) twice; rep from * around: 24 sts, counting each double YO as one st.

Rnd 6: *K2, drop 1 YO lp from needle, forming a long lp; (K1, P1, K1) into long YO lp; rep from * around: 40 sts.

Rnds 7 through 10: Knit.

Rnd 11: *K5, YO; rep from * around: 48 sts.

Rnd 12: Knit.

Rnd 13: *K2 tog, K1, SSK, YO, Ktbl, YO; rep from * around: 48 sts.

Rnd 14: Knit.

Rnd 15: *Sl 1, K2tog, PSSO, (YO, Ktb) 3 times, YO; rep from * around: 64 sts.

Rnd 16: Knit.

Rnd 17: *K4, YO, Ktb, YO, K3, YO; rep from * around: 88 sts.

Rnd 18: Knit.

Rnd 19: *K2tog, K3, YO, Ktb, YO, K3, SSK; rep from * around.

Rnd 20: Knit.

For Larger Size Only
Rnd 21: *K5, YO, Ktbl, YO, K5; rep from * around: 104 sts.

Rnd 22: Knit.

Rnd 23: *K2tog, K4, YO, Ktbl, YO, K4, SSK; rep from * around: 104 sts

Rnd 24: Knit.

Rep Rnds 19 and 20 (23 and 24) until the hat is 6 3/4" (7 1/2") from the CO edge or until it is 1" less than the desired total length.

Finishing

Rnds 1 and 2: *K1, P1; rep from * around.

Rnds 3 through 10: Knit (for rolled hem). BO.

#83–87 LITTLE PRINCESS

Designed by Patons Design Staff

Note: *Instructions are written for smallest size; changes for larger sizes are in parentheses.*

SWEATER AND SKIRT CHILD'S SIZES	2	4	6	8
Body Chest Measurements	22"	23"	25 $\frac{1}{2}$"	27 $\frac{1}{2}$"
Finished Chest Measurements	26 $\frac{1}{2}$"	28"	30"	32"

MUFF
Small
   8" x 8"
Large
   8" x 10"

LEGWARMERS
Small
   Fits 2 to 4 years
Large
   Fits 6 to 8 years

SCARF
6" x 60"

MATERIALS

Bulky weight yarn

Sweater
   3 $^1/_2$ (5 $^1/_4$, 5 $^1/_4$, 7) oz rose (MC)
   8 $^3/_4$ (10 $^1/_2$, 10 $^1/_2$, 13) oz white (A)

Skirt
   1 $^3/_4$ (3 $^1/_2$, 3 $^1/_2$, 3 $^1/_2$) oz rose (MC)
   1 $^3/_4$ (3 $^1/_2$, 3 $^1/_2$, 3 $^1/_2$) oz white (A)

Muff
   1 $^3/_4$ (3 $^1/_2$) oz rose (MC)
   3 $^1/_2$ (3 $^1/_2$) oz white (A)

Legwarmers
   1 $^3/_4$ (1 $^3/_4$) oz rose (MC)
   1 $^3/_4$ (3 $^1/_2$) oz white (A)

Scarf
   1 $^3/_4$ oz rose (MC)
   1 $^3/_4$ oz white (A)
   1 $^3/_4$ oz lilac (B)

Note: Photographed models made with Patons® Carmen #07729 Rose (MC), #07005 White (A) and #07307 Lilac (B)

3 stitch holders (for sweater)

1 yd $^3/_4$" wide elastic (for skirt)

12" x 20" piece quilt batting (for muff)

1 yd (1 $^1/_2$ yds) satin cord (for muff)

Size 10 (6 mm) knitting needles

Size 10 $^1/_2$ (6.5 mm) knitting needles (or size required for gauge)

Size L (8 mm) crochet hook (or size required for gauge for crochet scarf)

GAUGE

13 sts and 16 rows = 4" with larger needles in stock st (knit 1 row, purl 1 row)

For crochet scarf: 9 sts and 9 rows = 4" in patt

STITCH GUIDE

Yf: take yarn to front of work

Yb: take yarn to back of work

Loop Stitch (Lp St): K1; Do not drop original st off left-hand needle; yf; wrap yarn around thumb forming a 2" lp, yb; sl the st just made back on left needle and K2tog: Lp St made. Pull lp firmly to right side of work.

Sl 1yb: Slip next st as to purl with yarn at back of work

Sl 1yf: Slip next st as to purl with yarn at front of work, take yarn to back of work

SWEATER

INSTRUCTIONS

Back

With smaller needles and A, CO 39 (43, 47, 51) sts.

Row 1 (right side): K1; *Lp St, K1; rep from * across.

Row 2: Knit.

Row 3: K1; * K1, Lp St; rep from * to last 2 sts, K2.

Row 4: Rep Row 2.

These 4 rows form Lp St pat.

Rep last 4 rows once more, inc 4 sts evenly across last row: 43 (47, 51, 55) sts.

Change to larger needles.

Color Patt

Row 1 (right side): With MC, K3; *Sl 1yb, K3; rep from * across.

Row 2: With MC, K1, yf, Sl 1yf; *K3, yf, Sl 1yf; rep from * to last st, K1.

Row 3: With A, rep Row 1.

Row 4: With A, rep Row 2.

207

Instructions continue on next page. →

These 4 rows form Color Patt.

Continue in Color Patt until work from beg measures 6 1/2" (6 1/2", 8 1/2", 9"), ending by working a wrong-side row.

Shape Armholes
BO 5 (5, 5, 6) sts at beg of next 2 rows: 33 (37, 41, 43) sts.

Work even until armhole measures 5" (5 1/2", 6", 6 1/2") ending by working a wrong-side row

Shape Shoulders
BO 4 (5, 6, 6) sts at beg or next 2 rows, then BO 5 (6, 6, 7) sts at beg of following 2 rows. Place rem 15 (15, 17, 17) sts on a st holder.

Front
Work same as Back to Shape Armholes.

Shape Armholes
BO 5 (5, 5, 6) sts at beg of next 2 rows: 33 (37, 41, 43) sts.

Work even until armhole measures 2 1/2" (3", 3", 3 1/2"), ending by working a wrong-side row.

Shape Left Neck
Row 1: Work in patt across 12 (14, 16, 17) sts for Left Neck. Place rem sts on a st holder.

Continue in patt, dec 1 st at neck (inner) edge on next 2 rows, then every other row 1 (1, 2, 2) time(s) more: 9 (11, 12, 13) sts.

Work even until armhole measures same as Back to beg of shoulder shaping, ending by working a wrong-side row.

Shape Shoulder
BO 4 (5, 6, 6) sts at beg next row. Work one row even. BO rem 5 (6, 6, 7) sts.

Shape Right Neck
With right side of work facing, leave center 9 sts on stitch holder and rem 12 (14, 16, 17) sts to needle for Right Neck; work in patt across.

Dec 1 st at neck (inner) edge on next 2 rows, then every other row 1 (1, 2, 2) time(s) more: 9 (11, 12, 13) sts.

Work even until armhole measures same as Back to beg of shoulder shaping, ending by working a wrong-side row.

Shape Right Shoulder
BO 4 (5, 6, 6) sts at beg of next row. Work one row even. BO rem 5 (6, 6, 7) sts.

Sleeve (make 2)
With smaller needles and A, cast on 17 (21, 25, 25) sts. Work 8 rows of Lp St pattern (Rows 1 through 4 two times), inc 2 sts across last row: 19 (23, 27, 27) sts.

Change to larger needles and proceed in patt as for Back, inc one st each end of needle on next row, then every 4th row thereafter until there are 35 (39, 31, 31) sts, working inc sts into patt.

For Sizes 6 and 8 Only
Inc one st at each end of needle on every following 6th row from previous inc until there are 43 (47) sts, taking inc sts into patt.

Work even until piece measures 9" (10 1/2", 13", 15"), ending by working a wrong-side row. Place markers at each end of last row.

Work 6 more rows even.

Shape Sleeve Cap

BO 6 (7, 7, 8) sts at beg of next 4 rows. BO rem 11 (11, 15, 15) sts.

Finishing

Collar

Sew right shoulder seam.

With right of work facing, using larger needles and A for two smaller sizes and smaller needles and A for two larger sizes, pick up and knit 11 (11, 16, 16) sts down left front neck edge. K9 from front st holder, dec 1 st at center. Pick up and knit 11 (11, 16, 16) sts up right front neck edge. K15 (15, 17, 17), dec 2 sts evenly across. 43 (43, 55, 55) sts.

Lp St Border

Row 1: With smaller needles, knit.

Row 2 (right side): K1; *Lp St, K1; rep from * across.

Row 3: Knit.

Row 4: K1; * K1, Lp St; rep from * to last 2 sts, K2.

Rep last 4 rows once more, then first 2 rows once. BO.

Sew Left shoulder and collar seam.

Sew in sleeves, placing rows above markers along BO sts of Fronts and Back to form square armholes. Sew side and sleeve seams.

SKIRT

INSTRUCTIONS

Back

Starting at bottom with smaller needles and A, cast on 39 (43, 47, 51) sts.

Work 8 rows of Lp St patt (Rows 1 through 4 twice), inc 4 sts evenly spaced across last row: 43 (47, 51, 55) sts.

Change to larger needles and work as for Sweater Back until piece measures 3 1/2" (3 1/2", 5", 6"), ending by working a wrong-side row.

Dec one st each end of needle on next and every following 8th (8th, 6th, 6th) row until 37 (39, 41, 45) sts rem. Work even until piece measures 9" (10", 12", 14"). End by working a wrong-side row.

Change to smaller needles and MC.

Next Row: Knit, dec 3 sts evenly across: 34 (36, 38, 42) sts.

Work in stock st for 1 1/2". BO.

Front

Work as for Back.

Finishing

Sew side seams. Fold inside top edge to wrong side for waistband casing and sew in position, leaving an opening for elastic. Cut elastic to desired length and thread through casing. Sew opening closed.

Instructions continue on next page. →

MUFF

INSTRUCTIONS

Lining

With MC, CO 27 (33) sts.

Work in stock st for 16" BO. Set piece aside.

Cover

Note: Piece is worked sideways.

With A, CO 51 sts.

Row 1 (right side): K1; *Lp St, K1; rep from * across.

Row 2: Knit.

Row 3: K1; *K1, Lp St; rep from * to last 2 sts, K2.

Row 4: Knit.

These 4 rows form Lp Patt.

Rep last 4 rows once more, inc 4 sts evenly spaced across last row: 55 sts.

Color Pattern

Row 1 (right side): With MC, K3; *Sl 1yb, K3; rep from * across.

Row 2: With MC, K1, yf, Sl 1yf; *K3, yf, Sl 1yf; rep from * to last st, K1.

Row 3: With A, rep Row 1.

Row 4: With A, rep Row 2.

These 4 rows form Color Pattern.

Cont in Color Pat until piece measures 6" (8"), ending by working a Row 1 or Row 3 of Color Patt. Finish off MC.

Next Row: With A, knit, dec 4 sts evenly spaced across: 51 sts.

Rep 4 rows of Lp Patt twice (8 rows in all). BO.

Finishing

Cut batting to size of lining piece.

Sew CO and BO edges of lining tog to form a tube, with right side of work inside.

Wrap quilt batting around lining and baste edges of batting tog.

Sew side edges of cover tog to form a tube with right side facing outside.

Slip cover over batting and lining. Sew cover to lining, enclosing batting.

Slip cord through muff and adjust length to fit. Knot cord and slide knot inside.

LEGWARMERS

INSTRUCTIONS (make 2)

With A, cast on 33 (41) sts.

Row 1 (right side): K1; *Lp St, K1; rep from * across.

Row 2: Knit.

Row 3: K1; *K1, Lp St; rep from * to last 2 sts. K2.

Row 4: Knit.

These 4 rows form Loop Pattern.

Rep 4 rows of Lp Patt once more, inc 2 sts evenly across last row: 35 (43) sts.

Join MC and work Color Patt as given for Muff until piece measures 8" (9 ½"), ending by working a Row 2 or a Row 4 of Color Patt. Finish off MC.

Next Row: Knit, dec 2 sts across: 33 (41) sts.

Work 4 rows garter st (knit every row). BO loosely.

Finishing

Sew back seam; weave in ends.

SCARF

INSTRUCTIONS

(crochet version shown in photo)

Stripe Pattern

6 rows MC

6 rows A

6 rows B

Note: When changing colors, work to last 2 lps on hook of last st, then draw new color through rem 2 lps of first color.

With MC, ch 20.

Foundation Row: Sc in 2nd ch from hook and in each rem ch: 19 sc; ch 1, turn.

Row 1: Sc in first sc; *ch 1, skip next sc, sc in next sc; rep from * across, ch 1, turn.

Row 2 (right side): Sc in first sc, sc in next ch-1 sp; *ch 1, skip next sc, sc in next ch-1 sp; rep from * to last st; sc in last sc; ch 1, turn.

Row 3: Sc in first sc; *ch 1, skip next sc, sc in next ch-1 sp; rep from * across ending with sc in last sc; ch 1, turn.

Rows 2 and 3 form patt.

Rep Rows 2 and 3 once more; join A at end of last row. The first 6 rows of Stripe patt are now complete.

Rep Rows 2 and 3, keeping stripe patt, until piece measures about 50".

Next Row: Sc in first sc; *sc in next ch-1 sp, sc in next sc; rep from * across. Finish off. Weave in all ends.

SCARF

INSTRUCTIONS

(knit version not shown in photo)

Stripe Pattern

*10 rows MC

10 rows A

10 rows B

Rep from * for patt.

With larger needles and MC CO 20 sts.

Following stripe pattern, work in garter st (knit every row) until piece measures 50". BO. Weave in all ends.

#88 FELTED MOCS FOR THE WHOLE FAMILY

Designed by Theresa Belville for Little Turtle Knits

MATERIALS

Worsted weight 100% wool yarn
   1/2 (1, 1 1/2, 1 3/4, 2, 2 1/4, 3) oz main color (MC)
   1/2 (1, 1 1/2, 1 3/4, 2, 2 1/4, 3) oz contrast color (CC)

Note: *Photographed model made with Bartlett Fisherman's yarns in assorted colors*

14" Size 9 (5.5 mm) knitting needles (or size required for gauge)

Blunt yarn needle

Stitch markers

GAUGE

Before felting, 14sts and 20 rows = 4" in stock st

Note: *Instructions are written for size Newborn; changes for larger sizes are in parentheses.*

SIZES	Newborn	Infant	Toddler	Child	Teen	Woman	Man
Shoe Size		0 - 6	6 - 10	1 - 5	5 - 8	8 - 10	10 - 13

INSTRUCTIONS

Sole

Starting at sole with CC, CO 26 (30, 32, 42, 48, 54, 60) sts.

Foundation Row: K12 (14, 15, 20, 23, 26, 29), place marker, knit to end.

Row 1: Knit

Row 2: K1, inc, knit to st before marker, inc, K2, inc; knit until 2 sts rem, inc, K1.

Rep Rows 1 and 2, one (1, 2, 3, 3, 4, 5) more times: 34 (38, 44, 58, 64, 74, 84) sts.

Knit 2 (2, 2, 4, 4, 6, 6) rows, then purl 1 row. Finish off CC.

Sides

Row 1 (wrong side): With MC, purl.

Work even in stock st for 3 (3, 5, 7, 7, 9, 9) rows, ending by working a right-side row.

Knit 3 rows.

Instep

Row 1: K13 (14, 16, 22, 25, 29, 34), K2tog tbl, K4 (6, 8, 10, 10, 12, 12), K2tog, turn.

Row 2: P6 (8, 10, 12, 12, 14, 14), sl 1, turn.

Row 3: K2tog tbl, K4 (6, 8, 10, 10, 12, 12), K2 tog, turn.

Row 4: P6 (8, 10, 12, 12, 14, 14), sl 1, turn.

Rep Rows 3 and 4 until 20 (24, 30, 42, 46, 54, 56) sts rem, ending by working a Row 3. Do not turn, knit to end of row.

Knit 1 row, then CO 2 sts. Finish off MC.

Ankle Trim

Row 1: With CC, *K2, K2tog; put these 3 sts back on left needle; rep from * until 3 sts rem. BO.

Finishing

Hold piece with right sides tog and with matching yarn, sew seam down back of heel and along the sole.

Felting

This is the process by which you will shrink the mocs down to wearable size. This shrinking occurs through the application of agitation and temperature changes. The easiest way to achieve this is by throwing the mocs into the washing machine on a hot wash with high agitation, followed by a cold rinse. You will achieve the best results if you put some clean old jeans or tennis sneakers in the wash to provide friction for the wool fibers to rub against. Add a small amount (less than 1 teaspoon) of dish soap to the wash. Once the cycle has begun and the agitation has started, check on your mocs every 3-4 minutes to ensure they do not shrink too much. Depending on the yarn you use, you might achieve the desired results within the first 5 minutes of the wash, or you might have to run 2 or 3 washes followed by a cycle in the dryer on high heat. Be sure to remove mocs before spin cycles.

ADULT'S PULLOVER

MATERIALS

DK or sport weight yarn
43 ¾ (45 ½ oz, 47 ¼, 49) oz
champagne (MC)
1 ¾ oz red (A)
1 ¾ oz dk blue (B)

Note: Photographed model made with Patons Grace #60011 Champagne (MC), #60011 Cardinal (A) and #60110 Marine (B).

Cable needle

Stitch holder

Small safety pin

14" Size 7 (4.5 mm) knitting needles

14" Size 8 (5 mm) knitting needles
  (or size required for gauge)

One 14" Size 8 (5 mm) spare knitting
  needle

GAUGE

22 sts and 26 rows = 4" with larger
  needles and 2 strands of yarn held
  tog, in cable pattern

Note: Instructions are written for size Small; changes for sizes Medium, Large and X-Large are in parentheses.

ADULT SIZES	Small	Medium	Large	X-Large
Body Chest Measurements	30" - 32"	34" - 36"	38" - 40"	42" - 44"
Finished Chest Measurements	42"	44"	46"	48"

PANEL PATTERNS

Panel A (worked over 4 sts)

Row 1 (right side): C2B, C2F.

Row 2: P4.

Row 3: C2F, C2B.

Row 4: Rep Row 2.

These 4 rows form Panel A.

Panel B (worked over 10 sts)

Row 1 (right side): P1, K8, P1.

Row 2: K1, P8, K1.

Row 3: P1, C4B, C4F, P1.

Row 4: Rep Row 2.

Rows 5 and 6: Rep Rows 1 and 2.

Row 7: P1, T4B, T4F, P1.

Row 8: K1, P2, K4, P2, K1.

Row 9: T3B, P4, T3F.

Row 10: P2, K6, P2.

Row 11: K2, P6, K2.

Row 12: Rep Row 10.

Row 13: T3F, P4, T3B.

Row 14: Rep Row 8.

Row 15: P1, C4F, C4B, P1.

Row 16: Rep Row 2.

These 16 rows form Panel B.

STITCH GUIDE

C2B: Sl next st onto cable needle and leave at back of work, K1, then K1 from cable needle.

C2F: Sl next st onto cable needle and leave at front of work, K1, then K1 from cable needle.

C4B: Sl next 2 sts onto cable needle and leave at back of work, K2, then K2 from cable needle.

C4F: Sl next 2 sts onto cable needle and leave at front of work, K2, then K2 from cable needle.

T4B: Sl next 2 sts onto cable needle and leave at back of work, K2, then P2 from cable needle.

T4F: Sl next 2 sts onto cable needle and leave at front of work, P2, then K2 from cable needle.

T3B: Sl next st onto cable needle and leave at back of work, K2, then P1 from cable needle.

T3F: Sl next 2 sts onto cable needle and leave at front of work, P1, then K2 from cable needle.

Reverse Stockinette (rev stock st)

Row 1 (wrong side): Knit.

Row 2 (right side): Purl.

INSTRUCTIONS

Note: Garment is worked with 2 strands of yarn held tog throughout.

Back
Bottom Border

With 2 strands of A and smaller needles, CO 92 (96, 102, 106) sts; finish off A.

Row 1: With 2 strands of B, knit.

Row 2: Knit, inc 16 (18, 18, 20) sts evenly across: 108 (114, 120, 126) sts. Finish off B.

Row 3 (right side): With 2 strands of MC, knit.

Ribbing

Rows 1 through 16: *K3, P3; rep from * across.

Row 17: Work in ribbing as established, inc 7 sts evenly spaced across: 115 (121, 127, 133) sts.

Change to larger needles.

For Size Small Only

Row 1 (right side): P3; (work Row 1 of Panel A, P3) twice; (work Row 1 of Panel A, P2; work Row 1 of Panel B, P2) twice; work Row 1 of Panel A, P1; (work Row 1 of Panel A, P2; work Row 1 of Panel B, P2) twice; (work Row 1 of Panel A, P3) 3 times.

Instructions continue on next page. →

Row 2: K3; (work Row 2 of Panel A, K3) twice; (work Row 2 of Panel A, K2; work Row 2 of Panel B, K2) twice; work Row 2 of Panel A, K1; (work Row 2 of Panel A, K2; work Row 2 of Panel B, K2) twice; work Row 2 of Panel A, K3) 3 times.

For Sizes Medium, Large and X-Large Only
Row 1 (right side): P2 (5, 8); (work Row 1 of Panel A, P2; work Row 1 of Panel B, P2) 3 times; work Row 1 of Panel Pat A, P1; (work Row 1 of Panel A, P2; work Row 1 of Panel B, P2) 3 times; work Row 1 of Panel A, P2 (5, 8).

Row 2: K2 (5, 8); (work Row 2 of Panel A, K2; work Row 2 of Panel B, K2) 3 times; work Row 2 of Panel A, K1; (work Row 2 of Panel Pat A, K2; work Row 2 of Panel B, K2) 3 times; work Row 2 of Panel A, K2 (5,8).

For All Sizes
Work even in pattern as established until piece measures 26" (26", 27", 28") ending by working a wrong-side row.

Shoulder Shaping

BO 12 (13, 14, 15) sts at beg of next 4 rows, then BO 13 (14, 14, 14) sts at beg of next 2 rows. Place rem 41 (41, 43, 45) sts on a st holder.

Front

Work same as Back until piece measures 17 1/2" (17 1/2", 18", 18)" from beg, ending by working a wrong-side row.

Divide for Neck

Row 1 (right side): Work even in patt as established across 57 (60, 63, 66) sts for Left Front. Leave rem sts on needle for Right

Front to be worked later.

Row 2: Continuing on Left Front, with spare needle, CO 1 st; work in patt across.

Row 3: Work in patt to last 7 sts, work 2tog; work appropriate row of Panel A, P1.

Row 4: Work in patt across.

Rep Rows 3 and four, 15 (15, 16, 14) times more: 42 (45, 47, 52) sts.

Shape Top Neck

Row 1: Work in patt to last 7 sts, work 2tog; work appropriate row of Panel A, P1.

Row 2: K1, work in patt across.

Row 3: Work in patt to last st, P1.

Row 4: K1, work in patt across.

Rep Rows 1 through four 4 (4, 4, 7) times more: 37 (40, 42, 44) sts,

Work even in patt until Front measures same length as Back to beg of shoulder shaping, ending by working a wrong-side row.

Shape Left Shoulder

Row 1: BO 12 (13, 14,15) sts, work in patt across.

Row 2: Work even in patt.

Row 3: Rep Row 1.

Row 4: Work even in patt across. BO rem 13 (14, 14, 14) sts.

Right Front

With right side facing, begin at center of Dividing Row and sl next st onto a safety pin.

Join 2 strands of MC to rem sts.

Row 1: CO 1 st; work even in pattern across.

Row 2: Work in patt across.

Row 3 (right side): P1, work Panel A, work 2tog, work in patt across.

Row 4: Work in patt across to last st, K1.

Rep Rows 3 and four 15 (15, 16, 14) times more: 42 (45, 47, 52) sts.

Shape Top Neck

Row 1 (right side): P1, work Panel A, work 2tog, work in patt across.

Row 2: Work in patt to last st, K1.

Row 3: P1, work in patt across.

Row 4: Rep Row 2.

Rep Rows 1 through four 4 (4, 4, 7) times more: 37 (40, 42, 44) sts.

Work even in patt until Front measures same length as Back to beg of shoulder shaping, ending by working a right-side row.

Shape Right Shoulder

Row 1: BO 12 (13, 14, 15) sts, work in patt across.

Row 2: Work even in patt.

Row 3: Rep Row 1.

Row 4: Work even in patt. BO rem 13 (14, 14, 14) sts.

Sleeve (make 2)

With smaller needles and 2 strands of A, CO 55 sts; finish off A.

Border

Row 1: With 2 strands of B, knit.

Row 2: Knit, inc 8 sts evenly spaced across: 63 sts; finish off B.

Row 3 (right side): With 2 strands of MC, knit.

Ribbing

Row 1: P3; *K3, P3; rep from * across.

Row 2: K3; *P3, K3; rep from * across.

Rep Rows 1 and 2, seven times more; then rep Row 1 once more, increasing 7 sts evenly spaced across: 70 sts

Sleeve Body

Row 1 (right side): With larger needles, P1; (work Row 1 of Panel A, P3) twice; (work Row 1 of Panel A, P2, work Row 1 of Panel B, P2) twice; (work Row 1 of Panel A, P3) twice; work Row 1 of Panel A, P1.

Row 2: K1; (work Row 2 of Panel A, K3) twice; (work Row 2 of Panel A, K2; work Row 2 of Panel B, K2) twice; (work Row 2 of Panel A, K3) twice; work Row 2 of Panel A, K1.

Work in patt as established, inc 1 st at each end of next and following 6th (6th, 4th, 4th) rows until there are 94 (98, 80, 98) sts, taking inc sts into reps of Panel A bordered by 3 sts of reverse stock st.

For Sizes Large and X-Large Only
Inc 1 st at each end of every following 6th row until there are 104 (110) sts, taking inc sts into reps of Panel A bordered by 3 sts of reverse stock st on each side.

For All Sizes
Work even until sleeve measures 18" (18 ½", 19", 19") from beg, ending by working a wrong-side row. BO.

Instructions continue on next page. →

Finishing

Pin garment pieces to shape and cover with a damp cloth; allow cloth to dry.

Neckband

Sew right shoulder seam. With right side facing, with smaller needles and 2 strands of MC, pick up and knit 52 (52, 58, 64) sts down Left Front of V-neck, P1 from safety pin (mark this st); pick up and knit 51 (51, 57, 63) sts up Right Front of V-neck; decreasing 4 (4, 6, 2) sts evenly spaced, knit sts from Back st holder: 141 (141, 153, 171) sts.

Row 1 (wrong side): *P3, K3; rep from * to 4 sts before marked st, P2, P2tog, K1, P2togtbl, P2; (K3, P3) to last 3 sts, K3.

Row 2: Work in (K3, P3) ribbing to 2 sts before marked st, work 2tog, P1, work 2tog, work in (K3, P3) ribbing across.

Row 3: Work in (K3, P3) ribbing to 2 sts before marked st, work 2tog, K1, work 2tog; work in (K3, P3) ribbing across.

Rep Rows 2 and 3 once more, then Row 2 once. Finish off MC.

Change to 2 strands of B and knit 2 rows, dec 1 st each side of marked st, as before, on both rows.

Change to 2 strands of A and knit 1 row, dec 1 st each side of marked st, as before. BO.

Sew left shoulder and neck band seam.

Place markers 8 1/2" (9", 9 1/2", 10") down from shoulder seams on sides of Back and Front. Sew in sleeves between markers. Sew side and sleeve seams.

CHILD'S PULLOVER

Note: Instructions are written for size 4; changes for sizes 6 and 8 are in parentheses.			
Sizes	4	6	8
Body Chest Measurements	24"	26"	28"
Garment Chest Measurements	30 1/2"	32"	34 1/2"

MATERIALS

DK or sport weight yarn
   21 (22 3/4, 24 1/2) oz champagne (MC)
   1 3/4 oz red (A)
   1 3/4 oz dk blue (B)

Note: Photographed model made with Patons® Grace #60011 Champagne (MC), #60011 Cardinal (A) and #60110 Marine (B)

Cable needle

Stitch holder

Small safety pin

14" Size 7 (4.5 mm) knitting needles

14" Size 8 (5 mm) knitting needles (or size required for gauge)

One 14" Size 8 (5 mm) spare knitting needle

GAUGE

22 sts and 26 rows = 4" with larger needles and 2 strands of yarn held tog, in cable pattern

INSTRUCTIONS

Note: Garment is worked with 2 strands of yarn held tog throughout.

Back

With 2 strands of A and smaller needles, CO 66 (70, 76) sts; finish off A.

Border

Row 1: With 2 strands of B, knit.

Row 2: Knit, inc 12 (12, 14) sts evenly spaced across: 78 (82, 90) sts; finish off B.

Row 3 (right side): With 2 strands of MC, knit.

Ribbing

Row 1: *K2, P2; rep from * to last 2 sts, K2.

Row 2: *P2, K2; rep from * to last 2 sts, P2.

Rep Rows 1 and 2, five times more, then rep Row 2 once, increasing 7 (7, 5) sts evenly spaced across last row: 85 (89, 95) sts,

Body

Change to larger needles.

Row 1 (right side): P2 (4, 7); (work Row 1 of Panel A, P2; work Row 1 of Panel B, P2) twice; work Row 1 of Panel A, P1; (work Row 1 of Panel A, P2; work Row 1 of Panel B, P2) twice; work Row 1 of Panel A, P2 (4, 7).

Row 2: K2 (4,7); (work Row 2 of Panel Pat A, K2; work 2nd row of Panel B, K2) twice; work 2nd row of Panel A, K1; (work 2nd row of Panel A, K2; work 2nd row of Panel B, K2) twice; work 2nd row of Panel A, K2 (4, 7).

Work even in patt as established until piece measures 17" (19", 20 1/2"), ending by working a wrong-side row.

Shape Shoulders

BO 10 (11, 12) sts at beg of next 4 rows. BO 11 sts at beg of next 2 rows. Place rem 23 (23, 25) sts on a st holder.

Front

Work same as Back until piece measures 11" (12 1/2", 13 1/2"), ending by working a wrong-side row.

219

Instructions continue on next page. →

Dividing Row: Work in patt as established across 42 (44, 47) sts for Left Front; place rem sts on a spare needle for Right Front to be worked later.

Shape Right Neck

Row 1 (wrong side): With spare needle, CO 1 st, work in patt across.

Row 2: Work in patt to last 7 sts, work 2tog, work appropriate row of Panel A, P1.

Row 3: K1, work in patt across.

Rep Rows two and three 5 (4, 4) times more: 37 (40, 43) sts.

Shape Top Neck

Row 1: Work in patt to last 7 sts, work 2tog, work appropriate row of Panel A, P1.

Row 2: K1, work in patt to end of row.

Row 3: Work in patt to last 5 sts, work appropriate row of Panel A, P1.

Row 4: K1, work in patt to end of row.

Rep last 4 rows 5 (6, 7) times more: 31 (33, 35) sts.

Work even in patt until front measures same length as back to beg of shoulder shaping, ending by working a wrong-side row.

Shoulder Shaping

Row 1: BO 10 (11, 12) sts, work in patt across.

Row 2: Work even in patt.

Row 3: Rep Row 1.

Row 4: Work even in patt. BO all rem sts.

Right Front

With right side of work facing, slip next st to left of Left Front on Dividing Row onto a safety pin.

Row 1: Join 2 strands of MC to rem sts. CO 1 st, work in patt as established across.

Row 2: Work even in patt.

Row 3 (right side): P1; work appropriate row of Panel A, work 2tog tbl, work in patt across.

Row 4: Work in pat to last st, K1.

Rep last 2 rows 5 (4, 4) times more: 37 (40, 43) sts.

Shape Top Neck

Row 1 (right side): P1; work appropriate row of Panel A, work 2tog tbl, work in patt across.

Row 2: Work in patt to last st, K1.

Row 3: P1; work in patt across.

Row 4: Work in patt across, K1.

Rep last 4 rows 5 (6, 7) times more: 31 (33, 35) sts.

Work even in patt until Front measures same length as Back to beg of shoulder shaping, ending by working a right-side row.

Shoulder Shaping

Row 1: BO 10 (11, 12) sts, work in patt across.

Row 2: Work even in patt.

Row 3: Rep Row 1.

Row 4: Work even in patt. BO rem sts.

Sleeves (make 2)
Border
With smaller needles and 2 strands of A, CO 32 sts. Finish off A, join B.

Row 1: With 2 strands of B, knit.

Row 2: Knit, inc 6 sts evenly spaced across: 38 sts. Finish off B.

Row 3: With 2 strands of MC, knit.

Ribbing
Row 1: *K2, P2; rep from * to last 2 sts, K2.

Row 2: *P2, K2; rep from * to last 2 sts, P2.

Rows 3 through 12: Rep Rows 1 and 2 in sequence.

Row 13: Rep Row 1, inc 4 sts evenly spaced: 42 sts.

Sleeve Body
Change to large needles.

Row 1 (right side): P1; (work Row 1 of Panel A, P2; work Row 1 of Panel B, P2) twice; work Row 1 of Panel A, P1.

Row 2: K1; (work Row 2 of Panel A, K2; work Row 2 of Panel B, K2) twice; work Row 2 of Panel A, K1.

Work in patt as established, inc 1 st at each end of next and every other following row until there are 48 (54, 60) sts; then inc 1 st at each end every 4th row until there are 68 (72, 78) sts, taking inc sts into patt reps, bordered by 3 sts of reverse stock st on each side.

Work even until sleeve measures 10 ½ (12, 12 ½"), ending by working a wrong-side row. BO all sts.

Finishing
Pin garment pieces to shape and cover with a damp cloth; allow cloth to dry.

Neckband
Sew right shoulder seam. With right side of work facing, smaller needles and 2 strands of MC, pick up and knit 37 (41, 45) sts down Left Front of V-neck, P1 from safety pin (mark this st); pick up and knit 37 (41, 45) sts up Right Front of V-neck; K23 (23, 25) sts from Back st holder and dec 1 (dec 1, inc 1) st at center: 97 (105, 117) sts.

Row 1 (wrong side): *P2, K2; rep from * to 3 sts before marked st, P1, P2tog, K1, P2togtbl, P1, K2; *P2, K2; rep from * to end of row.

Row 2: Work in (K2, P2) ribbing to 2 sts before marked st, work 2tog, P1, work 2tog; work in (K2, P2) ribbing to end of row.

Row 3: Work in (K2, P2) ribbing to 2 sts before marked st, work 2tog, K1, work 2tog, work in (K2, P2) ribbing to end of row.

Change to 2 strands of B and knit 2 rows, dec 1 st each side of marked st, as before, on both rows.

Change to 2 strands of A and knit 1 row, dec 1 st each side of marked st, as before. BO.

Sew left shoulder and neckband seam,

Place markers 6" (6 ½", 7") down from shoulder seams on sides of Back and Front. Sew on sleeves between markers; sew side and sleeve seams.

#9 CLASSIC COLOR BLOCKS

MATERIALS

Bulky weight yarn
- 10 (15, 15, 20) oz dk brown (A)
- 10 (10, 15, 20) oz med brown (B)
- 10 (15, 20,25) oz dk blue/green (C)

Note: Photographed model made with Lion Brand® Wool-Ease® Chunky #127 Walnut (A), #173 Willow (B) and #180 Evergreen (C).

Size 9 (5.5 mm) straight knitting needles

Size 9 (5.5 mm) circular knitting needle

Size 10 ¹/₂ (6.5 mm) knitting needles (or size required for gauge)

GAUGE

14 sts and 18 rows = 4" with larger needles in stock st (knit 1 row, purl 1 row)

Note: Instructions are written for size Small; changes for sizes Medium, Large and X-Large are in parentheses.

SIZES	Small	Medium	Large	X-Large
Body Bust Measurements	38"	42"	46"	50"
Finished Bust Measurements	40"	44 ¹/₂"	49"	53"

PATTERN STITCHES

First Stripe Patt

For first half of sts on front and back:

6 rows B

*12 rows C

12 rows A

12 rows B

Rep from * for patt.

Second Stripe Patt

For second half of sts on front and back and for both sleeves:

*12 rows A

12 rows B

12 rows C

Rep from * for patt.

INSTRUCTIONS

Back

With smaller straight needles and C, CO 70 (78, 86, 94) sts. Work in K1, P1 rib for 1".

Change to larger needles and work in stock st.

Work First Stripe Patt over first 35 (39, 43, 47) sts, place marker. Join A and work Second Stripe Patt across. Work in stripe patts until piece measures 8 1/2" (9", 9 1/2", 10") from beg, ending by working a wrong-side row.

Shape Armholes

Cont in Stripe Patt, and dec 1 st each side every row 6 (6, 7, 9) times: 58 (66, 72, 76) sts.

Work even until piece measures 17" (17 1/2", 18 1/2", 19 1/2") from beg.

Shape Shoulders

BO 6 (7, 8, 9) sts at beg of next four rows, then BO 5 (6, 7, 7} sts at beg of next two rows. BO rem 24 (26, 26, 26) sts.

Front

Work same as back until piece measures 16" (16 1/2", 17 1/2" , 18 1/2") from beg, ending by working a wrong-side row.

Shape Neck

Work across first 24 (27, 30, 32) sts, join 2nd skein of yarn, BO center 10 (12, 12, 12) sts and work to end row. Working both

sides at once with separate skeins of yarn, BO 3 sts each neck edge once, BO 2 sts at each neck edge once, then dec 1 st at each neck edge every row twice; and at the same time, when piece measures same as back to shoulders, shape shoulders same as back.

Sleeves (make 2)

With smaller straight needles and C, CO 35 (39, 39, 41) sts. Work in K1, P1 Rib for 1".

Next Row (right side): Change to larger needles and A, and beg Stock St. Cont in Stripe Patt and inc one st each side every 4th row 7 (0, 4, 6) times, every 6th row 6 (8, 9, 7) times, then every 8th row 0 (3, 0, 0) times: 61 (61, 65, 67) sts. Work even until piece measures 16 1/2" (17 1/2", 18", 18 1/2") from beg, ending by working a wrong-side row.

Shape Sleeve Cap

Work same as back armhole shaping: 49 (49, 51, 49) sts. BO.

Finishing

Sew shoulder seams.

Neckband

With right side facing, with circular needle, and C, pick up and knit 58 (62, 62, 62) sts; join. Work rnds of K1, P1 rib for 3". BO in rib. Set in sleeves. Sew sleeve and side seams.

#92 THREE LITTLE FISHES

Designed by Patons Design Staff

MATERIALS

DK or sport weight yarn
   8 ³/₄ (10 ¹/₂, 12 ¹/₄, 14) oz med blue (MC)
   1 ³/₄ oz white (A)
   1 ³/₄ oz lt blue (B)

Note: *Photographed model made with Patons® Grace #60104 Azure (MC), #60130 Sky (A) and #60005 Snow (B).*

5 stitch holders

14" Size 3 (3.25 mm) knitting needles

14" Size 5 (3.75 mm) knitting needles (or size required for gauge)

24" Size 3 (3.25 mm) circular knitting needle

One 14" Size 5 (3.75 mm) spare knitting needle

GAUGE

24 sts and 32 rows = 4" with larger needles in stock st (knit 1 row, purl 1 row)

INSTRUCTIONS

Back

Starting at bottom of ribbing, with B and smaller needles, cast on 82 (86, 90, 98) sts.

Row 1: *K2, P2; rep from * to last 2 sts, K2.

Row 2: *P2, K2; rep from * to last 2 sts, P2; finish off B.

Rows 3 through 8: With MC, rep Rows 1 and 2.

Row 9 (right side): With larger needles, knit, increasing 2 (4, 6, 4) sts evenly spaced across row: 84 (90, 96, 102) sts.

Continuing with larger needles, work in stock st until piece measures 9" (10", 11", 12") from CO edge, ending by working a wrong-side row.

Shape Raglans

Row 1 (right side): BO 2 sts, knit across: 82 (88, 94, 100) sts.

Row 2: BO 2 sts, purl across: 80 (86, 92, 98) sts.

Row 3: K2, K2tog, knit to last 4 sts, sl 1, K1, PSSO, K2: 78 (84, 90, 96) sts.

Rows 4 through 6: Work even in stock st.

Rows 7 through 10: Rep Rows 3 through 6: 76 (82, 88, 94) sts.

For Sizes 6, 8 and 10 Only

Rows 11 through 14: Rep Rows 3 through 6: (80, 86, 92) sts.

For All Sizes

Row 1 (right side): K2, K2tog, knit to last 4 sts, sl 1, K1, PSSO, K2: 74(78, 84, 90).

Row 2: Purl.

Rep last 2 rows until there are 36 (38, 40, 42) sts, ending by working a purl row.

Place rem sts on a st holder.

Front

Work as for back to Raglan Shaping.

Shape Raglans

Row 1 (right side): BO 2 sts, knit across: 82 (88, 94, 100) sts.

Row 2: BO 2 sts, purl across: 80 (86, 92, 98) sts.

Row 3: K2, K2tog, knit to last 4 sts, sl 1, K1, PSSO, K2: 78 (84, 90, 96) sts.

Rows 4 through 6: Work even in stock st.

Rows 7 through 10: Rep rows 3 through 6: 76 (82, 88, 94) sts.

For Sizes 6, 8 and 10 Only

Rows 11 through 14: Rep Rows 3 through 6: (80, 86, 92) sts.

For All Sizes

Instructions continue on next page. →

Row 1 (right side): K2, K2tog, knit to last 4 sts, sl 1, K1, PSSO, K2.

Row 2: Purl.

Rep last 2 rows until there are 70 (74, 78, 80) sts, ending by working a purl row.

Shape Placket Opening

Row 1 (right side): K2, K2tog, K31 (33, 35, 36), turn. Place rem sts on a spare needle.

Row 2: Purl.

Row 3: K2, K2tog, knit to end of row.

Row 4: Purl.

Rep last 2 rows until there are 26 (28, 30, 31) sts, ending by working a purl row.

Shape Left Neck

Row 1 (right side): K2, K2tog, K15 (16, 18, 18) (neck edge); turn, place rem 7 (8, 8, 9) sts on a stitch holder.

Row 2: P2tog through back lps, purl to end of row: 17 (18, 20, 20) sts.

Row 3: K2, K2tog, knit to last 2 sts, sl 1, K1, PSSO: 15 (16, 18, 18) sts.

For Sizes 6, 8 and 10 Only
Rep last 2 rows once more: (13, 15, 15) sts.

Shape Left Shoulder

For All Sizes

Row 1 (wrong side): Purl.

Row 2 (right side): K2, K2tog, knit to last 2 sts, sl 1, K1, PSSO.

Rep last 2 rows until there are 5 sts, ending by working a purl row.

Row 1 (right side): K1, K2tog, sl 1, K1, PSSO.

Row 2: P3.

Row 3: K1, K2tog.

Row 4: P2.

Row 5: K2tog. Finish off.

Shape Right Shoulder

With right side of work facing, join MC to rem 35 (37, 39, 40) sts.

Row 1: Knit to last 4 sts, sl 1, K1, PSSO, K2.

Row 2: Purl.

Rep last 2 rows until there are 26 (28, 30, 31) sts, ending by working a purl row.

Shape Right Neck

Row 1 (right side): K7 (8, 8, 9) (neck edge), Slip these sts onto a marker, knit to last 4 sts, sl 1, K1, PSSO, K2.

Row 2: Purl to last 2 sts, P2tog.

Row 3: K2tog, knit to last 4 sts, sl 1, K1, PSSO, K2.

For Sizes 6, 8 and 10 Only
Rep last 2 rows once more.

For All Sizes

Row 1 (wrong side): Purl.

Row 2: K2tog, knit to last 4 sts, sl 1, K1, PSSO, K2.

Rep last 2 rows until there are 5 sts, ending by working a purl row.

Row 1 (right side): K2tog, sl 1, K1, PSSO, K1.

Row 2: P3.

Row 3: Sl 1, K1, PSSO, K1.

Row 4: P2.

Row 5: Sl 1, K1, PSSO. Finish off.

Sleeves (make 2)

With B and smaller needles CO 42 (42, 46, 46) sts.

Row 1 (right side): *K2, P2; rep from * to last 2 sts, K2.

Row 2: *P2, K2; rep from * to last 2 sts, P2. Finish off B.

Rows 3 through 8: With MC, work rows in K2, P2 ribbing as established.

For Sizes 4 and 8 Only
Row 9: Inc 1, [K13 (14), inc] 2 times; K12 (14), inc: 46 (50) sts.

For Sizes 6 and 10 Only
Row 9: Inc 1, [K7 (8), inc] 4 times; K8, inc: 48 (52) sts.

Upper Arm Shaping

For All Sizes
Change to larger needles.

Rows 1 through 5: Work in stock st, beginning with a purl row.

Row 6 (right side): Inc, knit to last st, inc.

Rep Rows 1 through 6 until there are 68 (74, 78, 84) sts.

Beginning with a purl row, work even in stock st until work measures 10 $\frac{1}{2}$" (12 $\frac{1}{2}$", 14", 16 $\frac{1}{2}$") from beg, ending by working a wrong-side row.

Shape Raglans

Row 1: BO 2 sts, knit across.

Row 2: BO 2 sts, purl across: 64 (70, 74, 80) sts.

Row 3: K2, K2tog, knit to last 4 sts, sl 1, K1, PSSO, K2.

Row 4: P2, P2tog through back lps, purl to last 4 sts, P2tog, P2.

Row 5: Rep Row 3.

Row 6: Purl.

Rep Rows 3 through 6, one (2, 1, 2) time(s) more: 52 (52, 62, 62) sts.

Final Shoulder Shaping

Row 1: K2, K2tog, knit to last 4 sts, sl 1, K1, PSSO, K2.

Row 2: Purl.

Rep last 2 rows until there are 10 (10, 12, 12) sts, ending by working a purl row. Place rem sts on a st holder.

Instructions continue on next page. →

Neck Edging

Sew raglan seams.

Row 1: With right side of work facing, with circular needle and MC, K7 (8, 8, 9) from Right Front st holder; pick up and knit 12 (12, 14, 14) sts up Right Front neck edge. K10 (10, 12, 12) from right sleeve st holder and dec 2 sts evenly across; K36 (38, 40, 42) from Back st holder and dec 4 sts evenly across. K10 (10, 12, 12) from left sleeve st holder and dec 2 sts evenly across; pick up and knit 12 (12, 14, 14) sts down Left Front neck edge. K7 (8, 8, 9) from Left Front stitch holder: 86 (90, 100, 104) sts. Do not join.

Working back and forth across needle in rows, proceed as follows:

Row 2 (wrong side): Knit. Finish off MC.

Rows 3 and 4: With A, knit. Finish off A.

Rows 5 and 6: With B, knit. BO all sts.

Placket Edging

Row 1: With right side of work facing, with smaller needles and MC, pick up and knit 36 sts evenly around placket opening (including sides of neck edging).

Row 2: BO as to knit. Weave in all ends.

Kangaroo Pocket

Note: *When working from chart, wind small balls of the colors to be used, one for each separate area of color in the design. Start new colors at appropriate points. To change colors, twist the two colors around each other where they meet, on wrong side, to avoid a hole. Work small areas of color in duplicate stitch (page 252).*

With MC and larger needles, cast on 59 (59, 65, 65) sts.

Work Chart in stock st to end of chart, reading knit rows from right to left and purl rows from left to right noting dec rows will be worked as follows: K2, K2tog, knit to last 4 sts, sl 1, K1, PSSO, K2.

BO rem 31 (31, 33, 33) sts.

Sew Pocket in position to Front as illustrated.

Sew side and sleeve seams.

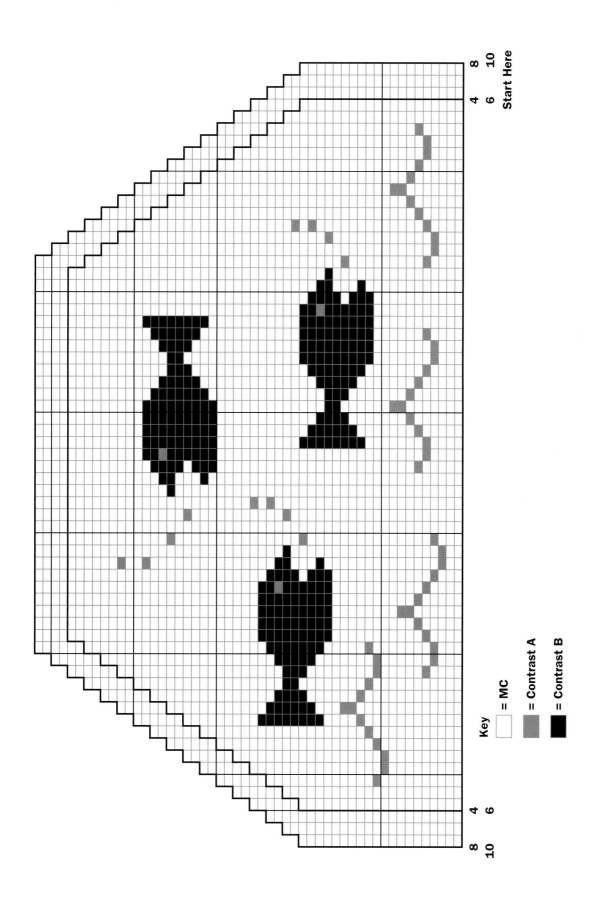

Key
☐ = MC
▨ = Contrast A
■ = Contrast B

MATERIALS

Bulky weight yarn
   24 (28, 32, 36) oz rose

Note: *Photographed model made with Patons® Divine #06406 Chantilly Rose*

Cable needle

2 stitch holders

Size 10 (6 mm) knitting needles

Size 10 ¹/₂ (6.5 mm) knitting
   needles (or size required for
   gauge)

GAUGE

12 sts and 16 rows = 4" with
   larger needles in stock st (knit
   1 row, purl 1 row)

Note: *Instructions are written for size Medium; changes for sizes Large, X-Large and XX-Large are in parentheses.*

SIZES	Medium	Large	X-Large	XX-Large
Body Bust Measurements	36	38	40	42
Garment Bust Measurements	42	44	46	48

INSTRUCTIONS

Back

With smaller needles, CO 60 (62, 68, 72) sts.

Work in K2, P2 ribbing for 3", inc 3 (4, 1, 0) sts on last row: 63 (66, 69, 72) sts.)

Change to larger needles and work in rev stock st (purl one row, knit one row) until piece from beg measures 18" (18 1/2", 18 1/2", 19"), ending by working a knit (wrong-side) row.

Armhole Shaping

BO 6 sts at beg next 2 rows: 51 (54, 57, 60) sts.

Cont in rev stock st until armhole measures 9" (9 1/2", 9 1/2", 10"); ending by working a wrong-side row.

Shoulder Shaping

BO 15 (16, 17, 18) sts at beg next 2 rows. Place 21 (22, 23, 24) sts on holder for back of neck.

Front

With smaller needles, CO 60 (62, 68, 72) sts. Work in K2, P2 ribbing for 3", inc 3 (4, 1, 0) sts on last row: 63 (66, 69, 72) sts.

Change to larger needles.

Row 1: P23 (23, 26, 26); (inc one st in next st, K1) 8 (9, 8, 9) times; inc one st in next st, P23 (24, 26, 27): 72 (76, 78, 82) sts.

Row 2: K23 (25, 26, 28); P8, (K1, P8) twice, K23 (25, 26, 28).

Row 3: P23 (25, 26, 28); work Row 1 of Cable Panel Patt, P23 (25, 26, 28).

Row 4: K23 (25, 26, 28); work Row 1 of Cable Panel Patt, K23 (25, 26, 28).

Cable Panel Patt is now in position. Continue in patt, keeping continuity of sts, until work measures 18" (18 1/2", 18 1/2", 19"), ending by working a knit row.

Armhole Shaping

BO 6 sts at beg next 2 rows: 60 (64, 66, 70) sts.

Cont in patt as established until armhole measures 5 1/2" (6", 6", 6 1/2") ending by working a knit row.

Neck Shaping

Work in Patt over 19 (20, 21, 22) sts, K2tog, turn; place rem sts on a holder. Continue in patt, dec one st at neck edge on next 2 rows, then every other row 3 times: 15 (16, 17, 18) sts.

Cont in rev stock st until work from beg measures same length as Back before shoulder, end by working a knit row. BO.

Instructions continue on next page. →

With right side facing, sl next 18 (20, 20, 22) sts to a st holder. Join yarn to rem sts, sl 1, K1, PSSO, work in patt to end of row.

Dec one st at neck edge on next 2 rows, then every other row 3 times: 15 (16, 17, 18) sts.

Work even in patt until piece measures same as Back to shoulder, ending by working a right-side row. BO.

Sleeve (make 2)

With smaller needles, cast on 36 (36, 40, 40) sts.

Work in K2, P2 ribbing for 5".

Change to larger needles and work in reverse stockinette st, inc one st at each end of needle on 5th and every following 6th row from previous inc until there are 54 (56, 56, 60) sts.

Cont until work from beg measures 22 ½" (23", 23 ½", 24") ending by working a knit row.

Shape Sleeve Cap

BO 4 sts at beg next 8 rows.

BO rem sts.

Finishing

Sew right shoulder seam.

Collar

With right side of work facing and smaller needles, pick up and knit 10 sts down left front neck edge, K18 (20, 20, 22) sts from front st holder, dec 5 (6, 5, 6) sts evenly across; pick up and knit 10 sts up right front neck edge, K21 (22, 23, 24) sts from back st holder, dec 2 (4, 2, 4) sts evenly across: 52 (52, 56, 56) sts.

Work in K2, P2 ribbing until collar measures 3". Change to larger needles and cont in ribbing until Collar measures 10". BO in ribbing.

Sew left shoulder and Collar, reversing seam for fold-back. Place markers 1 ½" down from BO edge at each side of sleeve. Sew in sleeves, placing rows above markers along BO sts at Front and Back armholes to form square armholes. Sew side and sleeve seams, reversing seams at cuffs for fold-back.

Designed by Rita Weiss

SIZE
12" x 74"

MATERIALS
Bulky weight yarn
   12 oz white

Note: Photographed model made with Lion Brand® Homespun® #300 Hepplewhite

Yarn needle

Size 13 (9 mm) knitting needles (or size required for gauge)

GAUGE
11 sts = 4"

INSTRUCTIONS

CO 33 sts.

Row 1: Knit.

Rep Row 1 until piece measures 74". Finish off; weave in yarn ends.

Fold piece in half. Starting at fold, and using yarn needle, sew a 11" seam to form the hood.

#95 SELF-STRIPING GLOVES

Designed by Rita Weiss

SIZE

Fits glove sizes 6 ¹/₂ to 7 ¹/₂

Note: Stripe pattern is achieved by using a self-striping yarn, not by changing colors.

MATERIALS

Worsted weight yarn
  3 oz self-striping

Note: Photographed model made with Red Heart® Super Saver® #317 Reef Stripe

Four 7" size 7 (4.5 mm) double-point knitting needles (or size required for gauge)

Stitch marker

6 safety pins or small stitch holders

Yarn needle

GAUGE

5 sts = 1" in stock st

INSTRUCTIONS

Right Glove

Starting at wrist, CO 36 sts loosely onto one needle. Divide sts evenly onto 3 needles, having 12 sts on each needle. Join, being careful not to twist sts, and work in rnds. Place marker to denote start of rnd after 3rd needle.

Work in K2, P2 ribbing for 2". Then knit 3 rnds even.

Thumb Gusset

Rnd 1: Knit to last 2 sts on 3rd needle. Place marker to separate sts of hand and thumb. Inc in next st, K1: 3 thumb sts. Sl marker on following rnds.

Rnds 2 and 3: Knit.

Rnd 4: Knit to marker; inc in each of next 2 sts, K1: 5 thumb sts.

Rnds 5 and 6: Knit.

Rnd 7: Knit to marker; inc in next st, knit to last 2 sts; inc in next st, K1: 7 thumb sts.

Rnds 8 and 9: Knit.

Rnd 10: Knit to marker; inc in next st, knit to last 2 sts; inc in next st, K1: 9 thumb sts.

Rnds 11 and 12: Knit.

Rnd 13: Knit to marker; inc in next st, knit to last 2 sts; inc in next st, K1: 11 thumb sts.

Thumb Dividing Rnd: Knit to marker; remove marker. Sl rem 11 sts onto holder to be worked later for thumb. CO 2 sts: 36 sts. Continue working in rnds and knit until work measures 1 1/2" above thumb (or desired length to base of fingers).

Fingers Dividing Rnd: K2. CO 2 sts and leave these 4 sts on needle for part of index finger. Sl next 5 sts to holder for one side of middle finger; sl next 4 sts to holder for one side of ring finger; sl next 8 sts to holder for little finger; sl next 4 sts to holder for other side of ring finger; sl next 5 sts to holder for other side of middle finger. Divide rem sts evenly on 2 needles for rem part of index finger. Sts for index finger should now be divided evenly on 3 needles.

Index Finger: Join and knit even in rnds until finger measures 2 1/2" (or desired length).

Dec Rnd: *K2tog; rep from * around: 6 sts. Cut yarn, leaving approx 6" end. Thread into yarn needle; draw through all sts. Draw up tightly and fasten securely.

Middle Finger: Sl sts from holders (one on each side of index finger) to 2 needles. Join yarn and with free needle pick up and knit 2 sts over CO sts at base of index finger. With free needle, knit next 5 sts (from one holder); CO one st. With rem free needle, knit next 5 sts (from other holder). Divide these 13 sts on 3 needles: 4, 4, 5. Join and knit in rnds until finger measures 2 3/4" or desired length.

Instructions continue on next page. →

Dec Rnd: *K2tog; rep from * to last st, K1: 7 sts. Finish in same manner as index finger.

Ring Finger: Sl sts from holders (one on each side of middle finger) to 2 needles. Join yarn and with free needle, pick up and knit 2 sts over CO sts at base of middle finger. With free needle, knit next 4 sts (from one holder); CO one st. With rem free needle, knit next 4 sts (from other holder). Divide these 11 sts on 3 needles: 4, 4, 3. Join and knit in rnds until finger measures 2 1/2" or desired length.

Dec Rnd: *K2tog; rep from * to last st, K1: 6 sts. Finish in same manner as index finger.

Little Finger: Sl sts from holder onto 2 needles. Join yarn and with free needle pick up and knit 2 sts over CO sts at base of ring finger. Divide these 10 sts onto 3 needles: 4, 4, 2. Join and knit in rnds until finger measures 2 1/4" or desired length.

Dec Rnd: *K2tog; rep from * around: 5 sts. Finish in same manner as index finger.

Thumb: Sl sts from holder to 2 needles. Join yarn and with free needle, pick up and knit 3 sts over CO sts. Divide these 14 sts on 3 needles: 4, 4, 6. Join and knit in rnds until thumb measures 2 1/4" or desired length.

Dec Rnd: *K2tog; rep from * around: 7 sts. Finish in same manner as index finger, Weave in all ends.

Left Glove

Work same as Right Glove to Dividing Rnd (for fingers).

Dividing Rnd (for fingers): K8, CO 2 sts. Leave these 10 sts on needle for part of index finger. Sl next 5 sts to holder for one side of middle finger; sl next 4 sts to holder for one side of ring finger; sl next 8 sts to holder for little finger; sl next 4 sts to holder for other side of ring finger; sl next 5 sts to holder for other side of middle finger; leave last 2 sts on needle for rem part of index finger. Divide sts for index finger evenly on three needles.

Work fingers and thumb same as Right Glove.

Designed by Patons Design Staff

SIZES

Hat
  Fits up to 23" head

Scarf
  8" x 95"

MATERIALS

Worsted weight yarn

Hat
  3 ¹/₂ oz natural (A)

Scarf
  7 oz natural (A)
  3 ¹/₂ oz taupe (B)
  3 ¹/₂ oz blue (C)
  3 ¹/₂ oz green (D)
  3 ¹/₂ oz red (E)
  3 ¹/₂ oz orange (F)

Note: *Photographed model made with Patons® Classic Merino Wool #229 Natural Mix (A), #227 Taupe (B), #218 Peacock (C), #240 Leaf Green (D), #206 Russet (E) and #238 Paprika (F)*

14" Size 7 (4.5 mm) knitting needles (or size required for gauge) for hat

14" Size 8 (5 mm) knitting needles (or size required for gauge) for scarf

Yarn needle

GAUGE

For Hat
  19 sts and 38 rows = 4" in patt with size 7 needles

For Scarf
  With Size 8 needles, 19 sts and 25 rows = 4" with size 8 needles in stock st (knit 1 row, purl 1 row)

Instructions continue on next page. →

STRIPE PATTERN

Row 1: With E, knit.

Row 2: With F, purl.

Row 3: With D, knit.

Row 4: With B, purl.

Row 5: With B, knit.

Row 6: With B, purl.

Row 7: With C, knit.

Row 8: With C, purl.

Row 9: With F, knit.

Row 10: With E, purl.

Row 11: With E, knit.

Row 12: With E, purl.

Row 13: With A, knit.

Row 14: With D, purl.

Row 15: With D, knit.

Row 15: With C, purl.

Row 16: With C, knit.

Rows 17 through 20: Rep Rows 15 and 16 in sequence.

Row 21: With A, purl.

Rows 22 through 42: With A, work 21 rows in stock st.

SCARF

INSTRUCTIONS

With B, CO 38 sts,

Row 1 (right side): (K1, P1) twice, (K2, P2) 7 times, K2, (P1, K1) twice.

Row 2: (P1, K1) twice, (P2, K2) 7 times, P2, (K1, P1) twice.

Rows 3 through 6: Rep Rows 1 and 2.

Work in Stripe Patt, keeping first and last 4 sts in (K1, P1) ribbing as established, until piece measures about 94" from CO row, ending by working a Row 21 of patt.

With B, rep Rows 1 through 6. BO in patt.

HAT

INSTRUCTIONS

With A, CO 99 sts,

Row 1 (right side): *K2, P2; rep from * to last 3 sts, K2, P1. This row forms seed st ribbing.

Rep Row 1 until piece measures 10 ½" from CO row, ending by working a wrong-side row.

Shape Top

Row 1: K2, P2, K1; *P3tog, (K2, P2) 3 times, K1; rep from * 4 more times, P3tog, (K2, P2) twice, K2, P1: 87 sts.

Row 2: (K2, P2) twice, K2; *P1, K1, (P2, K2) 3 times; rep from * 4 more times, P1, K1, P2, K2, P1.

Row 3: *K2, P2, K1, P1, K2, P2, K1, P3tog; rep from * 5 more times, K2, P1: 75 sts.

Row 4: K2, P1; *K1, P2, K2, P1; rep from * to end of row.

Row 5: *K1, P3tog, K1, P1, K2, P2, K1, P1; rep from * 5 more times, K2, P1: 63 sts.

Row 6: K2; *P1, K1, P2, K2, (P1, K1) twice; rep from * to last st, P1.

Row 7: (K1, P1) twice; *K1, P3tog, (K1, P1) 3 times; rep from * 4 more times, K1, P3tog, K1, P1, K2, P1: 51 sts.

Row 8: K1; *K1, P1; rep from * to end of row.

Row 9: K1; *(P1, K1) twice, P1, sl 1, K2tog, PSSO; rep from * 5 times more, K1, P1: 39 sts.

Row 10: Rep Row 8.

Row 11: (K1, P1) 3 times; *sl 1, K2tog, PSSO, P1, K1, P1; rep from * 4 more times, sl 1, K2tog, PSSO: 27 sts.

Row 12: P1; *K1, P1; rep from * to end of row.

Row 13: K1; *P1, sl 1, K2tog, PSSO; rep from * 5 more times, P1, K1: 15 sts.

Cut yarn, leaving a long end. Thread yarn into a tapestry needle and draw end through rem sts and fasten securely. Sew center back seam, reversing seam for cuff turnback.

SIZE
20" x 56"

MATERIALS
Use a variety of left-over yarn and coordinate colors, textures and blends. Weights can vary. Amount of yarn available will determine actual size. Lighter yarns can be worked with 2 strands held tog if desired. Include at least one eyelash yarn.

Note: Photographed model made with Tess' Designer Yarns Microfiber Ribbon Blue Razz, Moda Dea® Jai Alai®, Kathleen Hughes Hand Dyed Orignals Northern Lights, J&P Coats® Speed-Cro-Sheen®, Trendsetter Yarns Charm and assorted sport weight and worsted weight wool.

Size I (5.5 mm) crochet hook

36" size 15 (10 mm) circular knitting needle (or size required for gauge)

GAUGE
9 sts = 4" with worsted weight yarn in garter st (knit every row)

INSTRUCTIONS

Note: Entire shawl is worked in garter stitch.

Beg at pointed end of shawl, CO 30 stitches; do not join, work back and forth in rows.

Row 1: Knit.

Row 2: K1, inc in next st, knit to last 2 sts, inc in next st, K1.

Rep Row 2 for pattern, changing yarns randomly, until piece measures about 3" less than desired length.

Top Shaping
Row 1: K1, inc in each of next 2 sts; knit to last 3 sts, inc in each of next 2 sts, K1.

Rows 2 through 5: Rep Row 1. BO loosely.

Finishing
Weave in all yarn ends.

With crochet hook, join eyelash yarn with sl st in one corner of last row; work single crochet around shaped sides, being careful not to stretch work.

TEXTURED PONCHO AND BAG

Designed by Patons Design Studio

SIZE
27" long x 54" wide

MATERIALS
Worsted weight yarn
  42 oz grey

Note: Photographed model made with Patons® Classic Merino Wool #224 Grey mix

40" Size 7 (4.5 mm) circular knitting needle (or size required for gauge)

Size 7 spare circular knitting needle

16" Size 6 (4 mm) circular knitting needle

Stitch holder

Cable needle

GAUGE
20 sts and 26 rows = 4" with larger needles in stock st (knit 1 row, purl 1 row)

STITCH GUIDE

Bobble (MB): [(P1, YO) 3 times; P1] all in next st. Slip 6th, 5th, 4th, 3rd, 2nd and first sts separately over 7th st. One st rem: Bobble made.

M1: Make one st by picking up horizontal bar lying before next st and knitting into back of loop.

M1P: Make one st by picking up horizontal bar lying before next st and purling into back of loop.

T3B: Slip next st onto a cable needle and leave at back of work; K2, then P1 from cable needle.

T3F: Slip next 2 sts onto a cable needle and leave at front of work; P1, then K2 from cable needle.

Tw5B: Slip next 3 sts onto a cable needle and leave at back of work; K2, then P1, K2 from cable needle.

C4F: Slip next 2 sts onto a cable needle and leave at front of work; K2, then K2 from cable needle.

C5B: Slip next 3 sts onto a cable needle and leave at back of work; K2, then K3 from cable needle.

K1B: Knit into next st one row below, at same time slipping off st above.

Increase (inc): Knit (or purl) in front and in back of the same st.

DIAMOND PATT

(36-row patt rep)

Row 1 (right side): P6; *K1, P10; rep from * to last 7 sts, K1, P6.

Row 2: K6; *P1, K10; rep from * to last 7 sts, P1, K6.

Row 3: P5; *K3, P8; rep from * to last 8 sts, K3, P5.

Row 4: K5; *P3, K8; rep from * to last 8 sts, P3, K5.

Row 5: P4; *K5, P6; rep from * to last 9 sts, K5, P4.

Row 6: K4; *P5, K6; rep from * to last 9 sts, P5, K4.

Row 7: Rep Row 5.

Row 8: K2, M1, K2; *P5, (K2, M1) twice, K2; rep from * to last 9 sts, P5, K2, M1, K2.

Row 9: P5; *Tw5B, P8; rep from * to last 10 sts, Tw5B, P5.

Row 10: K5; *P2, K1, P2, K8; rep from * to last 10 sts, P2, K1, P2, K5.

Row 11: P4; *T3B, P1, T3F, P6; rep from * to last 11 sts, T3B, P1, T3F, P4.

Row 12: K4; *P2, K3, P2, K6; rep from * to last 11 sts, P2, K3, P2, K4.

Row 13: P3; *T3B, P3, T3F, P4; rep from * to last 12 sts, T3B, P3, T3F, P3.

Row 14: K3; *P2, K5, P2, K4; rep from * to last 12 sts, P2, K5, P2, K3.

Row 15: P2; *T3B, P1, P2tog, YO, P2, T3F, P2; rep from * to end of row.

Row 16: K2; *P2, K7, P2, K2; rep from * to end of row.

Row 17: P1; *T3B, P1, (P2tog, YO) twice, P2, T3F; rep from * to last st, P1.

Row 18: K1, P2; *K9, P4; rep from * to last 12 sts, K9, P2, K1.

Row 19: P1, K2; *P1, (P2tog, YO) 3 times, P2, C4F; rep from * to last 12 sts; P1, (P2tog, YO) 3 times, P2, K2, P1.

Row 20: Rep Row 18.

Row 21: P1; *T3F, P1, (P2tog, YO) twice, P2, T3B; rep from * to last st, P1.

Row 22: Rep Row 16.

Row 23: P2; *T3F, P1, P2tog, YO, P2, T3B, P2; rep from * to end of row.

Row 24: Rep Row 14.

Row 25: P3; *T3F, P3, T3B, P4; rep from * to last 12 sts, T3F, P3, T3B, P3.

Row 26: Rep Row 12.

Row 27: P4; *T3F, P1, T3B, P6; rep from * to last 11 sts; T3F, P1, T3B, P4.

Row 28: Rep Row 10.

Row 29: P5; *C5B, P8; rep from * to last 10 sts, C5B, P5.

Row 30: K2, K2tog, K1; *P5, K2, (K2tog, K1) twice; rep from * to last 10 sts, P5, K1, K2tog, K2.

Row 31: Rep Row 5.

Row 32: Rep Row 6.

Row 33: Rep Row 3.

Row 34: Rep Row 4.

Row 35: Rep Row 1.

Row 36: Rep Row 2.

Instructions continue on next page. ➔

CHECK PATT

(8-row pattern rep worked over 21 sts)

Row 1 (right side): *K3, P3; rep from * to last 3 sts, K3.

Row 2: *P3, K3; rep from * to last 3 sts, P3.

Row 3: Rep Row 1.

Row 4: Rep Row 2.

Row 5: *P3, K3; rep from * to last 3 sts, P3.

Row 6: *K3, P3; rep from * to last 3 sts, K3.

Row 7: Rep Row 5.

Row 8: Rep Row 6.

SEED ST PATT

(worked over odd number of sts)

Row 1: K1; *P1, K1; rep from * to end of row.

Rep row 1 for pattern.

BOBBLE EYELET BORDER

Row 1 (right side): Work 7 sts in seed st patt, knit to last 7 sts, work 7 sts in seed st patt.

Row 2: Work 7 sts in seed st patt, knit to last 7 sts, work 7 sts in seed st patt.

Row 3: Work 7 sts in seed st patt; *P1, YO, P2tog, P1, MB, P1; rep from * to last 10 sts, YO, P2tog, P1, work 7 sts in seed st patt.

Row 4: Rep Row 2.

PONCHO

INSTRUCTIONS

Back

CO 257 sts. Do not join; work back and forth in rows.

Row 1 (right side): K1; * P1, K1; rep from * to end of row.

Rows 2 through 6: Rep Row 1.

Row 7: Work 18 sts in seed st patt, inc, (work 20 sts in seed st patt, inc) 11 times, work 19 sts in seed st patt: 269 sts.

Bobble Eyelet Border

Row 1 (right side): Work 7 sts in seed st patt, knit to last 7 sts, work 7 sts in seed st patt.

Row 2: Work 7 sts in seed st patt, knit to last 7 sts, work 7 sts in seed st patt.

Row 3: Work 7 sts in seed st patt; *P1, YO, P2tog, P1, MB, P1; rep from * to last 10 sts, YO, P2tog, P1, work 7 sts in seed st patt.

Row 4: Rep row 2.

Diamond Panel

Row 1: Work 7 sts in seed st patt, purl to last 7 sts, work 7 sts in seed st patt.

Row 2: Work 7 sts in seed st patt, knit to last 7 sts, work 7 sts in seed st patt.

Row 3: Work 7 sts in seed st patt, work row 1 of diamond patt to last 7 sts, work 7 sts in seed st patt.

Row 4: Work 7 sts in seed st patt, work row 2 of diamond patt to last 7 sts, work 7 sts in seed st patt.

Rows 5 through 38: Continue working diamond patt (keeping 7 side sts in seed st patt as established) until 36 rows of diamond patt are complete.

Row 39: Work 7 sts in seed st patt, purl to last 7 sts, work 7 sts in seed st patt.

Row 40: Work 7 sts in seed st patt, knit to last 7 sts, work 7 sts in seed st patt.

Rows 41 through 44: Work 4 rows of bobble eyelet patt.

Row 45 (right side): Work 7 sts in seed st patt, P24; *K1B, P21, K1B, P11, M1P, P12; rep from * 3 times, K1B, P21, K1B, P24, work 7 sts in seed st patt: 273 sts.

Row 46: Work 7 sts in seed st patt, knit to last 7 sts, work 7 sts in seed st patt.

Diamond and Check Pattern

Row 1 (right side): Work 7 sts in seed st patt; *work row 1 diamond patt across next 24 sts, K1B, work row 1 check patt across next 21 sts, K1B; rep from * to last 31 sts. Work 1st row diamond patt across next 24 sts, work 7 sts in seed st patt.

Row 2: Work 7 sts in seed st patt; *work row 2 diamond patt across next 24 sts, P1, work row 2 check patt across next 21 sts, P1; rep from * to last 31 sts, work 2nd row diamond patt across next 24 sts, work 7 sts in seed st patt.

Rows 3 through 36: Cont working in patt (keeping 7 side sts in seed st patt and working K1B on right side rows as established) until 36 rows of diamond patt are complete.

Row 37: Work 7 sts in seed st patt, P3, P2tog, (P82, P2tog) 3 times, to last 9 sts, P2, work 7 sts in seed st patt: 269 sts.

Row 38: Work 7 sts in seed st patt, knit to last 7 sts, work 7 sts in seed st patt.

Rows 39 through 42: Work rows 1 through 4 of Bobble Eyelet Patt.

Row 43 (right side): Work 7 sts in seed st patt, P21, K1B, P11, M1P, P12, K1B, P21, (K1B, P24, K1B, P21) 4 times, work 7 sts in seed st patt: 270 sts.

Row 44: Work 7 sts in seed st patt, knit to last 7 sts, work 7 sts in seed st patt.

Check and Diamond Pattern

Row 1 (right side): Work 7 sts in seed st patt; *work row 1 of check patt across next 21 sts, K1B, work row 1 diamond patt across next 24 sts, K1B; rep from * to last 28 sts, work row 1 check patt across next 21 sts, work 7 sts in seed st patt.

Row 2: Work 7 sts in seed st patt; *work row 2 check patt across next 21 sts, P1, work row 2 diamond patt across next 24 sts, P1; rep from * to last 28 sts, work row 2 check patt across next 21 sts, work 7 sts in seed st patt.

Rows 3 through 36: Cont working in patt (keeping side sts in seed st patt and working K1B on right side rows as established) until 36 rows of diamond patt are complete.

Row 37: Work 7 sts in seed st patt, purl to last 7 sts, work 7 sts in seed st patt.

Row 38: Work 7 sts in seed st patt, knit to last 7 sts, dec 1 st at center. Work 7 sts in seed st patt: 269 sts.

Rows 39 through 42: **Work 4 rows of Bobble Eyelet patt.

Row 43 (right side): Work 7 sts in seed st patt, P24; *K1B, P21, K1B, P11, M1P, P12; rep from * 3 times, K1B, P21, K1B, P24, work 7 sts in seed st patt: 273 sts.

Row 44: Work 7 sts in seed st patt, knit to last 7 sts, work 7 sts in seed st patt.

Diamond and Check Pattern

Row 1 (right side): Work 7 sts in seed st patt; *work row 1 diamond patt across next 24 sts, K1B, work row 1 check patt across next 21 sts, K1B; rep from * to last 31 sts, work row 1 of diamond patt across next 24 sts, work 7 sts in seed st patt.

Row 2: Work 7 sts in seed st patt; *work row 2 diamond patt across next 24 sts, P1, work row 2 check patt across next 21 sts, P1; rep from * to last 31 sts, work 2nd row diamond patt across next 24 sts, work 7 sts in seed st patt.

Instructions continue on next page. →

Rows 3 through 36: Cont working in patt (keeping 7 side sts in seed st patt and working K1B on right side rows as established) until 36 rows of diamond patt are complete.

Row 37: Work 7 sts in seed st patt, P3, P2tog, (P82, P2tog) 3 times, to last 9 sts, P2, work 7 sts in seed st patt: 269 sts.

Row 38: Work 7 sts in seed st patt, knit to last 7 sts, work 7 sts in seed st patt.

Row 39: Work 7 sts in seed st patt, purl to last 7 sts, work 7 sts in seed st patt.

Row 40: Work 7 sts in seed st patt, knit to last 7 sts, work 7 sts in seed st patt.

BO.

Front

Work same as Back through Row 38 of Diamond and Check pattern.

Continuing with Diamond and Check Pattern
Rows 39 through 42: Work Rows 1 through 4 of Bobble Eyelet Patt.

Row 43 (right side): Work 7 sts in seed st patt, P21, K1B, P11, M1P, P12, K1B, P21, (K1B, P24, K1B, P21) 4 times, work 7 sts in seed st patt: 270 sts.

Row 44: Work 7 sts in seed st patt, knit to last 7 sts, work 7 sts in seed st patt.

Check and Diamond Pattern

Row 1 (right side): Work 7 sts in seed st patt; *work Row 1 of check patt across next 21 sts, K1B, work Row 1 of diamond patt across next 24 sts, K1B; rep from * to last 28 sts, work Row 1 of check patt across next 21 sts, work 7 sts in seed st patt.

Row 2: Work 7 sts in seed st patt; *work Row 2 of check patt across next 21 sts, P1, work Row 2 of diamond patt across next 24 sts, P1; rep from * to last 28 sts, work Row 2 of check patt across next 21 sts, work 7 sts in seed st patt.

Rows 3 through 36: Cont working in patt (keeping side sts in seed st patt and working K1B on right side rows as established) until 36 rows of diamond patt are complete.

Row 37: Work 7 sts in seed st patt, purl to last 7 sts, work 7 sts in seed st patt.

Row 38: Work 7 sts in seed patt, knit to last 7 sts, dec one st at center, work 7 sts in seed st patt: 269 sts.

Rows 39 through 42: Work 4 rows of bobble eyelet patt.

Row 43 (right side): Work 7 sts in seed st patt, P24; *K1B, P21, K1B, P11, M1P, P12; rep from * 3 times, K1B, P21, K1B, P24, work 7 sts in seed st patt: 273 sts.

Row 44: Work 7 sts in seed st patt, knit to last 7 sts, work 7 sts in seed st patt.

Diamond and Check Pattern

Row 1 (right side): Work 7 sts in seed st patt; *work Row 1 of diamond patt across next 24 sts, K1B, work Row 1 of check patt across next 21 sts, K1B; rep from * to last 31 sts, work Row 1 of diamond patt across next 24 sts, work 7 sts in seed st patt.

Row 2: Work 7 sts in seed st patt; *work Row 2 of diamond patt across next 24 sts, P1, work Row 2 of check patt across next 21 sts, P1; rep from * to last 31 sts, work Row 2 of diamond patt across next 24 sts, work 7 sts in seed st patt.

Rows 3 through 6: Work in patt (keeping 7 side sts in seed st patt and working K1B on right side rows as established) until 16 rows of diamond patt are complete: 297 sts.

Neck Shaping

Row 1 (right side): Work 7 sts in seed st; *work Row 17 of diamond patt across next 28 sts, K1B, work Row 1 of check pattern across next 21 sts, K1B; rep from * until 136 sts have been worked (neck edge). Turn. Place rem sts on spare needle.

Keeping patt as established, dec one st at neck edge on next 10 rows, then every other row 3 times: 123 sts.

Work even until Front measures same length as Back to BO edge, ending by working a wrong-side row. BO.

With right side of work facing, sl next 25 sts from spare needle onto a st holder. Join yarn to rem sts and work in patt across: 136 sts.

Dec 1 st at neck edge on next 10 rows, then on every other row 3 times: 123 sts.

Work even until Front measures same length as Back to BO edge, ending by working a wrong-side row. BO.

Collar

Sew shoulder seams. With right side of work facing and smaller size circular needle, pick up and knit 22 sts down left front neck edge. K25 from front st holder. Pick up and knit 22 sts up right front neck edge and 47 sts across back neck edge; join: 116 sts.

Work in rounds of K2, P2 ribbing until Collar measures 7". BO loosely in ribbing.

Tassel (make 4)

Cut a piece of cardboard 5" wide. Wind yarn around cardboard 40 times. Cut yarn leaving a long end and thread end through a needle. Slip needle through all lps and tie tightly. Remove cardboard and wind yarn tightly around lps 1 inch below fold. Fasten securely. Cut through lps at opposite end and trim ends evenly.

Sew one tassel to each corner of Poncho as shown in photo.

BLANKET BAG

MATERIALS
Worsted weight yarn
  7 oz cream

Note: *Photographed model made with Patons® Classic Merino Wool #202 Aran.*

14" Size 6 (4 mm) 14" knitting needles

14" Size 7 (4.5 mm) 14" knitting needles
  (or size required for gauge)

Cable needle

Button.

GAUGE
20 sts and 26 rows = 4" with larger needles in stock st (knit 1 row, purl 1 row)

INSTRUCTIONS

Front
With larger needles CO 68 sts.

Row 1 (wrong side): Knit.

Row 2: Purl.

Row 3: Knit.

Instructions continue on next page. ➔

Rows 4 through 39: Work Rows 1 through 36 of diamond patt.

Row 40 (right side): Purl.

Row 41: Knit.

Bobble Eyelet Border

Row 1 (right side): Knit.

Row 2: Knit.

Row 3: P3; *YO, P2tog, P1, MB, P2; rep from * to last 5 sts, YO, P2tog, P3.

Row 4: Knit.

These 4 rows complete bobble eyelet border.

Diamond and Check Patt

Row 1 (right side): P33, K1B, P34.

Row 2: K17, M1, K17, P1, knit to end of row: 69 sts.

Row 3: Work Row 1 of check patt across next 33 sts, K1B, work Row 1 of diamond patt across next 35 sts.

Row 4: Work Row 2 of diamond patt across next 35 sts, P1, work Row 2 of check patt across next 33 sts.

Rows 5 through 38: Work in patt until 36 rows of diamond patt are complete.

Top Border

Row 1 (right side): Knit, dec 1 st at center: 68 sts.

Row 2: Knit.

Row 3: P3; *YO, P2tog, P1, MB, P2; rep from * to last 5 sts, YO, P2tog, P3.

Row 4: (K9, k2tog) 6 times, K2: 62 sts.

Rows 5 through 13: Knit.

BO as to knit.

Back

Work same as front.

Strap

With smaller needles CO 9 sts.

Row 1: Knit

Rep Row 1 until strap (when stretched) measures 37". BO.

Twisted Cord

Cut 2 strands of yarn 8" long. With both strands tog hold one end and with someone holding other end, twist strands to the right until they begin to curl. Fold the 2 ends tog and tie in a knot so they will not unravel. The strands will now twist themselves tog. Adjust length if desired.

Finishing

Sew bottom and sides of front and back tog.

Sew CO and BO ends of strap to bag.

Sew twisted cord to center of top edge of bag to form button lp. Sew button to correspond to lp.

Abbreviations and Symbols

Knit patterns are written in a special shorthand, which is used so that instructions don't take up too much space. They sometimes seem confusing, but once you learn them, you'll have no trouble following them.

These are Standard Abbreviations

Beg . . . . .beginning
BO . . . . .bind off
CO . . . . .cast on
Cont . . . . .continue
Ch(s) . . . . .chain(s)
Dec . . . . .decrease
Fig . . . . .figure
G . . . . .gram(s)
Inc . . . . .increase(ing)
K . . . . .knit
K2tog . . . . .knit two stitches together
Lp(s) . . . . .loop(s)
Lpst . . . . .loop stitch
M1 . . . . .Increase one stitch
M(3, 6, 9) . . . . .Increase (3, 6, 9) stitches
Mm . . . . .millimeter(s)
Oz . . . . .ounces
P . . . . .purl
P2tog . . . . .purl two stitches together
Patt . . . . .pattern
Prev . . . . .previous
PSSO . . . . .pass the slipped stitch over
Rem . . . . .remain(ing)
Rep . . . . .repeat(ing)
Rev Sc . . . . .reverse single crochet
Sc . . . . .single crochet
Sk . . . . .skip

Sl . . . . .slip
Sl 1K . . . . .slip one stitch as to knit
Sl 1P . . . . .slip one stitch as to purl
Sp(s) . . . . .space(s)
SSK . . . . .slip, slip, knit
St(s) . . . . .stitch(es)
Stock st . . . . .stockinette stitch
Tbl .through back loop
Tog . . . . .together
YB . . . . .yarn in back of needle
YF . . . . .yarn in front of needle
YO . . . . .Yarn over the needle
YRN . . . . .Yarn around needle

These are Standard Symbols

* An asterisk (or double asterisks******) in a pattern row, indicates a portion of instructions to be used more than once. For instance, "rep from * three times" means that after working the instructions once, you must work them again three times for a total of 4 times in all.

† A dagger (or double daggers ††) indicates that those instructions will be repeated again later in the same row or round.

: The number after a colon tells you the number of stitches you will have when you have completed the row or round.

( ) Parentheses enclose instructions which are to be worked the number of times following the parentheses. For instance, "(K1, P2) 3 times" means that you knit one stitch and then purl two stitches, three times.

Parentheses often set off or clarify a group of stitches to be worked into the same space or stitch.

[ ] Brackets and ( ) parentheses are also used to give you additional information. For instance, "(rem sts are left unworked)".

Terms

Finish off—This means to end your piece by pulling the yarn through the last loop remaining on the needle. This will prevent the work from unraveling.

Continue in Pattern as Established—This means to follow the pattern stitch as if has been set up, working any increases or decreases in such a way that the pattern remains the same as it was established.

Work even—This means that the work is continued in the pattern as established without increasing or decreasing.

Right Side—This means the side of the garment that will be seen.

Wrong Side—This means the side of the garment that is inside when the garment is worn.

Right Front—This means the part of the garment that will be worn on the right side of the body.

Left Front—This means the part of the garment that will be worn on the left side of the body.

> The patterns in this book have been written using the knitting terminology that is used in the United States. Terms which may have different equivalents in other parts of the world are listed below.
>
> | United States | International |
> |---|---|
> | Gauge | tension |
> | Skip | miss |
> | Yarn over (YO) | yarn forward (yfwd) |
> | Bind off | Cast off |

Gauge

This is probably the most important aspect of knitting!

GAUGE simply means the number of stitches per inch, and the numbers of rows per inch that result from a specified yarn worked with needles in a specified size. But since everyone knits -some loosely, some tightly, some in-between-the measurements of individual work can vary greatly, even when the knitters use the same pattern and the same size yarn and or needle.

If you don't work to the gauge specified in the pattern, your project will never be the correct size, and you may not have enough yarn to finish your project. Needle sizes given in instructions are merely guides, and should never be used without a gauge swatch.

To make a gauge swatch, knit a swatch that is about 4" square, using the suggested needle and the number of stitches given in the pattern. Measure your swatch. If the number of stitches is fewer than those listed in the pattern, try making another swatch with a smaller needle. If the number of stitches is more than is called for in the pattern, try making another swatch with a larger needle. It is your responsibility to make sure you achieve the gauge specified in the pattern.

Metric Equivalents					
inches	cm	inches	cm	inches	cm
1	2.54	11	27.94	21	53.34
2	5.08	12	30.48	22	55.88
3	7.62	13	33.02	23	58.42
4	10.16	14	35.56	24	60.96
5	12.70	15	38.10	30	76.20
6	15.24	16	40.64	36	91.44
7	17.78	17	43.18	42	106.68
8	20.32	18	45.72	48	121.92
9	22.86	19	48.26	54	137.16
10	25.40	20	50.8	60	152.40

Knitting Needles Conversion Chart

U.S.	0	1	2	3	4	5	6	7	8	9	10	10½	11	13	15	17
Metric	2	2.25	2.75	3.25	3.5	3.75	4	4.5	5	5.5	6	6.5	8	9	10	12.75

Fringe

Basic Instructions

Cut a piece of cardboard about 6" wide and half as long as specified in the instructions for strands, plus ½" for trimming allowance. Wind the yarn loosely and evenly lengthwise around the cardboard. When the card is filled, cut the yarn across one end. Do this several times; then begin fringing. You can wind additional strands as you need them.

Single Knot Fringe

Hold the specified number of strands for one knot of fringe together, then fold in half.

Hold the project with the right side facing you. Using a crochet hook, draw the folded ends through the space or stitch from right to wrong side.

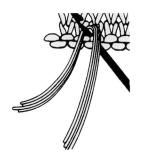 

Pull the loose ends through the folded section.

Draw the knot up firmly.

Space the knots evenly and trim the ends of the fringe.

Double Knot Fringe

Begin by working Single Knot Fringe. With right side facing you and working from left to right, take half the strands of one knot and half the strands in the knot next to it, and knot them together.

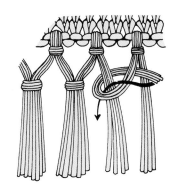

Triple Knot Fringe

First work Double Knot Fringe. Then working again on right side from left to right, tie the third row of knots.

Duplicate Stitch

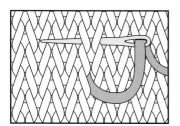 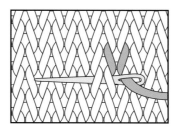 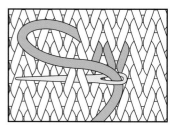

Bring needle up through center of stitch from back of work and * insert from right to left behind stitch immediately above.

Bring needle down through center of original stitch and out through center of next stitch to be worked.

Repeat from * to continue

I-Cord

Cord is worked from the right side only; do not turn. Stitches will fold toward the wrong side to form a double thickness cord.

CO 3 sts on one double-point knitting needle.

Row 1: With another double-point, K3; do not turn. Slide sts to opposite end of the needle.

Row 2: Take yarn around the back side of sts and with 2nd needle, K3; do not turn. Slide sts to opposite end of needle.

Rep Rows 1 and 2 until the cord is the desired length. BO,

Senior Technical Editor
Ellen W. Liberles

Technical Editors
Karen J. Hay and Kate Watt

Photography
James Jaeger
Carol Wilson Mansfield
Marshall Williams

Fashion Stylist
Christy Stevenson

Book Design
Graphic Solutions inc-chgo

Produced by
The Creative Partners, LLC™

The authors thank the following contributing designers:
Suzanne Atkinson, Orleans, Ontario, Canada
Donna Druchunas, Longmont, Colorado
Theresa Belville, Secane, Pennsylvania
Nazanin S. Fard, Novato, California
Sheila Jones, Port Orchard, Washington
Cynthia G. Grosch, Unionville, Connecticut
Laura Gebhardt, Pickering, Ontario, Canada
Marnie MacLean, Playa Del Rey, California
Marlaine Des Champs, Cohoes, New York
Joyce Bragg, Wilmington, North Carolina

ACKNOWLEDGEMENTS

The authors extend their thanks and appreciation to to the design departments at Coats & Clark, Lion Brand Yarn, Patons Yarns and S.R. Kertzer Ltd for sharing many of their most creative designs with us.

Whenever we have used a special yarn we have given the brand name. If you are unable to find these yarns locally, write to the following manufacturers who will be able to tell you where to purchase their products, or consult their internet sites. We also wish to thank these companies for supplying yarn for this book.

Artifiber
124 Sutter Street
San Francisco, CA 94104
www.artifibers.com

Bartlett Yarns, Inc.
20 Water Street
Harmony, ME 04942
www.bartlettyarns.com

Bernat Yarns
320 Livingston Avenue South
Listowel, Ontario
Canada N4W 3H3
www.bernat.com

Berroco, Inc.
14 Elmdale Road
Uxbridge, Massachusetts 01569
www.berroco.com

Brown Sheep
10062 Country Road 16
Mitchell, Nebraska 69357
www.brownsheep.com

Caron International
Customer Service
P. O. Box 222
Washington, North Carolina
27889
www.caron.com

Chester Farms
3581 Churchville Ave.
Churchville, VA 24421
www.chesterfarms.com

Classic Elite Yarns, Inc.
122 Western Avenue
Lowell, Massachusetts 01851
www.classiceliteyarns.com

J&P Coats
Coats and Clark
Consumer Services
P.O. Box 12229
Greenville, South Carolina
29612-0229
www.coatsandclark.com

S.R. Kertzer Limited
50 Trowers Rd
Woodbridge Ontario L4L 7K6
Canada
www.kertzer.com

Lily Yarn
320 Livingstone Avenue South
Listowel, Ontario
Canada N4W 3H3
www.sugarncream.com

Lion Brand Yarn
34 West 15th Street
New York, New York 10011
www.lionbrand.com

Naturally
S. R. Kertzer Limited
50 Trowers Rd
Woodbridge Ontario L4L 7K6
Canada
www.kertzer.com

Patons Yarns
2700 Dufferin Street
Toronto, Ontario
Canada M6B 4J3
www.patonsyarns.com

Plymouth Yarn Co., Inc
500 Lafayette Street
P.O. Box 28
Bristol, Pennsylvania 19007-0028
www.plymouthyarn.com

Red Heart Yarns
Coats and Clark
Consumer Services
P. O. Box 12229
Greenville, South Carolina
29612-0229
www.coatsandclark.com

Sirdar Yarn
Knitting Fever
315 Bayview Avenue
Amityville, New York 11701
www.knittingfever.com

Stylecraft Yarns
S. R. Kertzer Limited
50 Trowers Rd
Woodbridge Ontario L4L 7K6
Canada
www.kertzer.com

TLC Yarns
Coats and Clark
Consumer Services
P. O. Box 12229
Greenville, South Carolina
29612-0229
www.coatsandclark.com

Trendsetter Yarns
16745 Saticoy Street
Suite 101
Van Nuys, California 91406
www.trendsetteryarns.com

Twilleys of Stamford
S. R. Kertzer Limited
50 Trowers Rd
Woodbridge Ontario L4L 7K6
Canada
www.kertzer.com